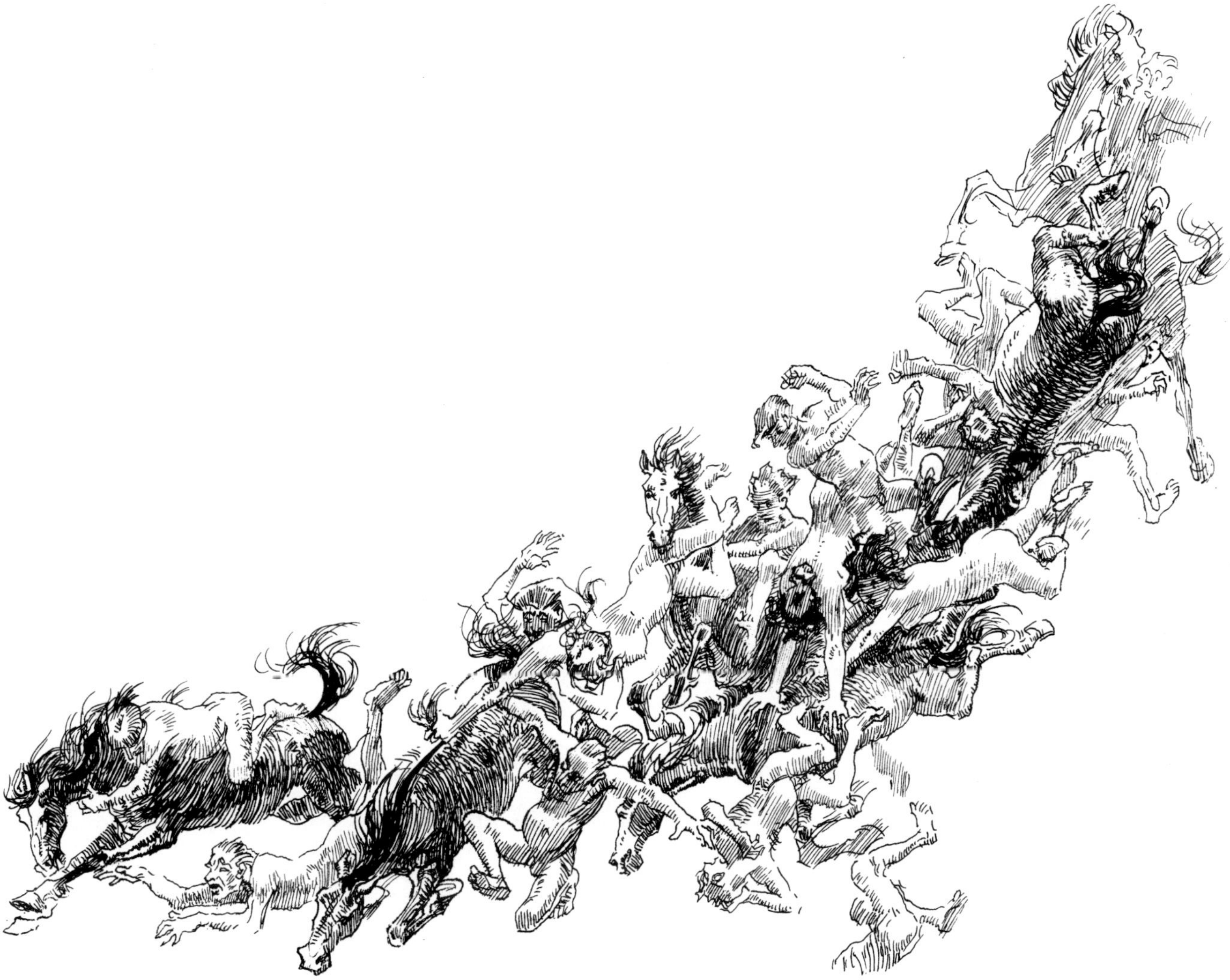

THE LOST ART OF HEINRICH KLEY

Vol. 2 • Paintings & Sketches

LOST ART BOOKS, the flagship series from Picture This Press, collects and preserves the works of illustrators and cartoonists from the late 19th through the mid-20th centuries. Too many of these artists have gone underappreciated for too long, with much of their work uncollected or unexamined for decades, if at all. The Lost Art Books series aims to preserve this cultural heritage by re-introducing these artists to new generations of working illustrators, historians, and admirers of things beautiful.

PICTURE THIS PRESS is dedicated to broadening the appreciation and awareness of the artists who work in the fields of illustration, cartooning, graphic arts, photography, and poster design.

OTHER LOST ART BOOKS

The Lost Art of Zim: Cartoons & Caricatures (2010)

The Lost Art of E.T. Reed: Prehistoric Peeps (2010)

The Lost Art of Frederick Richardson (2010)

The Lost Art of the Racy and Risqué (forthcoming)

The Lost Art of Matt Baker (forthcoming)

The Illustrated Bibliographical Dictionary of Cartoonists (forthcoming)

THE LOST ART OF

Vol. 2 • Paintings & Sketches

HEINRICH KLEY

Introduction by Alexander Kunkel • Appreciation by Jesse Hamm

Edited by Joseph V. Procopio

Editor's Note and Acknowledgments

This book was never meant to be. It was only after wading far into the deep end of my research that it became apparent that Kley could only be properly served by including about twice as many examples of his work as initially intended. My hope is to not find in a year's time that I actually need to publish a third volume, too. But there could be worse fates.

As with *Volume 1*, bibliographic information is provided, as available or deemed relevant, in the individual captions. Most of the material reproduced herein is taken from primary source material from my own collection.

Design guru Kieran Daly and his expert staff at Winking Fish again elevated the entire presentation to a level I only hoped for when starting this project. Several folks contributed scans of art from their collections, including Alexander Kunkel, Richard Hescox, Daniel Murphy from Grapefruit Moon Gallery, Andreas Deja's "Deja View" blog, and Heritage Auctions. Long-time champion of illustration art Roger Reed of Illustration House stepped up at the last moment to provide several wonderful pieces for this volume. Kunkel again proved himself a scholar and a gentleman in this volume's introduction and lengthy interview. I am especially grateful to scholarly powerhouse Jesse Hamm for his incisive appreciation of Kley's technique and what makes his art sing; I hope to have many more opportunities to collaborate with Hamm, a talented artist in his own right. Sara Duke at the Library of Congress was instrumental in securing reproductions to the Kley art in its collection. As always, Mark Wheatley provided encouragement and freely shared his technical expertise. Dave Nuttycombe and Steve Conley always make sure we put our best foot forward in all things video and Web related. Trusted friend and fine writer Nate Bruinooge provided careful reading of my work. And for me, all things begin and end with Ellen Levy, for which there wouldn't be much point otherwise.

To all of these folks: you are the giants on whose shoulders I stand. Thank you. —J.V.P.

Lost Art Books, an imprint of Picture This Press
Silver Spring, Maryland

www.PictureThisPress.com · www.LostArtBooks.com

Lost Art Book No. 5

Library of Congress Cataloging-in-Publication Data
Heinrich Kley (1863–1945)
the lost art of Heinrich Kley, volume 2: paintings and sketches / Heinrich Kley
1. Caricatures and cartoons. 2. Comic books, strips, etc.
I. Kley, Heinrich. II. Procopio, Joseph V. III. Hamm, Jesse. IV. Kunkel, Alexander.
Library of Congress Control Number: 2012946860

ISBN-13: 978-0-9829276-7-0 (paper)

COMICS & GRAPHIC NOVELS / General
ART / Popular Culture
ART / Individual Artists / General

Publishers—Joseph Procopio & Ellen Levy
Art direction—Joseph Procopio
Interior layout and design—Winking Fish
Cover design—Winking Fish

Printed in the United States of America

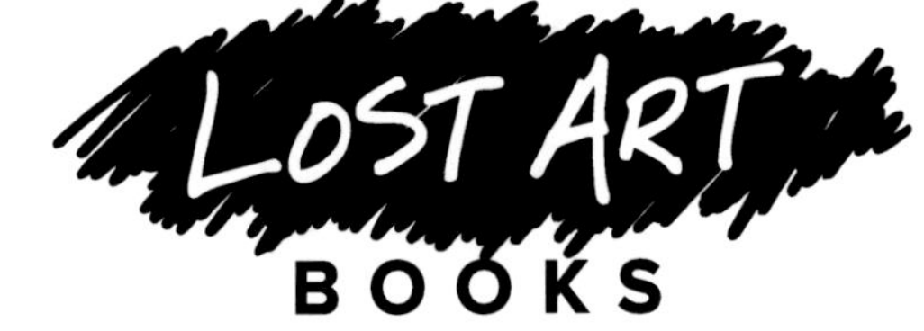

Contents

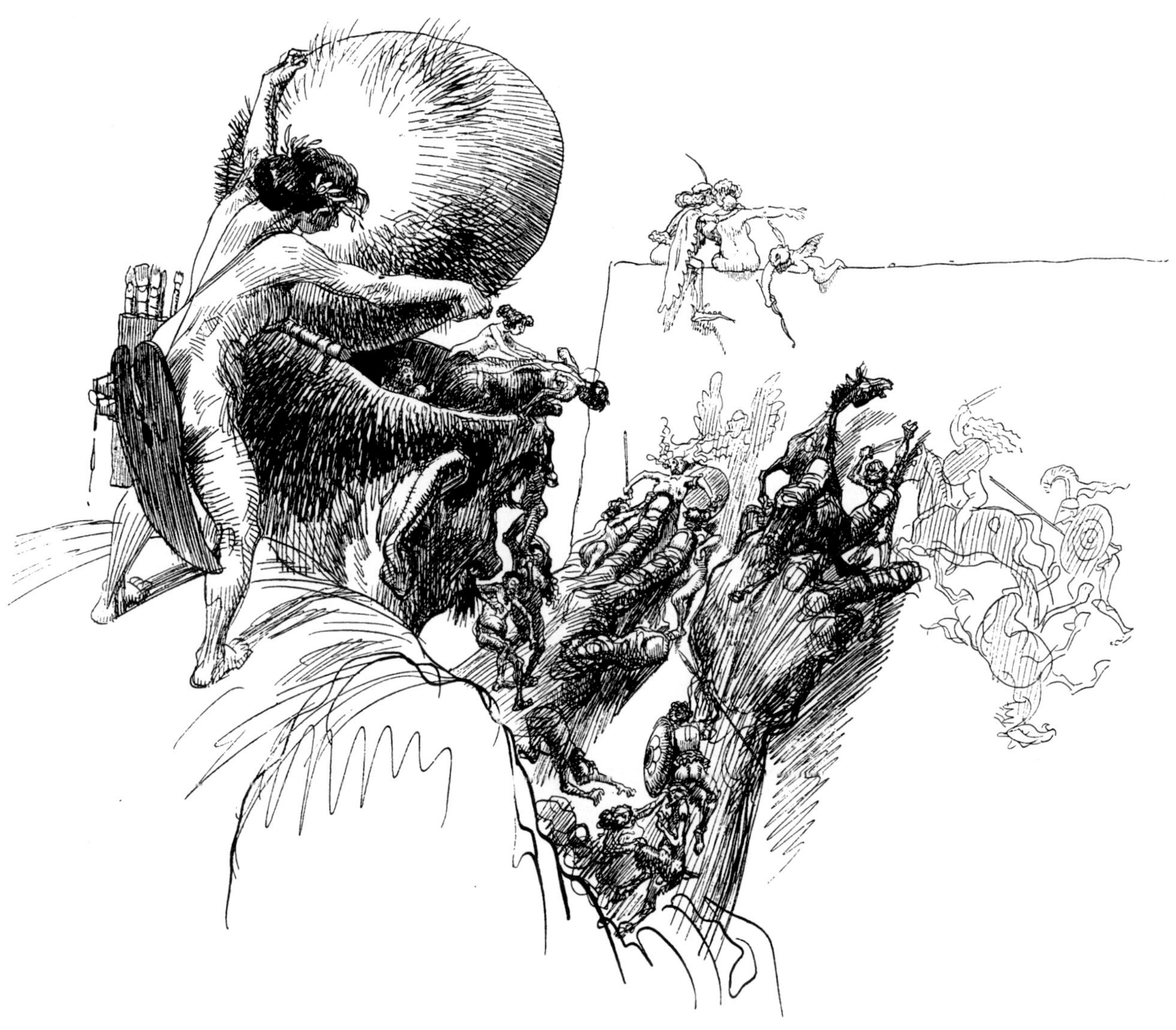

FOREWORD

Dreamer at the Drawing Board

Joseph V. Procopio
July 2012
Silver Spring, Maryland

Those familiar with Heinrich Kley's work know that he is an artist who delights in the human comedy, which in his eyes could run from the pitch black to the fatuous and frivolous. Fortunately for us, Kley wasn't a misanthrope, but if his art is to be any reflection, he definitely went through life at least bemused and perhaps sometimes a touch terrified by human folly.

It must be the tensions intrinsic in Kley's work that keep the heart of his art beating so strongly all of these decades later. His line has a deceptively dashed-off spontaneity that belies a level of craft only possible from years of sustained effort. His work and life stood astride centuries, a pen line pulled up and down through periods of cultural upheaval in a rapidly industrializing world that had yet to shed its 19th century vestments. A world afloat in utopian dreams abruptly smacked down by the horrors of the world's first "modern" war.

That life-giving tension also manifests in Kley's eccentric mix of agrarian fabulism and technological wonderment, natural eroticism and, at times, absurd violence. His work is rife with the tensions of a culture transitioning into the 20th century, but he never slips into

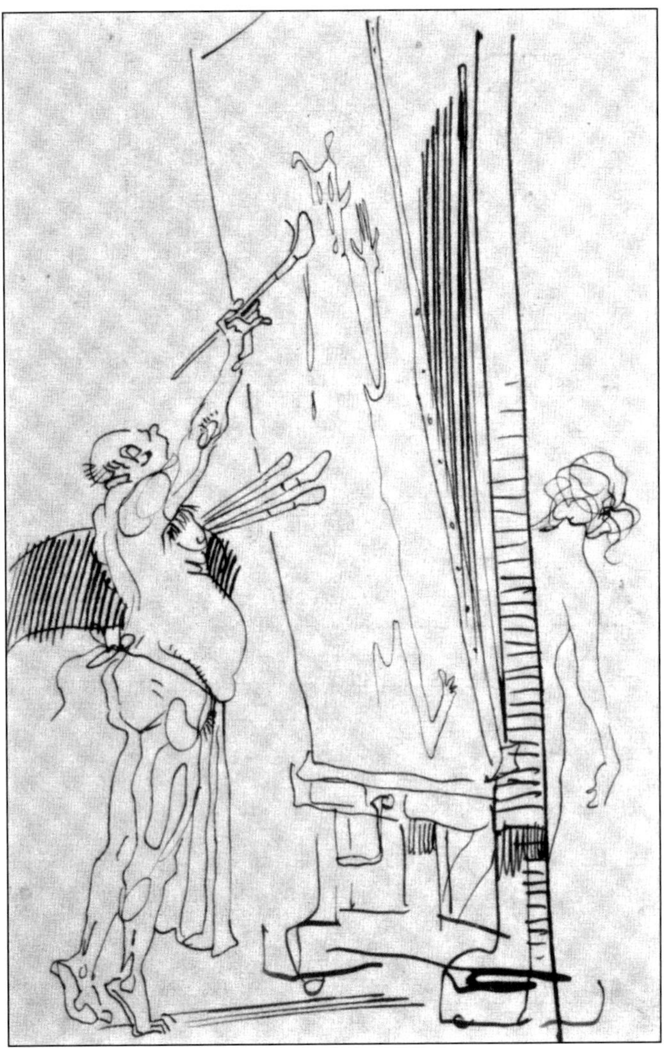

sentimentality for the past nor simple-minded pessimism toward the new. He plumbed the wellspring of a personal and collective psyche, and returned repeatedly with images that delight and disturb…of sensual reveries, frolicking beasts, demons, factories, guffawing satyrs, zeppelins. All somehow coexisted in Kley's world, even if they occasionally had to skirmish for the spotlight.

Kley was certainly fond of the tumult, whether it be a riot of figures tumbling headlong across the page or a lone protagonist flailing to keep balance in an off-kilter world. In a Kley drawing, adversaries grapple, horse herds gallop chaotically, anthropomorphic animals tug and push their way across a stage lit by Kley's unmistakable, fevered imagination. And though he never idealized it, Kley had an unquestionable affection for the human form, and was equally at ease depicting bodies naturalistically or in elastic exaggeration, as his wilder drawings so ably demonstrate. Bodies are very malleable objects, indeed, in Kley's world. Yet his well-observed drawings of man and beast show an amazing mastery of anatomy and mood, a "rightness" always undergirding the core of even his most exuberant drawings.

Kley obviously loved drawing animals, yet he rarely portrayed domestic ones, such as cats and dogs. He far preferred drawing alligators, monkeys, lions, or elephants, placing them in comically familiar human situations or coaxing them into physically unimagined feats. Kley was clearly a pioneer of anthropomorphizing animals in popular culture, and they provided one more outlet for his Id to run unfettered across the page. It's not surprising that, as scholars have noted, Kley was much beloved by the Walt Disney Studio's animators in the 1930s and 1940s, and an acknowledged influence during the making of *Fantasia* (as the dancing hippos and ominous trip to Bald Mountain attest).

Kley dreamt at his drawing board, and his art keeps dancing to this day across the page: sometimes waltzing to the clangorous, mechanistic rhythms of a world of ascendant industry, at others gliding gracefully, if a bit tipsily, in time to the heartbeat of Nature's bosom. Sometimes seemingly both at once. But no matter the tune, it would be difficult to find a better dance partner than Heinrich Kley.

***Joseph Procopio** is the founder and publisher of Lost Art Books.*

HEINRICH KLEY (1863–1945)

HIS LIFE AND WORK

Alexander Kunkel

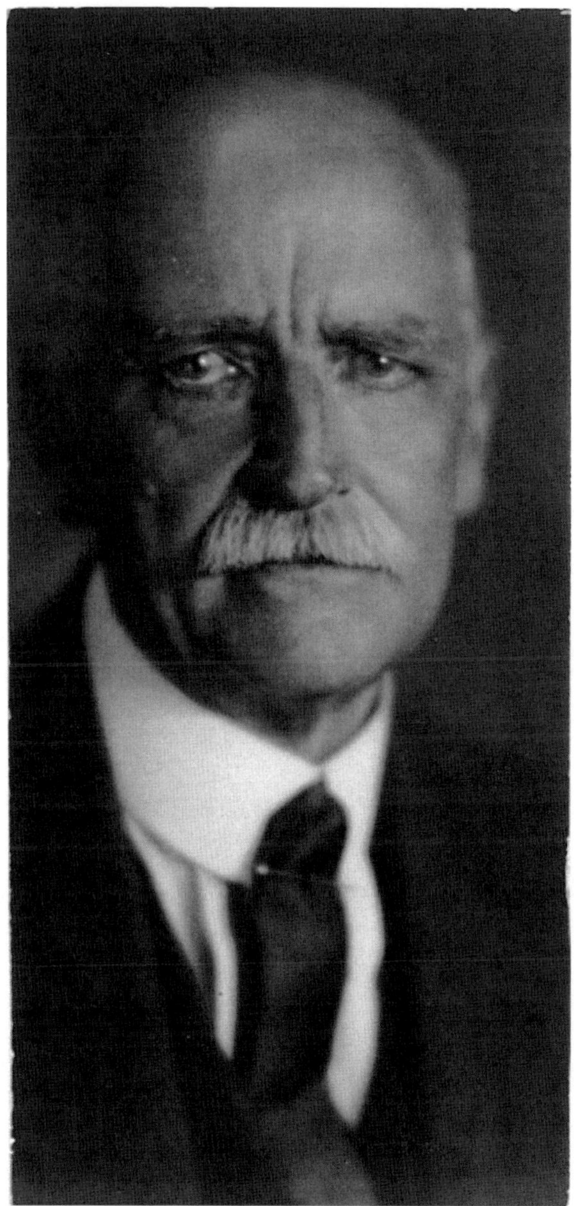

Family Background

Heinrich Kley was born on April 15, 1863, in Karlsruhe, Germany. He was the only child of silversmith Theodor Kley (1831–1870) and his wife Emma (1841–1908).[1] Following the death of his father, his mother married in 1874 the court musician Ferdinand Segisser (1822–1885) and had another son with him.

There is no other detailed information regarding Kley's childhood and youth. The relationship between Kley and his parents was already tense at the beginning of his art school studies, and was irreparably damaged by the end of them. Kley's parents opposed his relationship with Theophanie Kräuter (1861–1922), a half-orphan from a modest economic background. In order to gain financial independence from his parents, he worked in a pyrography business before and after classes. The situation, however, proved unsustainable in the long run. In 1884, in a state of utter physical and psychological exhaustion, Kley tried to commit suicide. After this, although his parents ceased to oppose Kley's activities, it appears that their differences remained irreconcilable. In any case, there is no available evidence suggesting that he maintained contact with his family following his marriage to Theophanie Kräuter in 1886.

Student Years

Kley's artistic talent must have been apparent from an early age, given that he joined the Karlsruher Kunstschule (Karlsruhe School of Fine Arts) even before graduating from secondary school, in 1880. After finishing his basic coursework, he joined the class of the history painter Ferdinand Keller (1842–1922). Leading up to his graduation in 1885, Keller did an excellent job of developing Kley's craftsmanship and academic knowledge. Kley, however, regarded Keller's solemn, lofty ideas on art as anachronistic, while Kley himself was more interested in realism.

While in art school, not only did Kley's fellow students regard him as the "element that gives fire and life to everything,"[2] but he was "also much loved and admired by older colleagues."[3] Despite being well-liked, Kley always maintained a certain degree of reserve. This was a character trait that was referred to by many of his companions throughout the decades.

Artistic Life in Karlsruhe

In connection with the celebration of the 500-year anniversary of the founding of the University of Heidelberg in 1886, Kley was given his first important assignment after finishing his studies. He created 25 illustrations for a publication intended to accompany the anniversary festivities. These illustrations mostly depict the events of the festivities, the highlight of which was a historic procession organized by the Karlsruhe Künstlerschaft (Karlsruhe Society of Artists). Kley documented the event in a Leporello album (a single folded sheet several feet long), which depicts hundreds of figures in costumes from the Middle Ages to contemporary times in a continuous procession. This album is the most important representation of his early drawing style.

Despite this early success, artistic life in Karlsruhe offered Kley only limited professional prospects.

Because of his contributions to two local court anniversaries (1892 and 1896) and two applied arts exhibitions (1891 and 1901), Kley was able to attract the attention of local authorities and secure larger commissions. In 1891/92, he painted "Die Einweihung des Merkur-Altars auf dem großen Staufen" ("The Dedication of the Mercury Altar on Mount Staufen"), and "Spazierfahrt Kaiser Wilhelms I und Kaiserin Augustas auf der Lichtenthaler Allee in Baden-Baden" ("Promenade of Emperor Wilhelm I and Empress Augusta along the Lichtenthaler Allee in Baden-Baden"),[4] which had been commissioned by the Karlsruhe postal authority for the imperial post office in Baden-Baden. In 1901/02, following a recommendation by the Department of Public Works of the city of Karlsruhe, he created the monumental wall painting "Heidelberger Sommertagszug" ("Heidelberg Summer Day Procession")[5] for the city hall in Heidelberg. In general, however, these kinds of acknowledgements of his talent were rare.

Work with architecture offices in the years around 1900 did not have a lasting influence on Kley's career, either. Rather, it proved to be an obstacle for Kley's artistic development, given that for the decorative works he created for private and public buildings were overly influenced in style and subject matter by other prominent predecessors.

The only lasting impact on his career came from the collaboration with the publishing house Hofkunsthandlung Velten. In 1897/98, Velten commissioned him to paint over 100 watercolors featuring views of German cities. These were characterized by precise draftsmanship and a painterly atmosphere and sold as color postcards all over Germany.

Periodical and Book Illustrations

To supplement his income, Kley also worked as an illustrator for popular periodicals. The traditional magazine *Über Land und Meer* (1886–98, with extended breaks) published stories dealing with cultural and political festivities in the South West of Germany. Humorous illustrations by Kley can be found in the somewhat old-fashioned *Meggendorfer Blätter* (1894/95). The avant-garde magazine *Jugend* (1897/98) also published some of his early works.

In addition, Kley also worked as a book illustrator. His thematic repertoire included chivalric novels (*Löwenburg, Eine Geschichte aus Schwabens Vergangenheit/Löwenburg, A Tale from Swabia's Past*, 1891), adventure novels (*The Swiss Family Robinson*, 1899), and heroic legends (*Heldensagen/Heroic Legends*, circa 1901), working in a strong academic style. Of course, these "bread and butter" assignments did little for his artistic development.

Attempts to Work as an Independent Painter

Despite his prolonged lack of success, Kley did not give up hope that he would one day be able to make a living as an independent painter. From 1888 onward, he participated in important international art exhibitions in Munich and Berlin with portraits, still lifes, and genre scenes; however, these efforts did not garner much encouragement. By joining the Karlsruher Künstlerbund (the Karlsruhe Association of Artists), formed in 1896 and modeled on the "Munich Secession," Kley hoped for an improvement in his situation. This organization engaged in a number of measures aimed at improving the reputation of local artists, both in Germany and abroad, and opening up new sources of income. One of these measures was organizing group exhibitions in which Kley, with mixed sales success, showed oil paintings with Dutch and Belgian motifs.

Nature Studies

Kley's Dutch and Belgian paintings were created in the years around 1900, and were the result of numerous trips to coastal villages of both countries, where he produced many nature studies. These works are evidence of his intensive efforts to develop his skills as a draftsman and resulted in an increasingly freer drawing and painting style that became the basis of his later work.

Career as Painter of Industrial Subject Matter

In 1901, a mere coincidence led to a decisive turn in Kley's professional career. The graphics department of the cast steel company Krupp in Essen (founded in 1812), which was responsible for the company's promotional and advertising material, contacted Kley after seeing his postcards published by Hofkunsthandlung Velten in Karlsruhe. He was hired to create a perspectival drawing of the factory grounds, two watercolors of places with symbolic meaning, and six watercolors with factory interiors. With their topographic accuracy and atmospheric liveliness, these works conveyed an impressive image of Germany's largest steel company. They were printed as postcards, used to illustrate a commemorative publication, and reprinted again as decorations for albums destined to be presents for important clients.

In the following years, Kley received other assignments to portray Krupp locations in Meppen (1905—ten watercolors of the shooting range), Kiel (1906/07—a perspectival drawing of the Germania shipyard) and Rheinhausen (1908—a perspectival drawing of the Friedrich-Alfred-Hütte iron works). These were also reproduced in numerous publications.

At the same time, Kley found inspiration in the various Krupp motifs for his independent artistic work. He repeated and made variations of some of his early watercolors with views of Krupp in Essen, either in the same medium or recreating them as oil paintings. What makes these depictions particularly attractive is the combination of precise draftsmanship and painterly atmosphere, visible in both the rendering of the complex industrial processes, and in the way that Kley captured the fascinating play of light and shadow during steel casting.

Compared with this, Kley's paintings of the activities at the Germania shipyard in Kiel, which had been taken over by Krupp in 1896, seemed somewhat prosaic. Here, the half-finished and finished parts from Essen and Rheinhausen were assembled into war ships and merchant vessels. The subject is usually the construction of the giant hulls on the lipways, or their completion at the waterfront, with human figures relegated to the background.

Workers also play only a minor role in the depictions of the Friedrich-Alfred-Hütte iron works in Rheinhausen, which had begun operations in 1897. Because of its complex layout, the area offered Kley favorable conditions for detailed views of the exterior of the facilities. This allows the viewer to get a good sense of the structure and size of the factory grounds, at the heart of which were the blast furnaces, whose clouds of smoke turned the light and air a peculiarly wan color.

With such drawings, watercolors, and oil paintings, Kley was gradually able to obtain a solid presence at art exhibitions from 1906 onward. Not long after, these works were reprinted or commissioned by illustrated magazines and newspapers. This helped Kley solidify his reputation as a painter of industrial scenes, whose works, by now, were also in demand on the art market.

His intention was neither to glorify industry, nor to point out its dark sides. Rather, he was interested in an atmospheric depiction of the complex production processes in factory halls and on the grounds.

However, a variety of workers' portraits from the steel casting factory in Essen show that Kley always harbored a certain skeptical attitude with regard to industrialization and its human consequences. This becomes even more palpable in Kley's grotesque pen-and-ink drawings, in which realism has been replaced by a vision of devil-like creatures interfering in the production process.

In one of his main works, the painting "Die Krupp'schen Teufel"[6] ("The Krupp Devils"), Kley returns to this idea and relativizes it: The demons do not appear as unholy meddlers, but are instead depicted as forces that can be satisfied and thus tamed. In the end, these later Kley works suggest reconciliation between man and technology is possible.

Relocation to Munich

In 1908, another coincidence occurred that had far-reaching consequences for Kley's career. His friend, the popular Munich-based actor Konrad Dreher (1859–1944) saw a few of

Kley's sketchbooks of humorous, satirical, and grotesque pen and ink drawings (Dreher was visiting with Kley after giving a performance in Karlsruhe). According to an interview Kley gave in the 1920s, he had created these drawings merely for his own relaxation, as well as for the amusement of his wife. Dreher suggested that Kley show these to the Munich-based publisher Albert Langen (1869–1909), who was looking for new staff to work on his magazine *Simplicissimus*. Langen was so excited that he not only published Kley's work in the magazine soon after, but even advised him to move to Munich. In the summer of 1909, Heinrich and Theophanie Kley moved to the Bavarian art capital.

Contributions to Simplicissimus

The satirical magazine *Simplicissimus* had been founded in 1896 by Albert Langen in Munich, and was characterized by a liberal bourgeois outlook. It was the leading opposition paper of the German Empire, and its popularity was largely based on the drawings of its staff artists Karl Arnold (1883–1953), Josef Benedikt Engl (1867–1907), Olaf Gulbransson (1873–1958), Thomas Theodor Heine (1867–1948), Bruno Paul (1874–1968), Ferdinand von Reznicek (1868–1909), Erich Schilling (1885–1945), Wilhelm Schulz (1865–1952), Eduard Thöny (1866–1950), and Rudolf Wilke (1873–1908). In order to ensure that the magazine's profile would be diverse, freelancers were hired in addition to the regular staff, including Käthe Kollwitz (1867–1945), Alfred Kubin (1877–1959), and Heinrich Zille (1858–1929).

Kley was hired as one of these freelancers for the weekly *Simplicissimus*. Between the summer of 1908 until the beginning of the First World War in 1914, every second or third issue featured one or more contributions by Kley. With a few exceptions, most of the 116 works were pen-and-ink drawings, which were for the most part printed on quarter or half-pages in the middle or back section of various issues. Contrary to most of the full-time staff contributions, there was no caption or dialogue to clarify the meaning of Kley's contributions, which usually only included a title to convey the sense of the picture.

Kley's works in *Simplicissimus* were—contrary to that of most of the regular staff—only rarely of a political nature. These drawings have a broad range with regards to content and theme, the various facets of which only become apparent in a broader overview. Fortunately, Kley could count on the support of his publisher for these apolitical, sometimes idiosyncratic drawings.

Albums Published by Albert Langen

When he began his work for *Simplicissimus*, Kley had reached an agreement with Albert Langen that he would publish an album with his humorous, satirical, and grotesque pen and ink drawings—a privilege that was otherwise reserved for full-time staff artists. The considerable success of his first volume (*Skizzenbuch*, 1909) in the press and the book trade moved the Albert Langen publishing house decide to publish two more volumes, *Skizzenbuch II* (1910) and *Leut' und Viecher* (1912), which featured a total of 340 works, apparently in random order. Only a relatively small number of these were printed in *Simplicissimus*, which means that these three volumes saved an important part of Kley's oeuvre from oblivion. In addition, they also made a decisive contribution to the reception of Kley's work in the field of animation.[7]

Contributions to Jugend

Like *Simplicissimus*, the magazine *Jugend*, which had been published since 1896 by Dr. Georg Hirth (1841–1916) in Munich, was also characterized by a liberal bourgeois bent. However, it did not define itself purely as an opposition paper. Rather, its intention was to influence the ethical and aesthetic development of society by providing a diversity of artists with a platform for their ideas. To achieve this goal, the magazine worked with a large number of freelancers.

From 1910 onward, Kley was one of those contributors. When he joined, he was given the honor of designing the traditional carnival issue of the magazine with 32 humorous, satirical, and grotesque contributions. Most of these works were pen-and-ink drawings, some of which were printed in color and can hardly be distinguished from true watercolors. The leitmotif of the issue was the synthesis of antiquarian and modern themes, as suggested by the issues cover, which featured a procession of creatures from myth and fable parading into a wintery Munich.

By the beginning of the First World War, the magazine had published 110 works by Kley at regular intervals. Stylistically and in terms of motifs, they can be compared for the most part with his works for *Simplicissimus* and the albums of the Albert Langen publishing house. A special issue also featured 11 depictions of industrial subjects by Kley. Occasionally, Kley's landscape and topographical imagery in watercolor and oils can also be found in *Jugend*. The small- to medium-size contributions were often printed with an accompanying text.

Assignments for Other Magazines and Publishers

His work for the magazines *Simplicissimus* and *Jugend* helped Kley gain popularity and secure assignments from other magazines. His humorous, satirical, and grotesque pen-and-ink drawings were especially well liked. They can be found in the short-lived Munich-based publications *Hyperion* (1908), and *Licht und Schatten* (1910–13), as well as in the *Berliner Illustrirte Zeitung* (*BIZ*), the illustrated paper that had the highest circulation in the German Empire. By the beginning of the First World War, *BIZ* had published 41 contributions by Kley. Most of these are either illustrations of human and animal stories or industrial depictions of the Vulcan shipyard in Hamburg, of Krupp in Essen, and of AEG in Berlin.

At the same time, Kley was encouraged to resume his activity as a book illustrator, and he received assignments for creating illustrated book covers through the Albert Langen publishing house. He was also hired by the publishers Georg Müller, Berthold Sutter, and Schaffstein. Between 1910 and 1914, he illustrated 10 publications for them. These ranged in genre from epics to stories, poems, historical subjects, fairy tales, and novellas. The illustration of works with a humorous, satirical, or grotesque character, in particular, must have provided the artist with great pleasure.

Collaboration with the Gallerist Franz Josef Brakl

Kley eventually formed a partnership with the extremely successful gallerist Franz Josef Brakl (1854–1935) in 1910 that allowed Kley to gain a solid reputation in the art market. Brakl specialized in the works of the "Munich School," of the artist group "Scholle," as well as in the works of the *Jugend* and *Simplicissimus* artists. He presented these in his elegant premises to an international audience—museums, art associations, merchant colleagues, and private collectors from Germany, Europe, and the United States. By the beginning of the First World War, Brakl had presented at least eight solo exhibitions of Kley's work. They were so successful that Brakl soon started referring to Kley as "his daily bread."[8] Of course, this did not prevent the gallerist from occasionally taking serious advantage of the artist, who tended to be somewhat helpless and naive in business matters. In spite of this, however, their relationship lasted into the early 1920s and was, all things considered, financially very beneficial for both sides.

Private Life

Through Konrad Dreher, Heinrich and Theophanie Kley were introduced into the social circles of other *Simplicissimus* and *Jugend* artists. However, with the exception of the sculptor Eduard Beyrer and his wife Elisabeth, there is little evidence that this resulted in any lasting, close friendships. Presumably, the artist's relationship with most of the members of these social circles was characterized mostly by a mutual collegial respect. Not infrequently, Kley showed interest in their work, as is evident in the bookplate-like drawings on flyleaves in books by the *Simplicissimus* editor Korfiz Holm and *Jugend* editor Karl Ettlinger. At the same time, they are proof of a genuine shared sympathy, as is also documented by mutual letters of gratitude and congratulation over a period of multiple decades.

First World War

The First World War did not immediately affect Kley. As a result of his age, he was not conscripted, nor did he volunteer. Because of years of heavy workloads, as well as the need to care for his wife, who had by now become gravely ill, Kley discontinued his work for *Simplicissimus* and the *BIZ* and put his artistic activities on hold. Only *Jugend* magazine occasionally still published contributions by him. This made Kley more and more financially dependent on selling works created in earlier years through Franz Josef Brakl.

Weimar Republic

At the beginning of the Weimar Republic, Kley briefly resumed his work for *Simplicissimus* (1918–20), and also made some contributions to other magazines (*Der Orchideengarten*, 1919–21; *Exlex*, 1918–20; and *Weltecho*, 1919).

He also once again became intensely engaged in book illustration (1921 alone saw the publication of five books illustrated by Kley, including fables, morality plays, travel and adventure novels, as well as political-visionary stories). His most ambitious project, however—an illustrated edition of *Faust*—was never published.

The humorous, satirical, and grotesque pen-and-ink drawings of the artist continued to be well liked: For his 60th birthday in 1923, the Albert Langen publishing house brought out the *Sammelalbum*, which contained over 240 works from the three albums published before the First World War.

Kley's personal situation in the first years of the Weimar Republic was quite difficult. The death of his wife in 1922 threw him into a state of crisis, which led him to break off contact with the people around him, and he gained a reputation as an oddball and loner. As a result of the hyperinflation of 1923, the artist also lost all his savings.

These and other factors led Kley to focus on his career as a painter of industrial motifs in the years that followed.

His most important client became the Mannheim-based civil engineering firm Grün & Bilfinger. He had been in contact with the company before the First World War, and during the 1920s Kley received commissions for watercolors with views of the hydroelectric plants and bridges the firm had built.

Kley also worked for the MAN (Maschinenfabrik Augsburg-Nürnberg) corporation. The Deutsches Museum in Munich had asked the company to commission and donate a monumental image depicting the "Kaiser-Wilhelm-Brücke über das Wuppertal bei Müngsten" ("Kaiser-Wilhelm-Bridge over the Wuppertal at Müngsten"),[9] which had been constructed by MAN at the end of the 19th century. Kley executed the painting in 1925. The company must have been satisfied with the result, because Kley continued to receive further commissions for watercolors and oil paintings depicting their machines and equipment into the early 1940s.

For the Berlin-based fire prevention company Minimax, Kley created a dozen humorous, satirical, and grotesque pen-and-ink drawings in 1926, in addition to watercolors depicting their factory grounds and halls. The drawings advertised a cylindrical hand-held fire extinguisher, and were among his most successful graphic works for advertising.

After marrying Emily Segisser (1878–1970) in 1928, Heinrich Kley was able to face life with renewed courage. Segisser had previously been married to an artist from Karlsruhe, and probably knew Kley from his hometown. She was a strong supporter of him and encouraged him to turn toward humorous, satirical, and grotesque pen-and-ink drawings again. With a few exceptions, he had made very few drawings in that vein following the death of his first wife and the ensuing period of grief.

From 1928 to 1933, Kley was again a strong presence in the pages of *Jugend*, contributing many drawings in his earlier style. In 1930, he executed his last big book illustration assignment for the animal fable "Reineke Fuchs" ("Reineke the Fox"). The artist also resumed his work for the *BIZ* around this time.

From 1928 until the end of his life, Kley was involved with the utopian project "Atlantropa." The project's originator—Herman Sörgel (1885–1952) an architect/engineer, and friend of Kley's—had suggested lowering the water level of the Mediterranean by building two dams at Gibraltar and the Dardanelles, thereby uniting Africa and Europe into a super continent. In Sörgel's mind, this would solve some of the urgent issues of the future, such as energy production, the creation of new human habitations, and a geopolitical balance vis-à-vis America and Asia. The artist's job was to visualize these ideas. Kley was a skilled creator of topographical and technical paintings, and he—like other reputable architects and city planners—willingly contributed his skills to this project, which seems rather eccentric by today's standards.

Third Reich

In the very first weeks of the Third Reich's rise to prominence, Kley stopped working for *Jugend* magazine. In the process of the Nazi government's consolidation of institutional powers (the so-called Gleichschaltung policy), the magazine had become a target. Kley was intent not to make matters worse with his irreverent pen-and-ink drawings. He also stopped working for the *BIZ*.

Due to his increasingly deteriorating state of health, Kley had to undergo numerous operations from 1934 onward. But these health setbacks only account for a small part of his diminished artistic output. Kley's declining artistic output was mostly due to his reserved attitude toward the Nazi government and his decision to wait until the end of 1938 before applying for membership in the Reichskammer der Bildenden Künste (Reich Chamber of Fine Arts). His application was accepted, despite the fact that authorities' had suspicions about his political attitudes. Once accepted in the Chamber, Kley was then able to again take on assignments from MAN (until 1942) as well as from the machine manufacturer Voith in Heidenheim an der Brenz (1940).

This, however, didn't stop the Reichsschrifttumskammer (Reich Chamber of Literature) from putting Kley's *Sammelalbum* on the "List of Harmful and Unwanted Publications" in 1939. As a result, the printing plates used for the *Sammelalbum* were destroyed, remaining copies in the book trade were seized, and copies found in private homes were confiscated. Despite this, following the invitation of his former colleague Karl Arnold, the artist resumed his work for *Simplicissimus* and, between 1941 and 1943, published 22 pen-and-ink drawings. For the most part, these are characterized by a rather harmless sense of humor, which, from a stylistic point of view, points to a waning of Kley's strength.

From 1943 until his death on February 8, 1945, Kley spent extended periods of time in hospitals, and even when at home he remained mostly confined to bed. During this time, he was cared for by his devoted wife, who also saved his artistic estate from destruction. She spent the last months of the war in the village of Polling, close to Munich. Until the end of her life, she made it her task to preserve the memory of her husband, and to make his work accessible to the public.[10]

Notes

1. The essay is based on the author's dissertation, *Heinrich Kley (1863–1945), Leben und Werk* (Weimar, 2010), hereafter cited as Kunkel. It contains all bibliographical and source references cited in this summary.

2. Franz Hein's *Wille und Weg, Lebenserinnerungen eines deutschen Malers* (Leipzig 1924, p. 100). (*Will and Way, Memoirs of a German Painter*), hereafter cited as Hein. Franz Hein (1863–1927) was a fellow student with Heinrich Kley at the Karlsruhe School of Fine Arts. In his memoirs, he provides insight into the private circumstances of the artist during his student years.

3. Hein, p. 73.

4. A reproduction of the work is in Kunkel, p. 40.

5. A reproduction of the work is in Kunkel, p. 48.

6. A reproduction of the work is in Kunkel, p. 94.

7. See the author's essay in *The Lost Art of Heinrich Kley, Volume 1* regarding Kley's influence on Walt Disney and his animators.

8. Anton Sailer's *Die Bretter waren sein Sprungbrett* (*The Planks Were His Jumping Board*). Published in *Süddeutsche Zeitung* (August 18, 1966, p. 13). The painter and art journalist Anton Sailer (1903–87) befriended Heinrich Kley in the 1920s and published numerous essays about him. The quote is taken from an article about Franz Josef Brakl, who, before embarking on career as an art dealer, was the director of the Gärtnerplatztheater in Munich.

9. A reproduction of the work is in Kunkel, p. 192.

10. In 1953, the Wilhelm-Busch-Museum in Hannover presented a retrospective exhibition on Heinrich Kley curated by Emily Kley. In 1954, it could be seen in an altered form in the Badischer Kunstverein (Art Association of Baden) in Karlsruhe. In 1962 and 1964, she organized two more exhibitions commemorating her husband, in collaboration with the Munich gallerist Wolfgang Gurlitt (1888–1965).

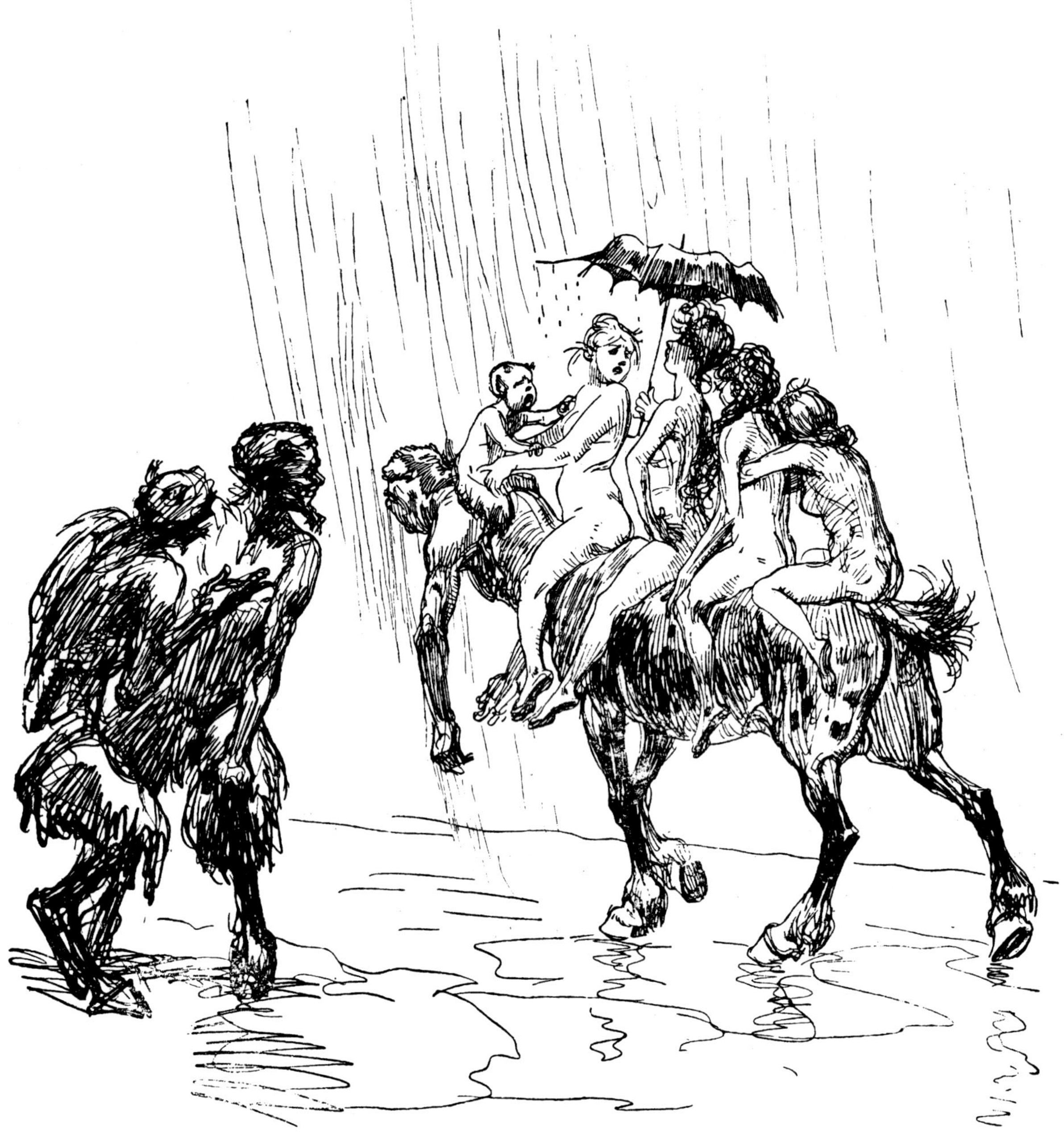

APPRECIATION

Kley's Distinction

Jesse Hamm

I was in my late teens at the San Diego Comic-Con International when I approached the booth of one of the largest publishers and asked the editor seated there to review my art. He consented, but before opening my portfolio, he paused and asked who my influences were. Too many names to list came to mind, so I combed back to my first happy encounters with art in the books my parents kept around the house, and one name emerged: "Heinrich Kley." The editor grinned with surprise at Kley's name and told me how refreshing it was to meet a young artist with taste: "Everyone else just names the Flavor-of-the-Month!" He described a recent show of Kley originals he'd seen at a gallery in New York, and we both enthused awhile over the German master's greatness. We soon returned to Earth, and when he opened my portfolio I realized then that the last thing you should do when trying to impress someone with your art is remind them of one of the finest draftsmen who ever lived. All of my drawings suddenly looked sad and empty, and the enthusiasm on the editor's face shrank to nothing. As I awaited my inevitable spanking, I gazed at the artwork displayed around the booth, and it occurred to me that this editor and his publisher had as much cause for shame as I did. For all our love of Kley and the heights he achieved, we trafficked in mediocrity.

Cartoonist Wally Wood, reflecting on his own fantasy masterpiece, "The Wizard King," reportedly said that it was "the closest I ever came to the real thing." His cryptic phrase, "the real thing," is an odd choice of words to describe a fantasy, but I think fans of the genre know what he meant. "The real thing" evokes what Tolkien called "eucatastrophe," what C. S. Lewis called "the Northernness," and what E. M. Forster, speaking not only of fantasy but any fiction that touches infinity, called simply "prophecy." If good fiction is an account in which everything is true but the facts, then perhaps good fantasy fiction is the most obviously true, since its facts are the most obviously false. At the heart of the best fantasies is a molten core of truth, blazing all the more clearly amid the dross of their fairytale falsehoods. At that convention in San Diego, where I stood surrounded by superheroes, monsters, and elves, all I could see was the dross. But in Kley's oeuvre, among satyrs, centaurs and fairies, we see the real thing.

Schooled in the late 19th century, a high point in the teaching of realistic art, Kley had a considerable advantage over artists of today. His teachers, Ferdinand von Keller and Carl Frithjof Smith, were themselves superb painters, and Kley spent at least five years training at schools whose standards at the time must have been rigorous. Judging by the ease with which he later drew animals, it's likely that life-drawing sessions at the Karlsruhe Zoo were common. It's also likely that his German upbringing would have instilled in Kley an iron work ethic. This was no art school dilettante, who needs to play a few more video games and smoke some joints before drawing his weekly webcomic. The young Kley would have turned out sketches by the tens of thousands, achieving a practiced authority seen more often today in blue-collar workers, like those taco cart chefs who can fold a burrito faster than you can sneeze. As his miraculous drawings demonstrate, he paid his dues.

But Kley's contemporaries received similar training without achieving his results. The period produced many great portrayers of fantasy: Gérôme, Alma-Tadema, Bouguereau, Doré, Pyle, Parrish, Dulac, Burne-Jones, Waterhouse, and so on...name after brilliant name, none of whom were able to bring their fanciful figures to life quite as vividly as Kley. I recall my mother's preference for Kley's equestrian drawings to those of Leonardo Da Vinci. She pointed out that Da Vinci's horses, while anatomically accurate, were rounded off and idealized. Though a horse-lover herself, Mom had been bucked off and kicked in the face by horses; she knew that Da Vinci's regal creatures failed to tell the whole story. Kley's horses instead had the abrupt angles, knobby joints, straining sinews, and nervous energy of the real thing. His humans, too, exhibit a naturalism absent from the work of his eminent peers. Kley's naked people look more like nudists than nudes. They lack the arched backs and pointed toes of nudes by Norman Lindsay or William Russell Flint; they seem instead like folks you'd see frying tofu burgers at a beach, wearing only Birkenstocks and barking at their kids. This contrast recalls the philosophical shift from Titian's supernal Venus of Urbino to Manet's earthy Olympia. Clearly, Kley followed Manet's outlook rather than Titian's. In this, among fantasists, he was largely alone.

Kley's naturalism was abetted by his peculiar technique. Most portrayers of fantasy seem eager to establish the reality of their scenes by fussing over every detail. But Kley's seemingly haphazard linework makes it seem as though he sketched his bizarre scenes from life,

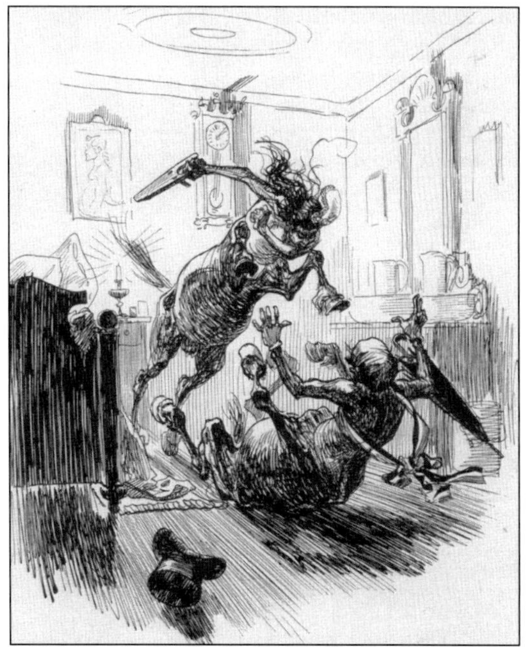

"The Battle-tested Veteran"
An interesting example of Kley's equestrian drawing, which also demonstrates his anatomical savvy and attention to detail by his inclusion of horse teats (a detail often missed by artists drawing horses, especially in fantasy scenes like this one) near the crotch of the female centaur.

"Ground Floor Acrobatics"

Another example of Kley searching for the right placement of feet. This one is notable because he just hatches over his prior attempts when he could easily have whited them out. His choice to obscure them without obliterating them implies that his intention was simply to serve the drawing (by focusing viewers on his final foot placement), rather than to hide his failed attempts due to vanity.

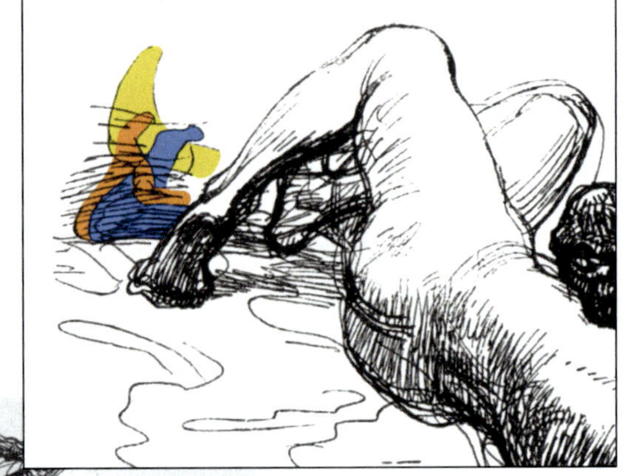

perhaps while watching them from a bench in the park. We often see false starts among his figures' limbs, as though he tried placing a foot here or there before deciding against it. This indicates that he sketched his drawings directly in ink, without pencil preliminaries—practically heresy in the fantasy art genre. Even other notably spontaneous artists tend to plan ahead before their bravura performances. J. S. Sargent was known to do numerous preliminaries for weeks, sometimes painting a face repeatedly before settling on the appropriate flurry of seemingly tossed-off strokes. Peter Arno and Charles Saxon, *The New Yorker's* maestros of spontaneity, both littered their floors with sketches of each cartoon before executing the final, apparently facile drawing. James Montgomery Flagg blocked in his ink drawings beforehand in pencil, and made extensive use of models. Today, even the most flamboyant comic book artists typically rely on a "wire-framing" method, whereby figures' poses and volumes are first established with sketches of boxes, ovals, and cylinders (representing a "wire frame" of the body) before clothing and other features are added. This helps the artist visualize figures in poses which are too acrobatic or violent to be modeled in real life. But then there was Kley, dashing it all in straight from his head, not even bothering to white out the occasional third or fourth leg. His strange, violent scenes also make the use of photo reference or life models unlikely, or even impossible. Not only does he populate his scenes with mythically implausible beasts, not only do his animals often gesture and walk and sit upright like humans, but we see subtler unlikelihoods throughout his work, such as snails and an elephant galloping (anatomical impossibilities), horses lying on the ground (a rarity in real life), or women wrestling and fighting in the nude (visible in some films today, but try finding such a sight in fin de siècle Germany!).

So by both method and subject matter, Kley bound himself to draw alla prima, without visual precedent in either preliminary sketch or reference model. No rehearsal, no safety net. A possible benefit of this approach is that it gave him greater access to his subconscious. Actors talk about the inspiration that occurs when ad-libbing on film, or when performing live before an audience: the brain panics, adrenaline flows, and ideas erupt that would never have found their way through the ordered pathways of a more sedate mind. Similarly, by performing "live," Kley probably gave fuller rein to his deepest impulses than he would have by beginning each piece with careful planning. My mother, a sign language interpreter, once told me that the greatest inspiration in her career came from a drunken bum she saw lying on the sidewalk outside the post office one day.

"The Joys of Skiing"

He was apparently deaf, and was signing "out loud" to himself about how badly he needed another drink. Mom said his signs rolled off his fingers with greater confidence and fluidity than she had ever seen, even among the deaf, and she made it a personal quest to achieve that grace in her own signing. It's tempting to joke that she should simply have taken up booze, and I doubt that advice would have been far wrong. The deaf drunk's advantage was liquid courage: It ensured he didn't care who saw him. Kley's bold approach also forced him to be courageous, likely granting him a similar advantage.

Kley's sketches have been rightly described as loose, but I think his admirers are incorrect when they describe his method as "fast" or "frantic." They probably assume his sketches were done rapidly because of their resemblance to gesture drawings. Gesture drawing is a method used by artists to sharpen their ability to imagine and delineate three-dimensional forms on the page. The artist places the tip of his pen on the page and scribbles lines around an imagined form—as though wrapping an invisible man in string—often without lifting the pen from the page. (Cartoonist John Buscema called this "one-line drawing." Prime examples of such, and of wire-framing, can be seen in his 1978 book *How To Draw Comics the Marvel Way.*) The rapidity of the method prevents the artist from considering each line by itself, disciplining him to see the volume instead of the lines that describe it. Gesture drawing is crucial to developing volumetric insight, and Kley doubtless relied on it heavily to achieve his skill at drawing convincing figures from any angle. However, most of the Kley drawings from his period as a cartoonist don't appear to me to be gesture drawings. When we compare his sketches with similarly loose work by other masters of drawing, such as Jules Feiffer or Frank Frazetta, telling differences emerge. In Frazetta's sketches, his contour lines are usually rounded and corner-free. They tend to be of varying thickness, implying the varied pressure of speedy strokes. His textures and shadings are almost all "scribbled"—that is, a quick back-and-forth zig-zag rather than hatched parallel lines. Feiffer's sketches are similar: The overall impression is one of speed. But in Kley's drawings, the contour lines are usually thin and of uniform thickness. He also includes delicate corners and angles that indicate a more carefully exploratory approach, and he frequently hatches, with parallel lines that are surprisingly straight and evenly spaced. This orderliness of line suggests a pace that was deliberate and unhurried.

An unhurried pace would have allowed Kley to enter that zone of calm focus we associate with a child at play: absorbed by his task, but unworried by it. Kley filled many of his drawings with a great level of detail, rendered with consistently high accuracy—a feat that demands tremendous creative energy. Personally, I find that if I spend my creative energy at the pace at which it comes, letting the satisfaction of each accomplishment fuel each next step, my energy replenishes itself, and I can continue working all day. But if I allow external pressures to hurry me beyond the pace of that refueling, I spend myself dry, tire, and lose focus, and the quality of the details begins to slip. Densely detailed drawings are especially vulnerable to this problem, given the many choices they represent and the threat they pose to deadlines. The temptation is to hurry, burn out, and fall back on shortcuts or sloppy hackwork. But Kley's densely detailed drawings, and the amazingly consistent level of concentration they

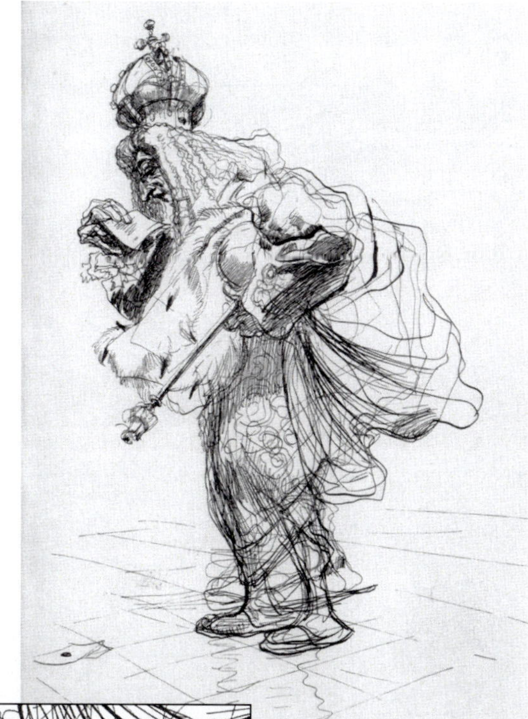

"His Most Exalted Highness"

A color-coded example of Kley searching for the right placement of feet and limbs.

"Poppy Day" (top), "The Pickpocket," and "At the Hofbräu" (bottom)

Good examples of what I suspect Kley's process to have been most of the time: light contour drawing followed by hatching and scribbles. Especially notable here are the orderly, parallel hatchings of lines (most visible on the background figures) that defined the forms before he scribbled in texture and shading.

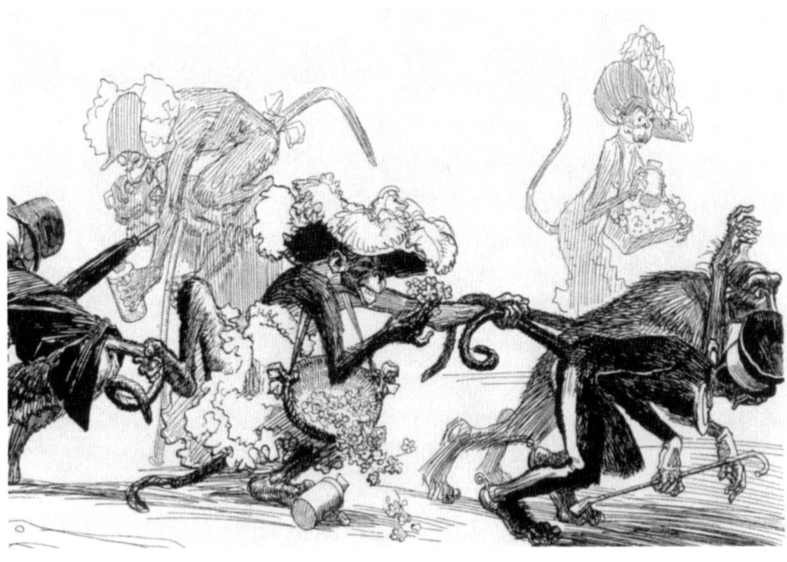

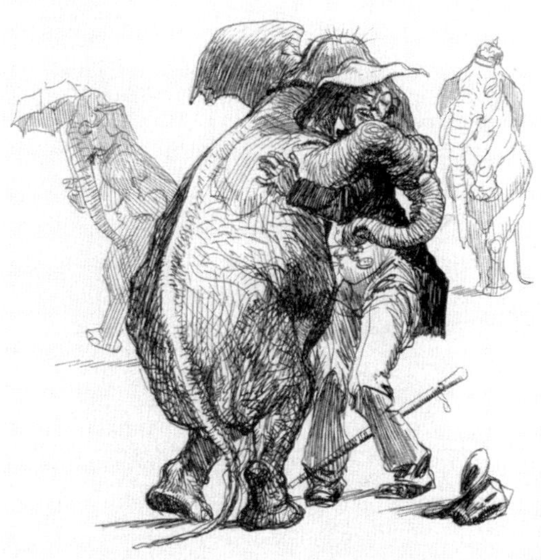

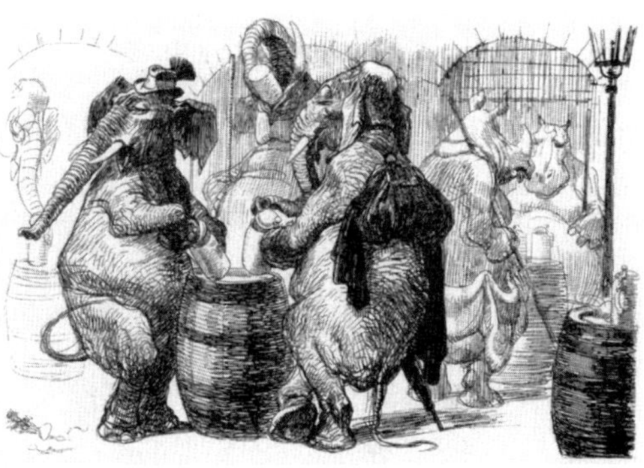

represent, indicate that he disciplined himself to remain calmly "in the zone" from start to finish.

Kley's working methods are unknown to me, but his less-finished drawings, and the less-finished figures at the outer edges of his more-finished drawings, offer some clues to their creation. Apparently, he would begin with gentle outlines of the figures' contours, followed by hatchings of parallel lines to lightly define the planes of the forms, and then add "washes" of looping, back-and-forth scribble lines, to denote shadows of various densities, finishing with the thickest, darkest strokes of black. This approach would have allowed him to include nuances of form and shadow, controlling the lighting in a way that rapid gestural lines would tend to interrupt. It would also allow him to carefully block in props and backgrounds that a more frantic pace would have precluded.

Kley's sketches do feature a greater variety of objects than are present in most other artists' sketches and cartoons. He was clearly a devotee of what I call "pure drawing"—that is, drawing motivated mainly by the desire to portray visual phenomena (textures, shapes, lines, activity, and volumes), rather than by the pictured object's sentimental appeal. Many artists take up drawing in order to render pretty women, or some other subject fascinating in its own right, and not for the sake of drawing itself. Such artists tend to avoid drawing subjects that fall beyond their area of interest, or draw such subjects in a perfunctory and mediocre way. This is especially true in the fantasy genre. But Kley drew everything with creativity, skill, and careful attention. Buildings, furniture, machinery, flora, fauna, men and women (young and old), beauties, horrors, props of all kinds, fanciful or mundane—nothing fell outside his wheelhouse. The world he shows us is therefore all the richer and more credible than his whimsical subjects seem to deserve.

Returning to Kley's general outlook, we find a strange departure from the arc followed by Manet and subsequent modern artists. Manet, Courbet, Millet, and other mid-19th century realists moved away from the practice—traditional from the Greeks through the Renaissance—of idealizing humanity. During Kley's era, people were increasingly pictured in less noble states than was traditional in fine art, and his drawings certainly reflect this shift. Far from the Renaissance ideal, or even the wan nobility of a Sargent or Whistler, Kley's figures lie around carousing in the nude, and find themselves in awkward and even humiliating positions. But by the time of Klimt, Kollwitz, Kokoschka, and Schiele, Kley's fellow Germanic masters of drawing, portrayals of people reached a nadir of lostness. Drawn figures in cutting-edge art became sickly and corpse-like; grieving, staring, masturbating, their faces sagging with ennui. They usually appear without backgrounds, and at eye level, so not even the viewer's vantage point can place them in a context—physical or moral—larger than themselves. When they revel, sin, or suffer, it's in a vacuum; there's no "good" to grant their sad condition the honor of tragedy by its remoteness, nor their pleasure the honor of joy by its accord. This is where Kley parts company with his brethren.

Kley's people—and their animal counterparts—are engaged with the world. They have more in common with Hieronymus Bosch's people than the Moderns', which is to say that even in their mortification they occupy a context. Though Kley shared the Moderns' refusal to deify Man, he didn't share their refusal to deify God. I don't know what his religious beliefs were, if any, but his artwork seems to assume at least one "God": the artist himself, and the viewer who shares his vantage point—a holy trinity of two persons, against whose opinions the characters are weighed. Unlike the Germanic masters listed above, Kley rarely crops his figures, often places them in environments, and almost never lets them look the viewer in the eye. They perform for us at a distance, visible from head to toe in their little world, looking anywhere but at us, apparently unaware of our omniscient gaze. The absurdity or grace of their poses suggests the approval or disapproval of their God, and their prop-filled environments allow Kley to make pointed juxtapositions that reveal his divine opinion of the pictured events. In one scene, shoppers ignore religious icons in favor of foreign novelties; in another, clergymen picnic happily beneath a statue of the crucified Christ; elsewhere, a demon winces with disgust at the smell of an industrial smokestack. In essence, Kley uses physical landscapes to show us his moral landscape (inscrutable though it often is). If Classical artists placed humanity on a pedestal, and the Moderns removed that pedestal, Kley shows humanity beside the pedestal, and our absurd attempts to climb on or off.

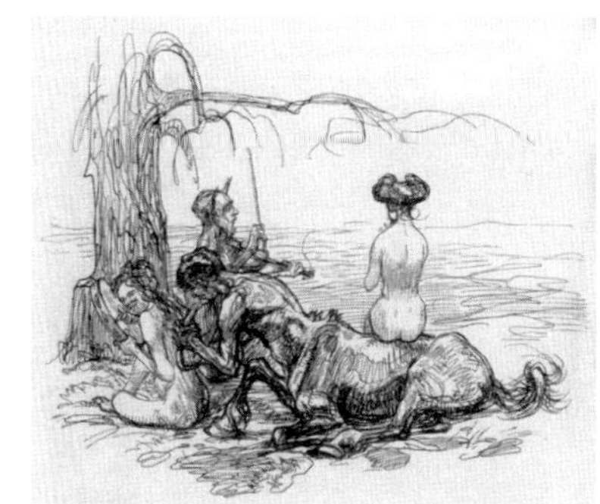

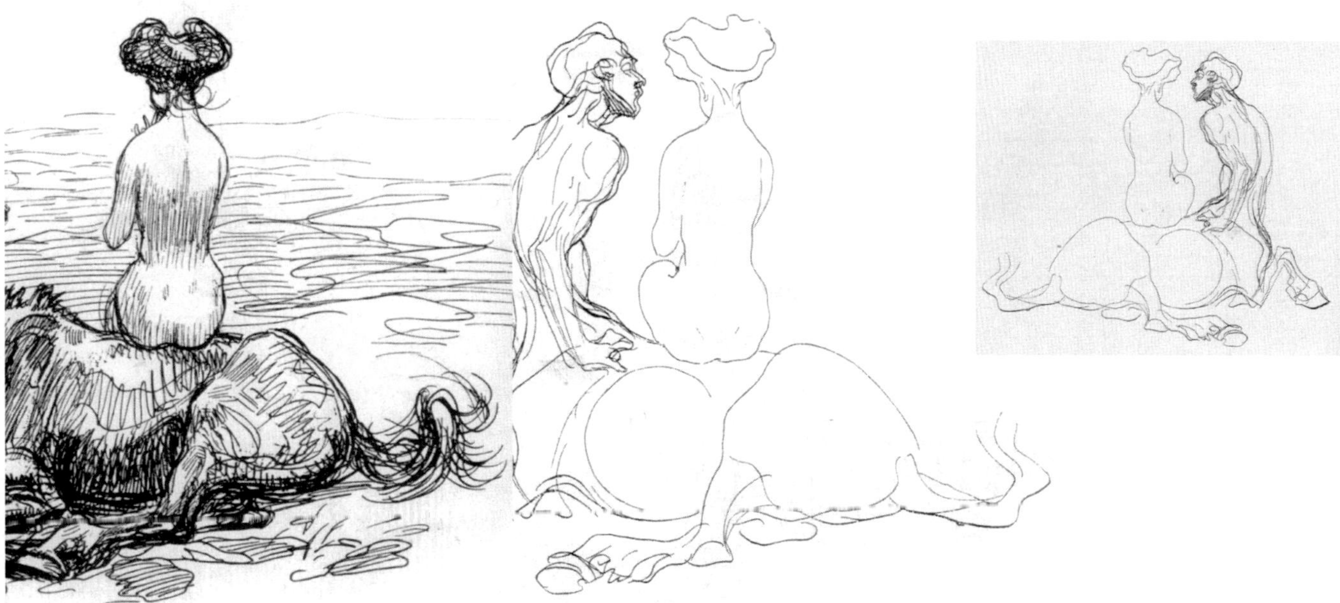

A reconstruction of how Kley's drawings may have progressed, comparing a finished drawing (left) with a less finished, unrelated-but-similar sketch (right), which is flopped to aid the comparison. We can see how he might have mapped out his forms with light contours before building up the volumes and shadows with hatched lines and scribbles.

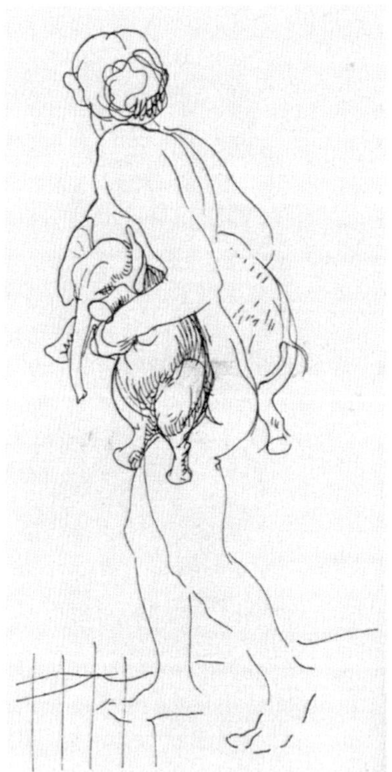

Another example of the contour sketching that may have occurred at the beginning of the drawing process. Note the broken contour of the woman's back foot, indicating the way Kley searched out its position. ▶

Thus, Kley turned away from the philosophical trends of his fine art milieu, and into the lowly realm of cartooning, where his brand of irreverent moralizing has always been welcome. What distinguishes his work from other cartoonists', apart from his monumental skill, is that it defies categorization. His art is often described as erotic, humorous, or satirical, but on the whole it occupies none of those categories. Despite his many nudes, genitals rarely appear in Kley's art, areolae are virtually absent, and pubic hair is rarely seen: groins are obscured by limbs, or fade gradually into shadow. Flirtation is common, but sex itself hardly makes an appearance, and the characters physiques and behavior rarely seem designed to arouse the viewer. Similarly, surprisingly few of his drawings attempt to evoke laughter; most are content to be quirky or odd. Even there, the oddness is not of a flavor distinct enough to be claimed by any one subculture. Beardsley and Charles Addams may be claimed by the goths, Gary Larson by the nerds, Crumb by stoners, Sendak by dreamers, but Kley belongs to no one. He makes occasional stabs at satire or social comment—the fat pastor asleep beneath a bleeding crucifix is one, a critic peeing ink onto a painting is another—but in general Kley's message is too obtuse to fit the mold of satire. His pictures resemble fairytales rather than fables: more interested in framing life than explaining it. In one drawing—"Die Weinlese" ("Gathering Grapes")—several figures harvest grapes from the grape-clad body of a larger figure. Grapes

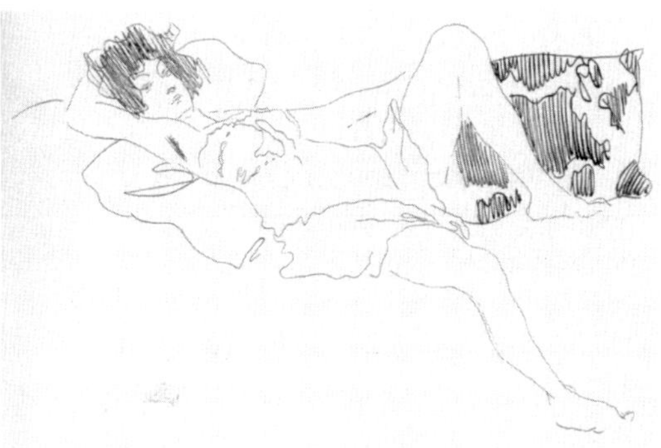

▲ A prime example of the delicate contour sketching that probably undergirded Kley's more developed drawings.

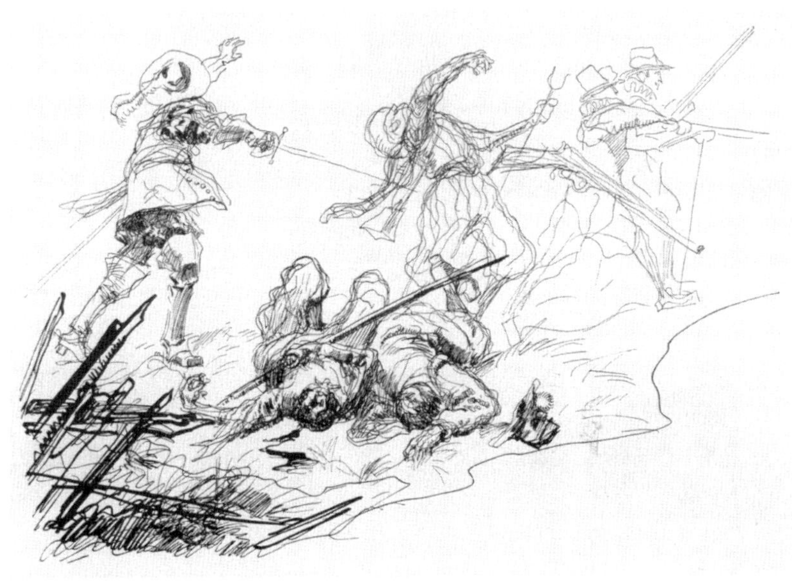

The progression of detail here, from the far figures at the right to the near figures at the left, is another good example of Kley's apparent process: light contour drawing followed by shading and textures. ▶

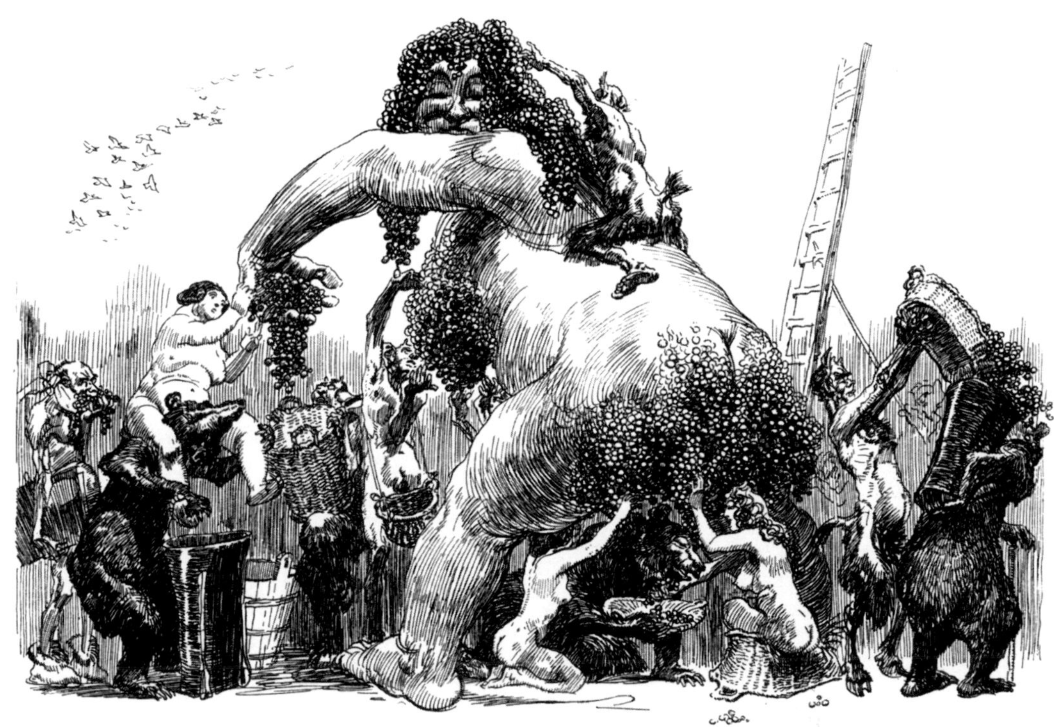

"Gathering Grapes"

grow from her head and breasts, possibly representing womanhood or motherhood...but they also grow from her buttocks, representing who-knows-what. Among the harvesters are Kley's usual nude women and satyrs, perhaps representing bacchanalia, but we also see a potbellied man in slippers and some humanoid bears, representing...what? Representing nothing specific, other than life's grand pageant, and a mood of happy work. This is not the sort of cartoon we would ever find in *The New Yorker*, or stuck to a refrigerator or cubicle wall. It's like the imaginings of someone drifting off to sleep: nearly coherent, but wandering toward absurdity. Most of Kley's work is this way, thankfully. Like a book that doesn't match the shape of any bookshelf, and must therefore remain out where it can be browsed, Kley's art has weird edges that prevent it from fitting neat categories, inviting us to peruse and consider it again and again. Other books of cartoons or drawings can be deemed read and done, but we never finish reading Kley; we only take breaks. We don't own his images, we visit them, and in this way they offer the "real thing" that the best fantasy strives to reveal.

***Jesse Hamm** is a cartoonist and illustrator in Portland, Oregon. His artwork and essays can be found at www.JesseHamm.com.*

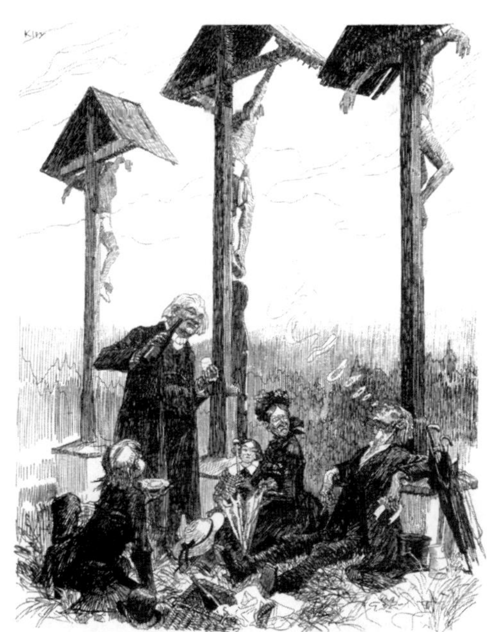

"Picnic"

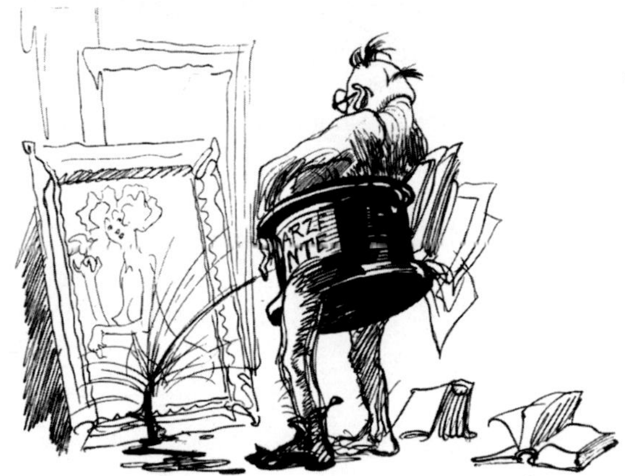

"Art Criticism"

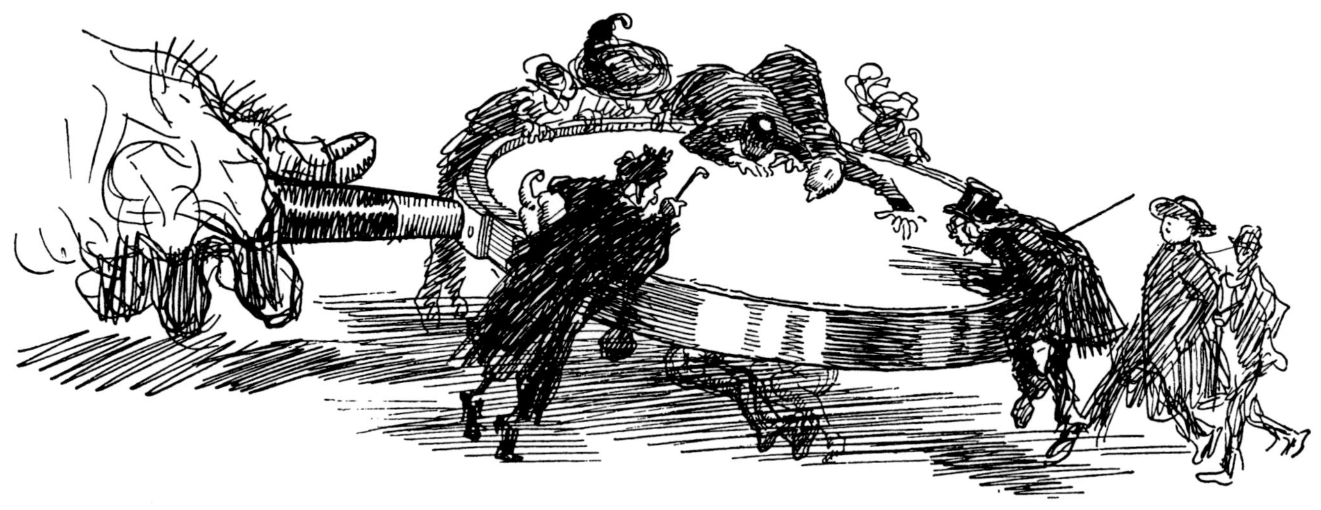

INTERVIEW

Heinrich Kley: Exploring The Enigma

Alexander Kunkel
interviewed by
Joseph V. Procopio

Much of what has been written about Kley in the past century or so, in English or German, has been piecemeal conjectures or flat-out falsehoods. That all changed in the past couple of years when German art historian Alexander Kunkel devoted his doctoral thesis to Kley's life and work, finally providing the scholarly attention this artist so richly deserves. Kunkel has subsequently organized exhibits of Kley's work, and is now recognized as the preeminent authority on this subject. Although *The Lost Art of Heinrich Kley, Volumes 1 & 2* include definitive biography and analysis of Kley for the first time in English, the following interview attempts to complement that information by exploring with Kunkel some facets of the enigmatic artist not easily covered in these books' other essays.

When did you first encounter Heinrich Kley's work?
I was about 16 years old, still going to school, and I happened upon an antiquarian book shop here in Munich where they sold a lot of illustrated books from the late 19th and early 20th century. This is where I found one of the albums that were published before World War I. I think it was *Skizzenbuch* or *Skizzenbuch II.*

I was just fascinated by Kley's very loose line, which did not remind me of anything else I had seen up to that moment. Even though I had been familiar with late 19th century art, I was really astonished when I saw Kley for the first time. So I bought that copy of Skizzenbuch right on. Years later, of course, I started to do some more intensive research on Kley.

Right...I think I was about the same age, actually. Like most Americans familiar with Kley, I came across one of the Dover reprints, and I was fascinated by it. Just the exuberance of his line, and the subject matter was so fanciful and imaginative. What else attracted you to Kley's art? What qualities do you like best in his work?
Kley, on the one hand, had really great craftsmanship. He was a draftsman capable of depicting any kind of subject…there is really no single subject that seems to be too hard to draw for him.

But this versatility is just part of his appeal. Irrespective of that, even though you see hundreds of lines in a Kley drawing, they all seem to be very light and have a kind of inner logic, despite being very dazzling and furious. Everything is combined in a way that has the feel of a single entity, of a whole. So you have a combination of a very personal style with extraordinary technical skills.

But on top of all of that is Kley's great imagination, his great fantasy, his wonderful ideas. His drawings contain a lot of puns and play on words, which inspire a whole other level of consideration in his drawings, how he translates those puns into drawing.

There's a kind of intellectual process when trying to understand the true meaning of a Kley drawing. Like an intellectual puzzle game, which I like a lot. And he obviously had a great sense of humor. His humor can be very light and broad, but it can also be very deep, very tentative. This is why I don't tire of looking at these drawings again and again. I think this explains why a lot of other people might feel similarly about his work.

There's a philosophical complexity or depth to some of his work...
Yes. And it's never "over-ripe." It's never too obvious or cheap. He would not go for the easy laugh, yet a broad audience would still understand. It's a bit more thoughtful. And Kley has a kind of "aristocratic" sense of humor, even though it still appeals to a wide range of people. It's never too plain. It's never too easy.

Yes... There's an esoteric or idiosyncratic quality to it.
Absolutely.

What was the most surprising or interesting thing you learned about Kley while doing your research?
Let's put it like this: There was nearly no scholarly work on Kley when I started my research. There were only some two or three little articles that were published during Kley's lifetime, containing very general information. The most helpful article I could start with was simply the entry in the art historical dictionary, Thieme-Becker, which provided some general information: where Kley lived, what kind of topics he painted, and in what exhibitions he participated...things like that. So, I really had to start basically from nothing.

With Kley, it was not like researching one of those great artists whose life has been described many times by various authors, and during your own research you find something completely new and astonishing. Kley was nearly unknown, had completely fallen into oblivion, so this was the heart of what was so surprising and interesting about my research. It was like a puzzle or a mosaic, you know? You put one stone next to the other, and then you have to rearrange everything because you can see, well, it doesn't really work out very well like this, so let's try this instead...

...you have a combination of a very personal style with extraordinary technical skills.

It sounds like you really had to unravel Kley's life story. What can you tell me about Kley's work habits? Technique? Artistic influences?
Let's start with the last one. As you know, he was an academically trained artist, so Kley had a very typical kind of education. And his teacher, Ferdinand von Keller, had I think two or three great artistic qualities. One was that he really had a great sense for colors. Not only the different kinds of effects, but an understanding of how to paint with color.

But von Keller also had a great, almost baroque sense of composition. Very complex compositions, with many elements, but with a unity or integrity to the whole. He had a kind of great sense for the entirety of a work. And von Keller was also a great animal painter. He painted some historical subjects in which horses play essential roles, where there's a lot of strength, power, and real vitality in the horses.

I think these are qualities that were an eye-opener for Kley, and that formed his artistic approach.

And then, of course, I assume that Kley was a very curious person. And by that I mean he must have visited a lot of local art exhibitions as well as the large exhibitions held in the great artistic centers of Germany—Munich, Berlin—especially when he was in his student years. Munich and Berlin would hold great

...Kley definitely had a very broad knowledge about the art of his time as well as that of the old masters and of 19th century artists.

artistic exhibitions once a year or even more often, apart from just the permanent collections that were always on display in those cities' museums. So Kley definitely had a very broad knowledge about the art of his time as well as that of the old masters and of 19th century artists.

There are so many allusions in a lot of Kley's drawings...he doesn't quote or copy anything, but he must have been exposed to certain paintings, certain masters, certain styles, such as the symbolist paintings by Arnold Böckling or Franz von Stuck.

So, what about Kley's technique? I don't think that Kley's foremost strength was painting in oil. It would take a lot of time for him to work in that medium, and compared with his watercolors and drawings, the oil paintings look a little bit dry. One can see that the true medium in which he must have preferred to work in was watercolor and pen-and-ink.

You really get a sense of energy in those watercolors and pen-and-inks...
Exactly. He could be more spontaneous. He didn't have to think for weeks about one subject. Sometimes when I try to imagine how he was as a person or as an artist, I picture him as someone who had thousands of ideas in his mind, and he would look for the best medium to bring them down onto paper in a very quick, very short period of time. I definitely don't imagine he was someone who enjoyed painting on an oil for months and months. It's a more painstaking process, and it is obvious, if you look at the drawings, that he enjoyed and preferred drawing rather than painting in oil.

So, his industrial paintings, were those watercolors or were they oils?
Actually, he started to paint them as watercolors. The first commission was a series of eight watercolors that were then reproduced as postcards, as illustrations in albums, and things like that. This was about 1901, 1902. In 1905 he would get another commission from the Krupp Company, in which he depicted a kind of military practicing ground.

I think at this time Kley probably thought, "Well, if I can do paintings as watercolors, why shouldn't I try doing oils?" This would have been around 1905 or 1906...not necessarily his formative years, but those years were when he tried to establish himself in a certain kind of niche.

One has to remember that there were really thousands of academic painters at this time in Germany and throughout Europe, and when we look at Kley's early career, he paints, rather ordinary subjects. There are some genre paintings and portraits, there are still lifes, there are landscapes that he would do well, but not extraordinary enough that anybody would remember. These paintings are really very nice, but there were a lot of other skilled artists at that time that could have done them just as well. So for Kley, these industrial paintings were a chance for him to establish himself—to acquire a reputation as a specialist in the field, which in the end he managed to achieve.

One has to keep in mind that...I don't want to say that around the year 1900 drawings and watercolors were considered as something minor in comparison with oils, but obviously, if you go to a museum, you normally see only oil paintings, not drawings or watercolors on the wall. Part of the reason for this has to do with the question of conservation. Drawings and watercolors are very fragile. You can hardly expose them to light for more than a month. And you could ask more money for oils than for watercolors and drawings.

Sure. There was a financial as well as a cultural bias toward oil painting.
Yeah, definitely. Kley always had this kind of ambition to be regarded as a painter, as well, even though he must have known that his true talents were drawing and watercolors, not painting. But he really wanted to prove that he could also create great paintings. And this explains why he did these really large paintings. You can see in my dissertation on Kley an example of one of these large paintings Kley did for a festival hall in Heidelberg. It's approximately 3.8 meters by 11 meters, the *Heidelberger Sommertagszug*. Kley would later do other large paintings...Two meters by 1 meter, or 2 meters by 3 meters...really large canvases. These were a kind of tour de force in which

Kley wanted to prove that he was really capable of creating large paintings.

He seemed to have a penchant for wanting to do tour de force-type pieces. I have a copy of the concertina-style book he drew near the time he was studying at the Karlsruhe School of Fine Arts, the one that is a long, continuous drawing that when unfolded measures something like 5 meters...
Yes...This was his first really big commission. And you can see in that piece, which depicts this long historical procession, that even at this very early point in his career, when he was just 23 years old, Kley had a great feeling for composition. There are other painters or artists that would have produced a very monotone illustration of something like that, right? But even in that piece there is always some movement in it, and the subjects are shown from all sorts of angles, so that it never gets boring. This is an important quality. Like I said, Kley had a kind of baroque affinity for composition, always some variety in it. He wasn't repetitious in his compositions.

The piece is not clichéd...Kley avoided taking the same approach to ideas over and over again...
Exactly. And in regards to Kley's work habits, one has to believe that he was someone who would draw, I'm pretty sure, every day. Out of some kind of inner necessity. For somebody like Kley, producing art, well...it's like how other people need to breath...such artists simply must paint or draw. They are compelled to it. And we do know from an old fragment of a letter from his last years that he would get up at 4:30 in the morning to start painting, and he would paint to perhaps the late afternoon. He was a very disciplined worker.

You can also see that from his style. This is a style you only develop if you paint or draw a lot. Otherwise, you do not have this kind of very personal style, with no sense of hesitation in his drawings. It's like every line is perfectly right from the very beginning.

There's such a confidence in his line. In his drawings you'll see a single, uninterrupted line that forms a perfectly sensuous outline of a woman's form, and it's all done with such utter confidence.
Yes, yes.

Often with artist's of this caliber, you'll find they excel in other arts, too. Did Kley write? Play music? Act in plays?
He definitely had a great affection for the theater. If you look at the albums [the published sketchbooks], you will find a lot of drawings that have something to do with the ballet or with people standing on stage, or dancing.

Kley also definitely had a great interest in music, as well. You'll notice a lot of musical topics as you look through his work. But we do not know whether he played any instrument himself...and while he definitely did not write poetry, he would write postcards, and adorn them with little drawings to illustrate anecdotes or other events from his own everyday life. And in these letters and postcards Kley would often depict himself while he was working or while sitting in the beer garden, things like that. And he would write little rhymes...They are very funny if you understand them. Little puns...He had a good sense for word play, and he would play with different dialects.

...one has to believe that he was someone who would draw every day. Out of some kind of inner necessity.

He definitely had a great sense for language even though his letters and postcards, if you read them, were written very quickly, always a little bit in haste. It's funny...like with his drawings, he would not really think about what he was writing...he didn't really write in a very careful, well thought-out manner, but in a very spontaneous way. And from time to time you see that there are little errors in the spelling or there's a word missing in the sentence. He didn't really seem to care a lot about correct spelling and whatnot.

I think that Kley was someone who just did not want to lose a lot of time with things like that, and he would really rather focus on work, and so usually just wrote little cards, instead of long letters, to acquaintances and friends.

Well, there's nothing belabored about his art, so it makes sense that there would be nothing belabored about his correspondence or his writing either. It sounds like he was very much a live-in-the-moment kind of person.
Exactly. He definitely would not write a diary or something like that. And he was also someone who—and we know this from various sources all throughout his lifetime—that he was someone people were attracted to because of his great sense of humor. They say he was very entertaining company.

But Kley was not someone who was good in following up, not someone who would really try hard to keep up friendships for an entire lifetime. He was more like, perhaps, a butterfly who is flying from blossom to blossom. He was always aware that people would like to be close to him and have fun with him, but he only had very few people that he would stay in touch with throughout his lifetime.

...in the first decades of his career, he was in a very precarious economic situation.

So it sounds like he was sociable, but didn't invest the time to maintain long relationships.
Yes. We have anecdotes that, from time to time at social gatherings, Kley would suddenly stand up and announce, "My dear friends, enough is enough," or something to that effect. "I wish you a nice evening...see you next time." He was never the last one to leave the table.

That's funny. But it does sound like he had a vitality about his personality, that people liked his company.
Absolutely, absolutely. We know that was true from Kley's earliest days, that when he was still a student in Karlsruhe he was very popular. One of his university fellows wrote a memoir—decades later—in which he describes Kley as someone that people nearly automatically paid attention to when he entered the room or started talking. And Kley even mocked himself a little bit for his talent for not always attracting the kind of company he might really like. Very "un-choice" company sometimes. Seemingly every kind of person gravitated toward Kley.

And though it might seem a bit harsh when he would announce "I am leaving now," Kley felt like he really needed to defend himself, to not get lost in this kind of socializing. To be honest, in the end I don't think he was very interested in other people.

That's interesting...
He was definitely very much interested in, let's say, the eternal experiences human beings have, and this is evident in all of his drawings.

So is that part of what helps explain why his work is still interesting today?
Yeah, because he's definitely interested in the human being in general, but not in particular.

Right. He was interested in the human condition, but not necessarily particular friendships or relationships...
Exactly, apart from a very few people.

That raises something I am curious about: Kley never had any children, correct?
Right, but we do know from various sources that children did like him a lot, and that Kley himself liked children a lot, too. I know you have seen from your own research that he illustrated a lot of children's books. But why he didn't have children, we do not know. What we do know is that in the first decades of his career, he was in a very precarious economic situation.

There are postcards on which he depicts himself standing on the street looking into his wallet and counting coins, and in the text he writes that he's unfortunately not able to attend the theater performance because he just has no money. And this is even though he was in his late 30s already.

Sounds like he was definitely still struggling around that time...
And though his drawings might suggest otherwise, Kley definitely was someone with very bourgeois manners and habits. He was definitely someone who wanted everything around him to be appropriate. He was absolutely not a bohemian. Definitely not. I hope this is not disappointing for you.

No, not at all. I think it's fascinating...
But he is definitely not someone who...well, you have seen the photographs of him. If you didn't know he was an artist, you might think that he was a burgher, or a banker, a lawyer, whatever. Maybe a scientist, but definitely not a bohemian, or something like that.

So given his long period of financial struggle, did Kley ever try another profession? Did he have other jobs?
No, definitely not. He always wanted to be a painter. That's for certain, and he accepted nearly any kind of commission in those times. Illustrations for publishers, then illustrations for magazines. And artists of the time also tried to exhibit at these annual art shows, always in the hope of gaining an audience and establishing a reputation. But, no, he was definitely someone who always wanted to be an artist, who always managed to work as an artist, even if it meant commissions that weren't always artistically fulfilling.

I also wanted to circle back to his personal life. I know he was married twice. And his first wife died of an illness of some sort?
Yeah, but we don't know from what. It's hard to say what illness she died of, but we do know—and coming back to your question regarding children—that his first wife must have been the ideal company for him through all kinds of different phases in life. He really must have loved her like crazy, and there are so many wonderful drawings in which he depicts himself together with her, with captions that tell us that he was a really very loving husband.

In the last five or six years before her death, he really must have cared for her and sacrificed everything for her.

It sounds like he was extremely devoted to her...
Yes, and this must really...the death of his first wife was really a horrible shock for him. So, it definitely does not seem like a lack of love would explain why they did not have children. Perhaps it was due to their economic situation or to some physical condition, but we do not know.

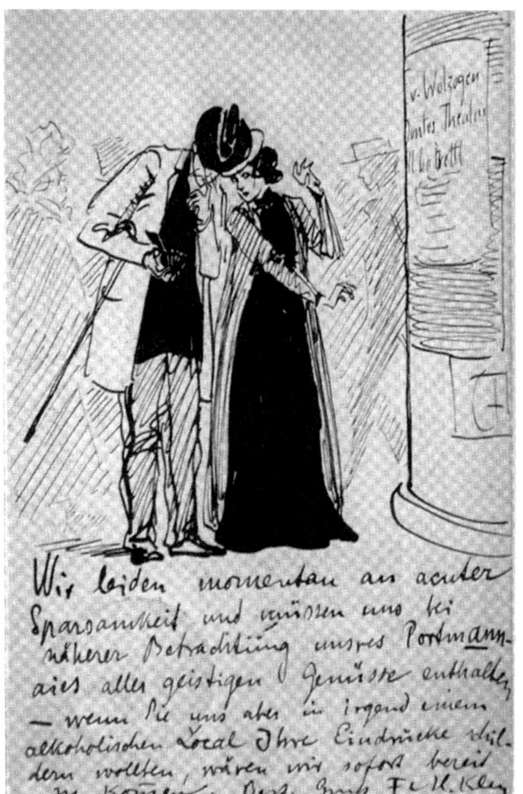

I want to get a better sense of who Kley was as a person. I know he would occasionally withdraw from the public, as he did during World War I for instance, when he quit publishing for several years...
Well, actually, there were several factors at work here. We do know that to some degree it was just a coincidence that he withdrew at the same time as World War I took place. He was in Munich at the outbreak of the war, and that's when his wife became very ill. But his disappearance, obviously, always aroused a lot of questions. What was his attitude toward World War I? Why did he do a lot less illustrating for magazines and things like that?

It helps to keep in mind that from around 1908 up through 1914, Kley illustrated a lot of books. And he did a lot of illustrations for the magazines. He did hundreds of drawings for *Jugend*, and *Simplicissimus*, and other illustrated magazines. At the same time, he would paint these large oil paintings, the industrialist motif subjects. I'm hesitant to say this, but perhaps he had come to a point of burnout.

He might simply have been exhausted or depleted at that point.
Exactly. Just very exhausted, very tired. At the same time, when the world war started, people looked for other things...I don't want to say

that Kley fell out of fashion then, but let's say people had other concerns than the kinds of drawings Kley did. This may also be why he more or less dropped out of the field in the 1920s, according to a pretty interesting critique that was published in a newspaper in 1923. It was just a little review of the last of the Kley albums published in Germany in 1923, the *Sammel Album*, which contains nearly 250 drawings, most of which were printed before World War I. This article describes the album as merely a historical document for the sense of humor people used to have before World War I. It was not that Kley's work was anachronistic at this time, but that World War I period was just such a break in so many aspects. Somehow the world Kley belonged to was gone.

"...I've already shared where I was born and in what year, and I don't think you need to know much more about me. At my age, I really do not care a lot what people think about me."

I think it was a common experience at that time for a lot of artists in Britain and Paris and Germany...

Exactly, the world that was the basis for their artistic work, it had just disappeared. Imagine: nearly all those artists that were really great in the 1920s, like Otto Dix or...take George Grosz, for instance, as someone who then moved to the United States. In comparison with what Grosz did in the Berlin of the 1920s, what he later did in New York in the 1940s and early 1950s...I mean, it's okay, but if that was all he had done, no one would talk about George Grosz today. Grosz from that period is still okay. It's good craftsmanship, but unspectacular.

Banal...

Yes...I'm sorry to say.

So, Kley obviously had something of a public following if he was able to publish these collections of his work, and it sounds like they were popular enough that they eventually published four of them. Was he well known by his peers in artistic circles?

He was a frequent contributor to the magazines *Jugend* and *Simplicissimus*, and they were very widely read. Each of them had a circulation of more than 100,000 copies a week.

These were not "working-class" magazines, but rather, let's say, aimed at the elite...the intellectual and the artistic elite of the time would have bought these magazines. These magazines were in cafés and also public libraries, places like that. So in reality, far more than 100,000 people actually read and looked at these magazines. I'm very sure that a lot of people would have said, if you had shown them a Kley drawing, "Oh, yes, I know this artist, I know his style." But in the end, Kley was—well, he wasn't a shy person, but he was not someone who would strive for celebrity, for fame.

He was absolutely not interested in socializing in that way. If you look at his life, perhaps this would have been completely different if he had had more success when he was younger, 20 or 25, or something. But by the time he had his real success, he was already in his late 40s.

That's late in life...

It was really a very long way to go until Kley got a reputation or some fame. So by the point he started to make a lot money, he was not someone who would make a great deal out of that.

It is very interesting that in the 1920s there were some art critics that wanted to interview him, who sent him letters with questions, and whatnot. We have two or three of Kley's responses to these letters in which he says something like, "Well, I've already shared where I was born and in what year, and I don't think you need to know much more about me. At my age, I really do not care a lot what people think about me."

This was not arrogance on Kley's part...he was simply not interested in what his contemporaries thought about him.

Right. It wasn't important to him to self-promote. Does this help explain why he slid into obscurity after his death?

There was just no information about him, and he was really someone who would not seek the limelight. He was the opposite of a self-promoter. But not because he considered himself too intellectual…it just was not his goal. This reminds me of one of the books published in America on Kley in the 1940s that said that Kley would rather have his art speak for itself. I think that assessment of the matter is a little bit too poetic, or a little bit naïve, but Kley was definitely not one to seek attention at all costs.

That makes sense, and leads nicely into the next question about why Kley seemed to be better known in the United States for many decades than he was in Germany. Part of the explanation seems to be that Kley didn't self-promote, didn't leave a lot of information behind. But what else do you think accounts for that obscurity in his native land?
Yes, there are a couple of reasons he was better remembered in America. First of all, there was a magazine, *The Golden Book*, that you might know from the 1920s, that published some of his drawings from the German albums released before World War I. But *The Golden Book* did not provide any biographical information on Kley. It didn't even try to contact him. It is questionable whether he would have answered them, but they did not even approach Kley as far as I know.

And then there was this other magazine, *The Coronet* magazine, that in 1937 published three consecutive issues with Kley drawings, something like three dozen or so. Mainly animals and erotic topics. *The Coronet*, however, claimed that Kley had died years before in an insane asylum…which was obviously completely stupid. Just sensational. If you make Kley out to be a lunatic or whatever, then it makes for an even more interesting story, which was obviously complete rubbish.

There were also the albums printed in America during the 1940s by Mr. Borden, which definitely helped raise awareness of Kley in the United States. And Kley had this special audience from California, with the illustrators and artists that worked in animated movies and whatnot. They obviously saw a lot of qualities in Kley that somehow were useful as an inspiration for their own work. They admired his great craftsmanship and his very personal style. So Kley developed a niche fan base among these California animators. They really appreciated what he did, even though he was from another country and that these things

…the sense of humor in the 1940s—when Germany had lost the war, had been completely destroyed, was being occupied by four different nations—people had other worries at that time.

were some 30 years old. They recognized the quality of Kley's drawings. They do have a timeless quality.

But why wasn't Kley as well remembered in Germany? Well…In Germany, as I mentioned, he had nearly fallen into oblivion in the 1920s and 1930s, at least for the particular drawings that would have seemed out of step with people's sense of humor after World War I. And after the end of World War II, his industrialist paintings—even though in reality they have no political meaning, no ideological meaning—they fell out of favor. Some Germans thought they might have somehow been associated with Nazi ideology or ideas. Which was absolutely untrue. But regardless, people still didn't want to pay the paintings any attention. Germans had a vague notion that Kley's industrialist paintings might somehow be "inappropriate."

And as I said earlier, the sense of humor in the 1940s—when Germany had lost the war, had been completely destroyed, was being occupied by four different nations—people had other worries at that time. They didn't care about their grandfather's sense of humor.

Another factor that led to Kley slipping between the cracks of history was that he was not a "degenerate" artist. After World War II, many art critics and historians tried to re-establish or rehabilitate the reputation of degenerate art by artists like Erich Heckel, Ernst Ludwig Kirchner, or Emil Nolde. These kinds of expressionists and pre-abstract artists. And Kley simply wasn't a part of the group that got rehabilitated. And when you consider the main artistic movements in the 1950s, 1960s—ranging from abstract art to pop art—those were definitely not the tastes that Heinrich Kley served. None of this was helpful to Kley's reputation.

Although we've touched on it tangentially throughout the interview, why do you think Kley's work is still interesting today?
I think it's a timelessness. And it is smart without being too intellectual.

Right. It goes to that bourgeois quality you spoke of before...
Exactly. [Laughter] It is very thoughtful, but it's also very light. Kley has a very broad range of different moods. Some of the drawings are just joyful, wonderful, humorous things, like the dancing elephants. But yet there are also these political caricatures that capture the spirit of an age. Some people will not know much about the time period or history; they go for the funnier things in Kley. And there are those people that have, let's say, more historical knowledge, and they're fascinated by the historical insight these pieces provide. It's a very broad range of qualities that make him interesting today.

Can you elaborate on the Walt Disney connection? It sounds like Kley's second wife actually had a correspondence with Disney at one point?
Yes. Walt Disney had a large collection of illustrated books from the 19th and early 20th century, as well as some fairy tale collections. The German books were the most important of those in Walt's collection. Disney had contact with a lot of antiquarian book dealers that would watch out for interesting books for him and make recommendations on what he should buy. Incidentally, I actually don't think that Walt Disney was a passionate art or book collector, or anything like that. He would look at these books as a source of inspiration, source of information. And he would just try to squeeze out of them whatever content he could use for his own projects.

Right.
And if Disney had assumed that Kley had passed away in the 1920s or 1930s (as many people had been suggesting), then he would definitely see no reason to send someone to find out what happened with Kley's estate.

That said, in 1964 Disney gave a TV interview in which he referred to Heinrich Kley by name and held up one of the Kley albums, saying something like, "Without the wonderful drawings of Heinrich Kley, I could not conduct my art school classes."

An acquaintance of Emily Kley, Heinrich's widow, told her about this TV appearance. So she wrote Disney, but by that time she would have been in her mid-80s or so, very old. She wrote to Disney in English because she did write and speak English fluently, and she told him that she had heard about his interest in Kley, and asked if he would like to know more about him. After that letter we have no more written source material on the matter, but what we assume is that perhaps a secretary of Walt Disney must have contacted one of the antiquarian book dealers in Munich, asking him to visit the widow to see what was still available in the estate. Original drawings, watercolors, things like that. But none of this is documented. Walt Disney died two years later in 1966, but we know he did acquire a big bunch of original drawings and watercolors that were then still in the Kley estate. These pieces were not, let's say, the top of the top.

I know that people from the Walt Disney Archive do not like to hear that, but these were pieces that Kley mostly did in the 1920s and 1930s. The drawings Kley did before World War I, however, were extremely popular. We still have the business records of Kley's art dealer, and there are hundreds of original drawings noted there as sold to this person or this collector or this public collection. So all that we consider to be, let's say, the best 10 percent of Kley's work was almost certainly sold right after it was created.

And these pieces were not very expensive. You could have a fine drawing at that time for something like 100 Reichsmark, which nowadays would be something like $2,000.

That's fantastic.
Something like a highly original, funny drawing of a dancing elephant for $2,000. Many people bought original art back then, and there were clients that bought 20 or even 30 drawings at once. And, of course, the art dealer Kley collaborated with was one of the most prominent of his time. We have his records and catalogues, and we can reconstruct that Kley had something like a dozen solo exhibitions within five years or so.

Kley's art dealer, Franz Josef Brakl, once said something along the lines of "Heinrich Kley is like my daily bread." Nearly every day there was a client who asked about or who purchased a drawing by Kley. Almost like the gallery was instead a bakery…

So, Kley must have been doing drawings specifically for the art market at that time? He wasn't just selling the illustrations he produced for books and magazines.
Well, one of the big problems with Kley is that he rarely ever dated his works. He signed nearly everything, but he almost never dated anything. So we don't know if a drawing published in 1910 was drawn that year or in 1905. I think that at the very beginning Kley sold a lot of drawings that he had already created for commercial clients and such purposes. He likely had built up a large stock of original drawings. Why should he start more drawings for the art market if there were still a lot of these things available in his chest of drawers?

But as Kley's commercial success continued, Brakl was definitely one of those art dealers who would say, you have to paint such-and-such amount within the next two months because I'm planning the next exhibition, and we need to keep this good thing going.

As a result, Kley started to repeat some of his subjects. There were obviously subjects that were very popular, like the large devil standing next to the chimney. I mean, even in the record book of Kley's art dealer, these topics come up two or three times. And it's not that these pieces were bought back by the dealer…Kley just made several versions of them.

And I wonder if the drawings were sometimes commissioned, if certain subjects were requested by patrons…
Exactly. And Kley was someone who would have no problem with redoing these things. His attitude seemed to be that if somebody wanted a specific drawing, was willing to pay a good price, and he could whip it out in an hour or two, then why shouldn't he do it? And this attitude can be traced back to his earlier life experiences. He had to work so long to get some financial success, that when it finally came, he definitely did not run away from it. It's not a very romantic explanation, but it's the way it was for Kley...

To support oneself and one's family as an artist is difficult, and it's interesting that he managed to finally achieve some financial success, albeit late in his life. It seems like such financial success typically either comes at a much younger age, or it doesn't come at all.
Yes, and even then it only lasted for some five or six years. So, comparatively, a very short time. As mentioned earlier, in World War I, Kley's production really slowed down a lot, and he was basically living off of what he had saved. He was not somebody who spent a lot of money…

He was someone who really had his habits, his manners, and so his lifestyle did not change when he became better known or better paid.

Would you say he was frugal?
Well…he did like to eat, he did like to drink. You can see this in the drawings of himself, where he has a very big tummy!

So he was not a starving artist!
He was not someone who would buy fancy clothes, stay in five-star hotels, who would only go to the best restaurants, things like that. He was someone who really had his habits, his manners, and so his lifestyle did not change when he became better known or better paid.

He would live in something like a four-room apartment that was situated in a very fine part of town. And I think, even in the times when he had little money, he always appeared as if he lived in a very good area. He had a slightly aristocratic idea of himself.

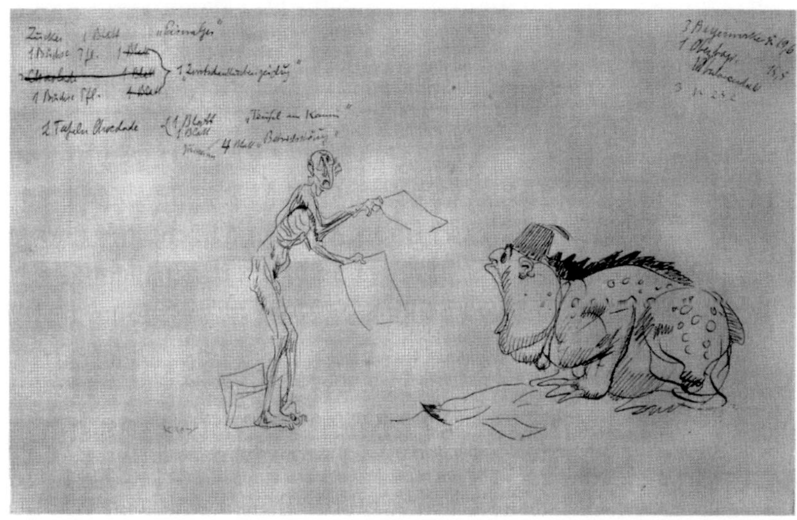

But he was also very generous with others… even though he only had little to give, he was a very generous person. And he was someone who could hardly say "no." For instance, he wanted to break up with his art dealer many times over the years. His dealer would sell pieces for prices other than what they had agreed upon or he would fail to pay Kley the whole amount owed, things like that. When Kley tried to end things, the art dealer would send his daughter, a child, to Kley's house to try to convince him to work with her father again. Kley could hardly resist, and so she always ended up with some drawings to take home. Kley was really bad at saying no.

We have nearly no material that shows Kley preparing drawings. The majority of his drawings must have been done without any kind of model.

So even though he might have had limited means at times in his life, he wasn't an extravagant spender, which allowed him to maintain a certain quality of life, it sounds like.

Yes, exactly. For instance, Kley would have dressed very soberly, but everything would be perfectly correct or appropriate, of good quality for what it was. Unfortunately, we do not have any photographs of his studio or of his apartment. But there are some pieces of furniture that recur in his drawings, and assuming Kley was using his own apartment furniture for reference, these pieces were absolutely ordinary, modest pieces of furniture. Really nothing splendid. This is another way in which we infer that Kley was a modest person.

So, what are the unanswered questions in your mind about Kley?

There are still some things in his biography we do not know. For instance, it is very interesting that we have nearly no material that show Kley preparing drawings. The majority of his drawings must have been done without any kind of model. Really pure imagination, because even if you go to the circus, you're hardly likely to see crocodiles dancing in the aisles. And this is one of his really fantastic, almost unbelievable qualities for me: That he knows the anatomy of every single animal that he depicts, and he depicts dozens and dozens of different animals.

Even the anthropomorphic animals still have the right anatomy underneath. You can see the underpinnings are all still correct.

Yes, exactly. Despite the movements depicted, the anatomy is perfectly convincing. And Kley had other qualities that made him really distinct in comparison with other illustrators, like, for instance, Grandville in France in the 1840s. When Grandville depicted an animal, it behaved like a human being. He would simply put the head of the animal on top of a coat or a nude, or something like that. You see the head of an animal, perhaps its tail or hand or something, but it's never the full anatomy. And it's never that lively…it lacks that imagination one finds in Kley.

And if you compare Kley with other draftsman from his time, like T.S. Sullivan, Kley is always a little bit more fluid. Obviously, depicting animals that behave like human beings has a very long tradition. It goes back to ancient cultures, like in Egypt where the goddesses are half man, half animal. So this is nothing new at all. But it is the way Kley depicted them that was completely new. And if you look at the drawings in which, for instance, Sullivan depicts something like a crocodile jumping into the water, it looks like a frozen picture. It looks like a still from a movie, as if someone had pressed a button and froze the frame. But Kley had a special drawing technique that put everything in motion.

Let's put it like this, lions have a kind of "extra life" or a kind of inner life. There is a movement when looking at a lion, and the eye tries to focus everything into a certain form, but this does not work. I think Kley captures this quality, and this is why one can look at these drawings again and again and never get tired of them.

I agree. I like your phrase, "extra life." I usually say something like the drawing captures some essential "energy" of the subject, that the drawings vibrate somehow.

Exactly. They vibrate, and also I'd say the drawings have a "pure quantity" of lines, you know? Every line has a kind of inner logic. Even though they look very spontaneous, they are very…they reflect a kind of unconsciousness that's a part of Kley's artistic training. He definitely did not think about each line before drawing it. And he definitely wasn't retracing a pencil drawing that he had done beforehand.

I wondered about that. Are there examples of his preliminary pencil work? Pre-drawing underneath the final inks?
No. Apart from perhaps some of the illustrations he did for books. But all the "free" drawings that were perhaps used in the illustrated magazines, or autonomous, free-standing artworks—he definitely did not work over top of pencil drawings or things like that.

He would, from time to time, work with whiteout to eliminate certain lines that he was not completely happy with. But even that was a very rare exception. From time to time, he even uses whiteout as a kind of heightening, extra optical effect. It was not necessarily used for correction, but rather to give some more life to the drawing. There is a drawing [page 58] in which you can see this whiteout effect… the one of a young naked lady—which is, by the way, a portrait of his first wife—standing on a large pillow. And the gentleman in that picture is a self portrait.

Interesting...
I mean, the setting is probably a little too opulent to be the salon of Mr. Kley. This was something he would have embellished for the picture. But in this particular drawing you can see clearly how he would use whiteout in order to give a kind of stimulating quality to his drawing.

Do you think that there are still some artists that are influenced by Kley's drawings?
I don't know whether Kley's drawings are still a great source of inspiration for living artists today, apart from some American illustrators, perhaps? But I do think that every art student—or even mature artist—can learn a lot from Kley in terms of ideas, technique, and approaches to the art of drawing. He definitely ranks among the great masters of this medium, and thus will always have a prominent status within this special field of art.

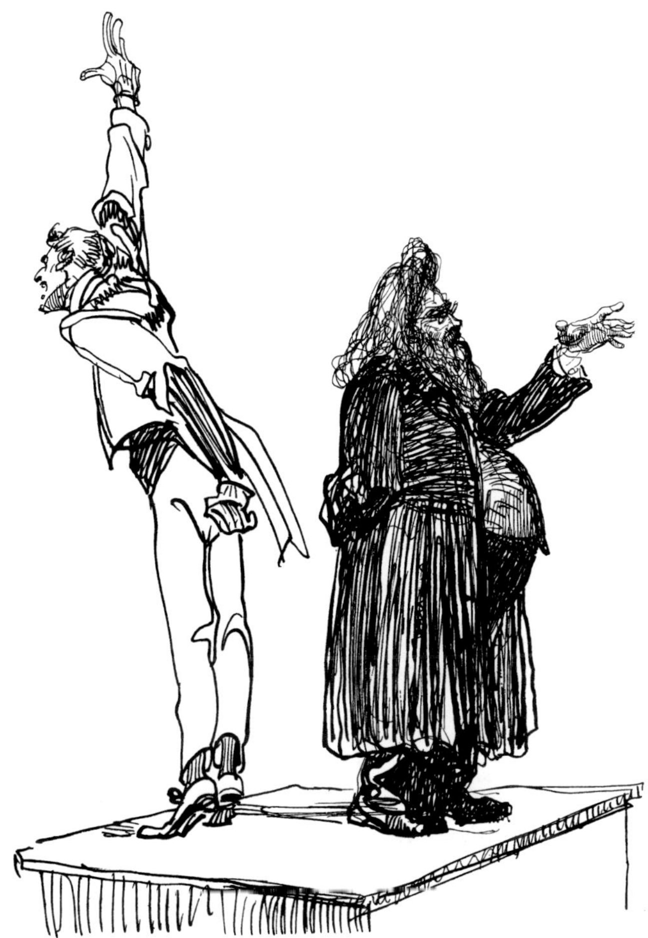

This interview was conducted on May 1, 2012, and was copyedited for clarity by Procopio and Kunkel.

Alexander Kunkel *is an art historian living in Munich, Germany. He wrote his doctoral dissertation on Heinrich Kley's influence on Walt Disney Studios.*

Joseph Procopio *is the publisher of* ***Lost Art Books****.*

Kley Timeline • 1863–1945

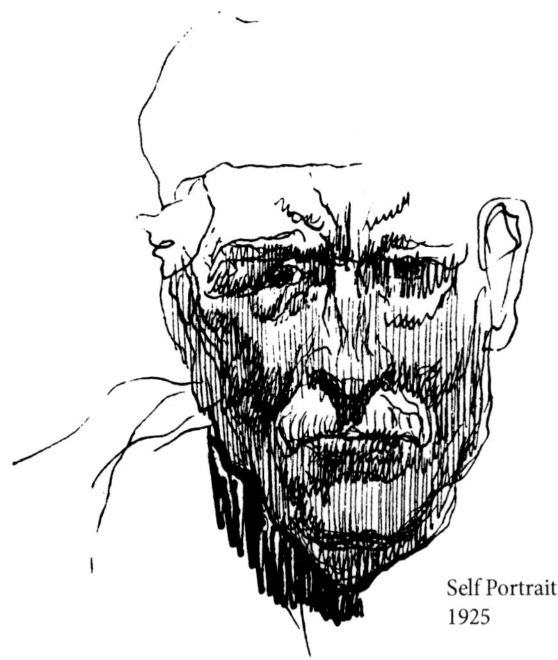

Self Portrait
1925

1863–1879

Heinrich Kley is born on April 15, 1863, in Karlsruhe, Germany. He is the only child of the silversmith Theodor Kley (1831–1870) and his wife Emma (1841–1908), née Roos. After the death of his father at age seven, his mother marries the court musician Ferdinand Segisser (1822–85).

1880–1885

Before graduating from secondary school, Kley joins the Karlsruher Kunstschule (Karlsruhe School of Fine Arts), where he studies under the history painter Ferdinand Keller.

1886

To celebrate the 500-year anniversary of the founding of the University of Heidelberg, the Karlsruhe Künstlerschaft (Karlsruhe Society of Artists) organizes a historic procession, which Kley documents in a Leporello-bound book. In addition, he provides illustrations for a chronicle of the celebration, as well as for the magazine *Über Land und Meer.*

Marriage with Theophanie Kräuter (1861–1922). They never have children.

1888–approximately 1908

Kley participates in art exhibitions in Karlsruhe, Munich, Berlin, and Vienna.

In addition to his work for illustrated magazines (*Über Land und Meer*, *Meggendorfer Blätter*, and *Jugend*), he works as a book illustrator of chivalric and adventure novels, as well as collections of heroic legends.

As a result of his contributions to the arts in Karlsruhe (he is, in addition to other activities, one of the founding members of the "Karlsruher Künstlerbund," the "Karlsruhe Association of Artists"), Kley receives commissions from the court, public authorities, and private companies. Among other things, he creates well over 100 watercolors for the imperial art dealer Velten. Featuring topographical motifs from German cities, these are reprinted and sold as postcards.

From 1896 onward, Kley undertakes numerous visits to Holland and Belgium. During his stays, he creates topographical, landscape, and genre studies, which help him develop a less restrained approach to drawing and painting. In order to amuse his wife, as well as for his personal relaxation, the artist produces a number of humorous, satirical, and grotesque pen-and-ink drawings in his sketchbooks.

1902

Kley creates a perspective drawing for the Krupp Company in Essen, along with six watercolors featuring interior scenes from the cast-steel factory, which convey the atmosphere and technical capabilities of the company. In the years that follow, Kley creates further motifs at Krupp locations in Meppen (shooting range), Kiel (Germania shipyard), and Duisburg (Friedrich-Alfred-Hütte iron works). The company uses these for publicity purposes.

From 1906 onward

Kley develops an interest in motifs of the Krupp Corporation outside his assignments, and establishes himself as a painter of industrial subjects.

1908

The actor Konrad Dreher sends the publisher Albert Langen one of Kley's sketchbooks, featuring his humorous pen-and-ink drawings. He convinces the artist to join his Munich-based magazine *Simplicissimus* as a freelance employee. Until the beginning of the First World War, Kley's contributions are published in every second or third issue.

1909

Heinrich and Theophanie Kley move from Karlsruhe to Munich.

The Albert Langen publishing house issues the album *Skizzenbuch* (Sketchbook), featuring 100 pen-and-ink drawings by the artist.

1910

The magazine *Jugend* presents 32 of Kley's humorous pen-and-ink drawings and watercolors in a carnival-themed issue. He keeps working as a freelance employee for the publication without any significant interruptions until the beginning of the 1930s.

Kley works as a freelance artist for the *Berliner Illustrierte Zeitung* (*Berlin Illustrated Newspaper*) until the beginning of 1914.

The artist becomes increasingly interested in illustrating books such as novellas, fairy tales, poems, and epics.

The gallery owner Franz Josef Brakl presents a solo exhibition of Kley's works in February. The two enter into a mutually beneficial business relationship.

The Albert Langen publishing house issues the album *Skizzenbuch II*, featuring 100 pen-and-ink drawings by the artist.

1911

Jugend magazine publishes an industry-themed issue with eight watercolors and paintings by Kley.

1912

Simplicissimus publishes Kley's illustrated sequence "Die Tanzschule" ("The Dance School"), which features a narrative in twelve drawings created in watercolor and pen and ink.

The Albert Langen publishing house issues the album *Leut' und Viecher* (*People and Beasts*), featuring 140 pen-and-ink drawings by the artist.

1913

Brakl opens a new gallery building and presents an exhibition with over 250 of Kley's works. The centerpiece of the exhibition is the monumental painting "In des Teufels Küche" ("In the Devil's Kitchen,") also known as "Die Krupp'schen Teufel" ("The Krupp Devils"). For the first time in his main body of work as a painter, the artist integrates grotesque elements into a realistic depiction of industry.

1914–1918

At the beginning of the First World War, Kley ceases all magazine work, which the exception of *Jugend*, and largely withdraws from the public. Following the end of the war, the artist temporarily resumes his work for *Simplicissimus*. He publishes a number of caricatures dealing with recent events.

1919

Kley works as a freelance employee for the short-lived publications *Welt-Echo* (*World-Echo*), *Exlex*, and *Der Orchideengarten* (*The Orchid Garden*).

1920

Kley documents the building of a hydroelectric plant in Jettenbach am Inn for the Mannheim-based civil engineering firm Grün & Bilfinger. In the following years, the company becomes one of the most important clients of the artist.

1921

Kley works intensively as an illustrator of satirical and grotesque novels, historical anthologies, and works of science fiction.

1922

Theophanie Kley passes away after a long illness.

1923

The Albert Langen publishing house issues the *Sammel-Album* (*Collector's Album*) with older pen-and-ink drawings by Kley.

As a result of hyperinflation, the artist loses all of his savings. The business relationship with Brakl ends.

1924

Kley paints the monumental painting "Kaiser-Wilhelm-Brücke über das Wuppertal bei Müngsten" ("Kaiser-Wilhelm-Bridge over the Wuppertal at Müngsten") for the Deutsches Museum in Munich. The work is commissioned and donated by the MAN (Maschinenfabrik Augsburg-Nürnberg) corporation. He keeps receiving assignments from the company into the 1940s.

1928

Heinrich Kley marries Emily Segisser (1878–1970), née Schmidt.

The architect and engineer Herman Sörgel presents his Atlantropa project to the artist and convinces him to join the utopian enterprise as an employee.

1933

Following the rise to power of the National Socialists, Kley once again ceases his work for all magazines and largely withdraws from the public.

In the following years, the artist's increasing health problems necessitate numerous operations.

1937

Without his knowledge, the American *Coronet* magazine publishes dozens of Kley's pen-and-ink drawings.

Kley participates in the inaugural exhibition of the Haus der Deutschen Kunst in Munich with an oil painting. His works will be featured in exhibitions of the institution until 1941.

1938

Kley applies for membership in the Reichskammer der bildenden Künste (Imperial Chamber of Fine Arts). His application is accepted, despite the fact that he is not considered to be a sympathizer of National Socialism.

1939

The Reichsschrifttumskammer (Reich Chamber of Literature) puts Kley's *Sammel-Album* on the "List of Harmful and Unwanted Writings" and has the Gestapo destroy the printing plates used for the publication by the Albert Langen publishing house.

1941

Without the artist's knowledge, the American publisher Emanuel Borden issues an album with pen-and-ink drawings by Kley.

1945

Heinrich Kley dies on February 8 in Munich. His remains are cremated, and the urn is sent to Polling bei Weilheim, the village to which his widow has fled. The artist finds his final resting place in the cemetery of the village church.

Paintings, Drawings, and Sketches

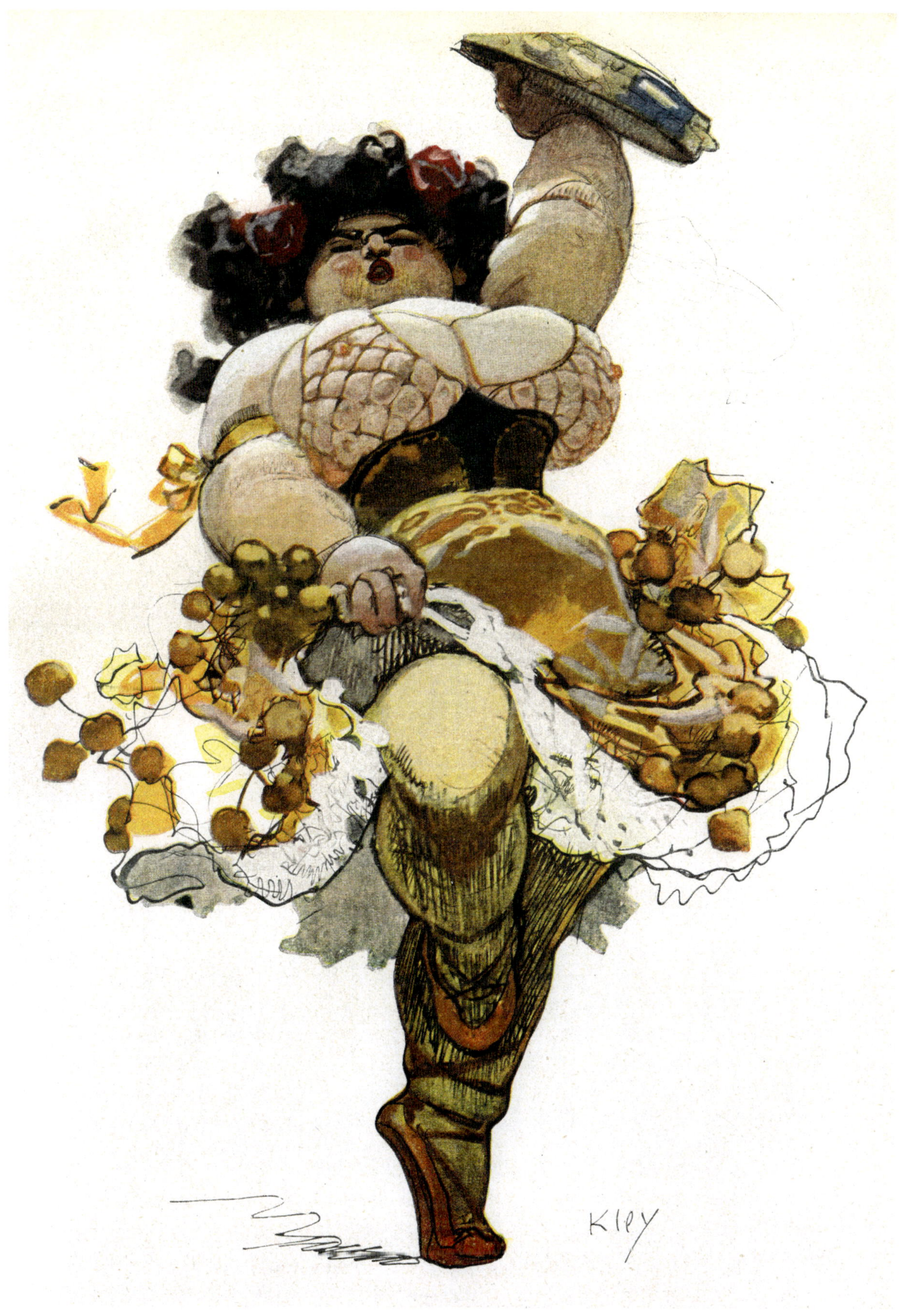

Jugend (No. 5) • 1910

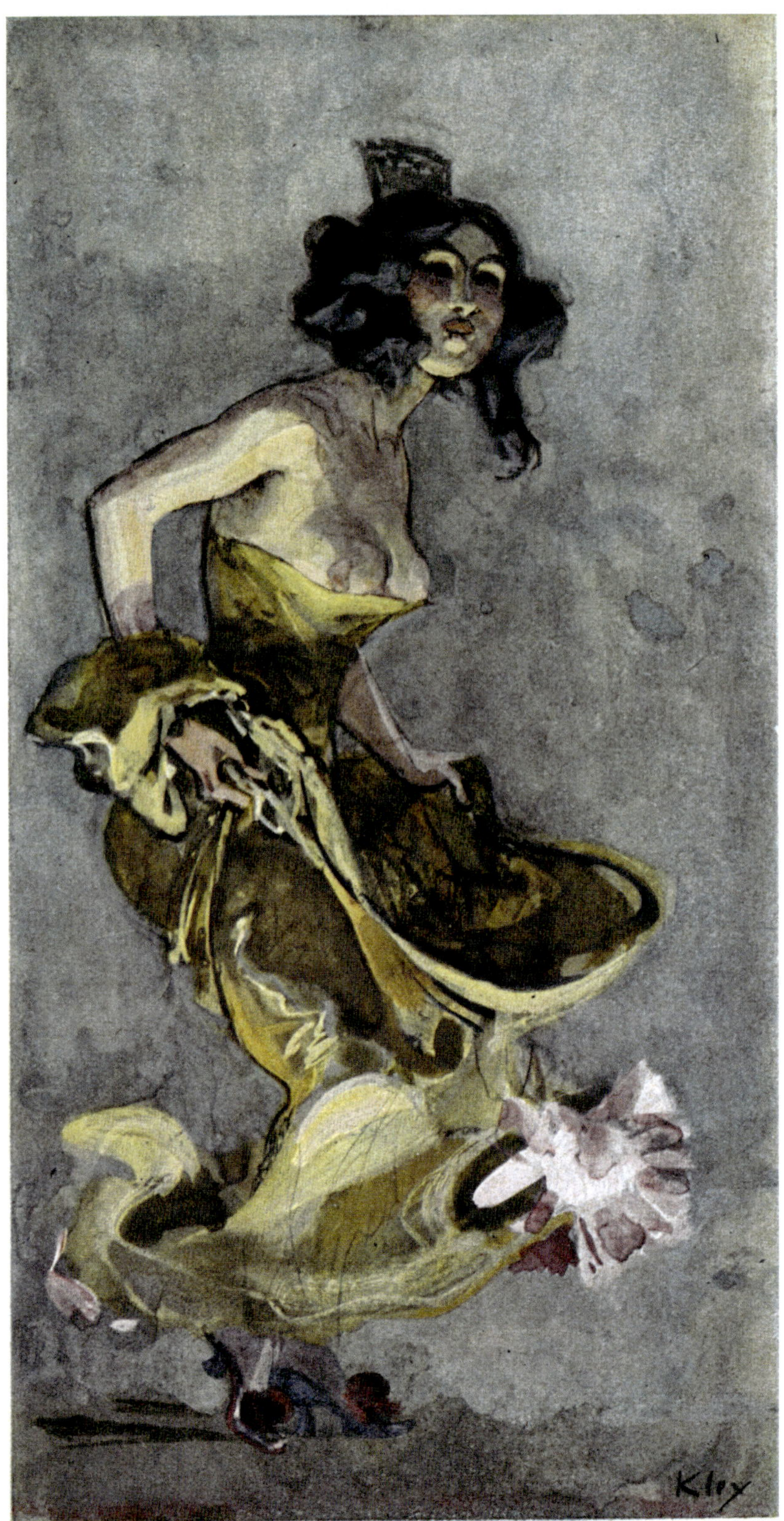

The Yellow Dancer
"What follows is the 'Dance of the Thousand Fears,' accompanied by the music of Viennese composer Arnold Schönberg. Here's a brief summary of the idea: while going to bed, the Sultan Suleiman feels a flea biting him. Enraged, he pulls his dagger and chases the vicious insect until he finds and kills it. My dance is meant to express the emotions of the flea!"

Jugend • 1911

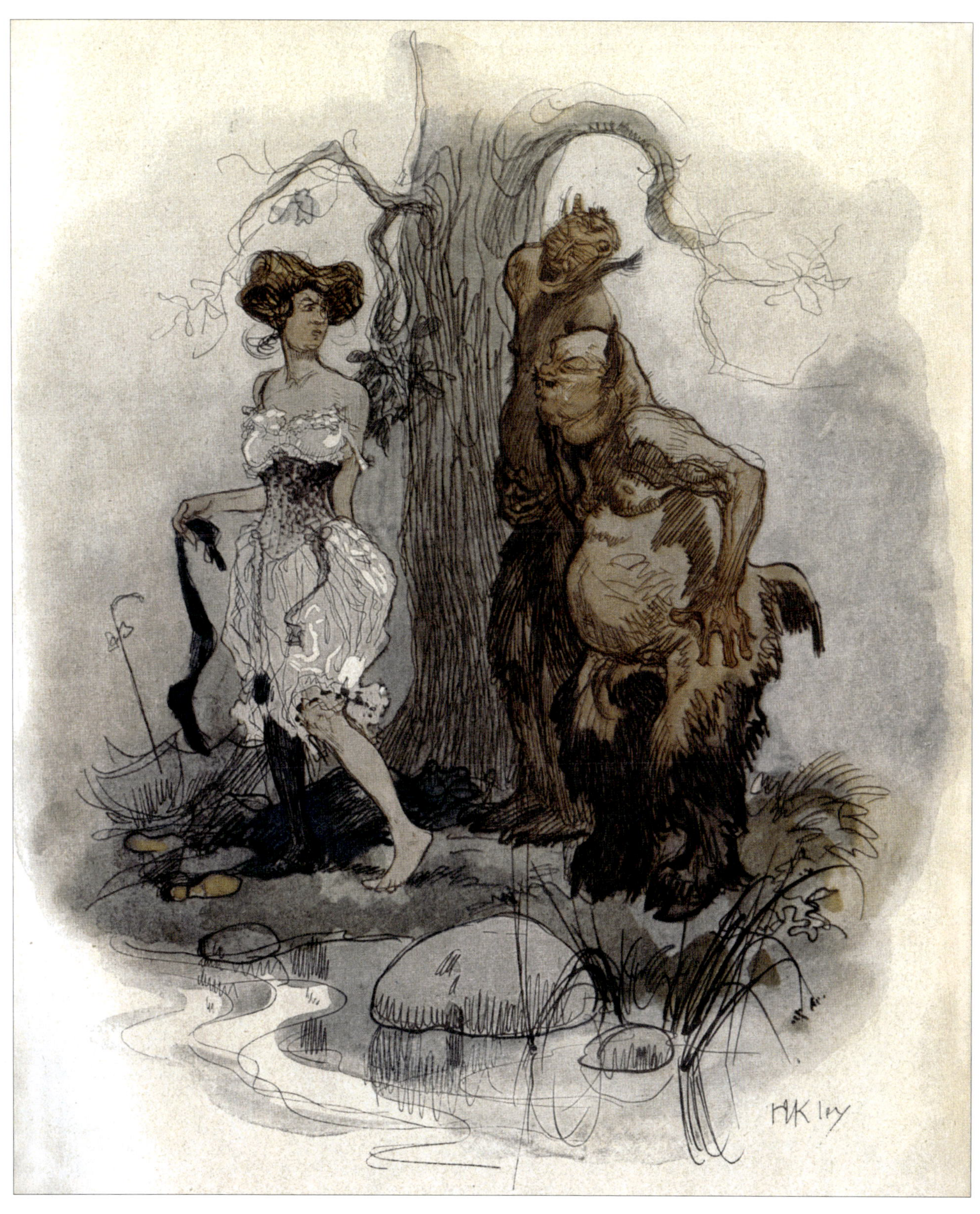

Surprise
Ueberraschung
Jugend • 1910

Prawn Catchers near Nieuport
Krabbenfänger bei Nieuport
Postcard
Artist postcard from the family magazine, *Das Buch für Alle*

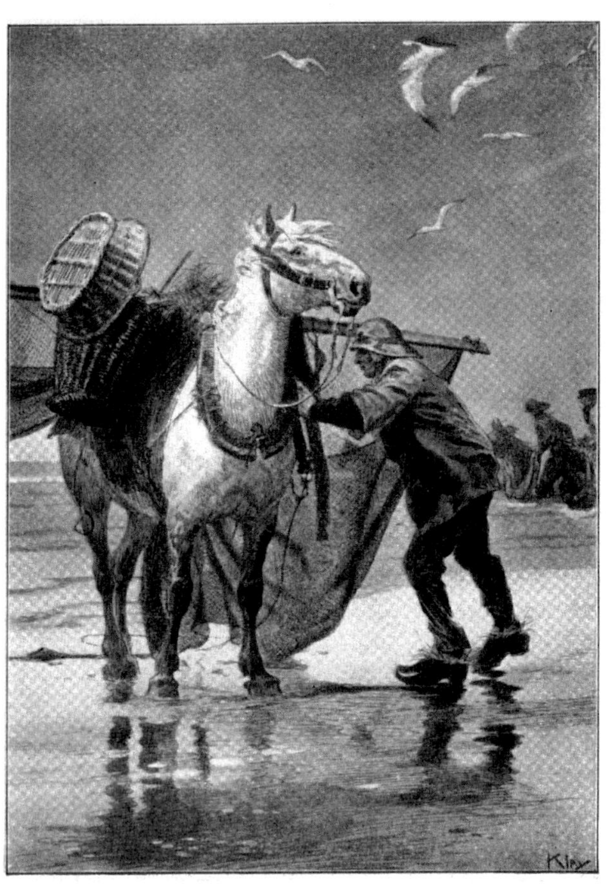

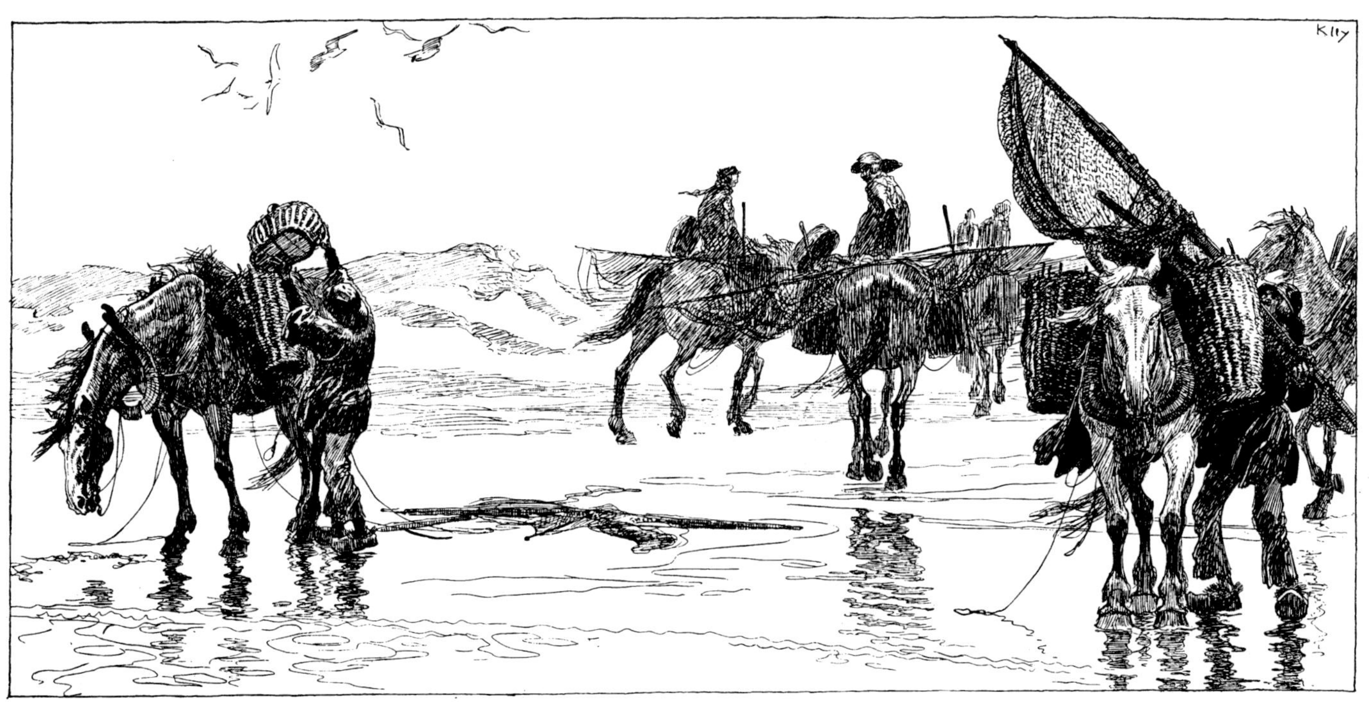

Prawn Fishers in Coxyde near Nieuport
Crevettenfischer in Coxyde bei Nieuport
Jugend • 1915

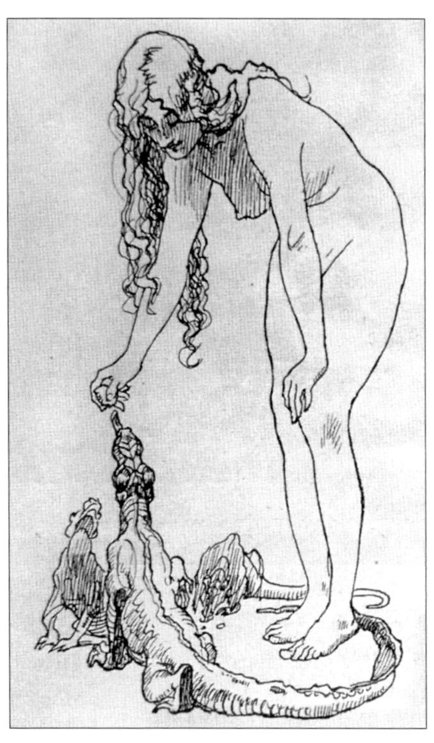

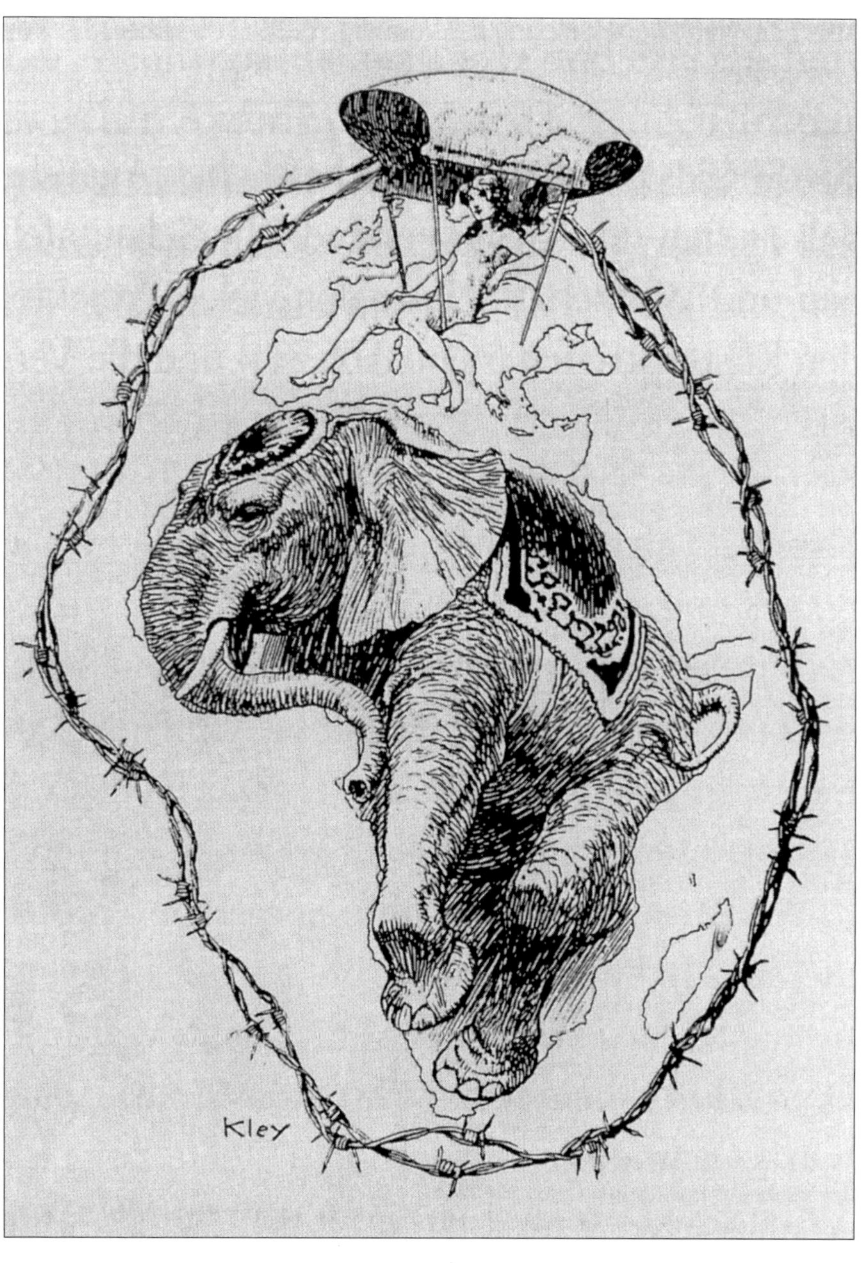
Kley

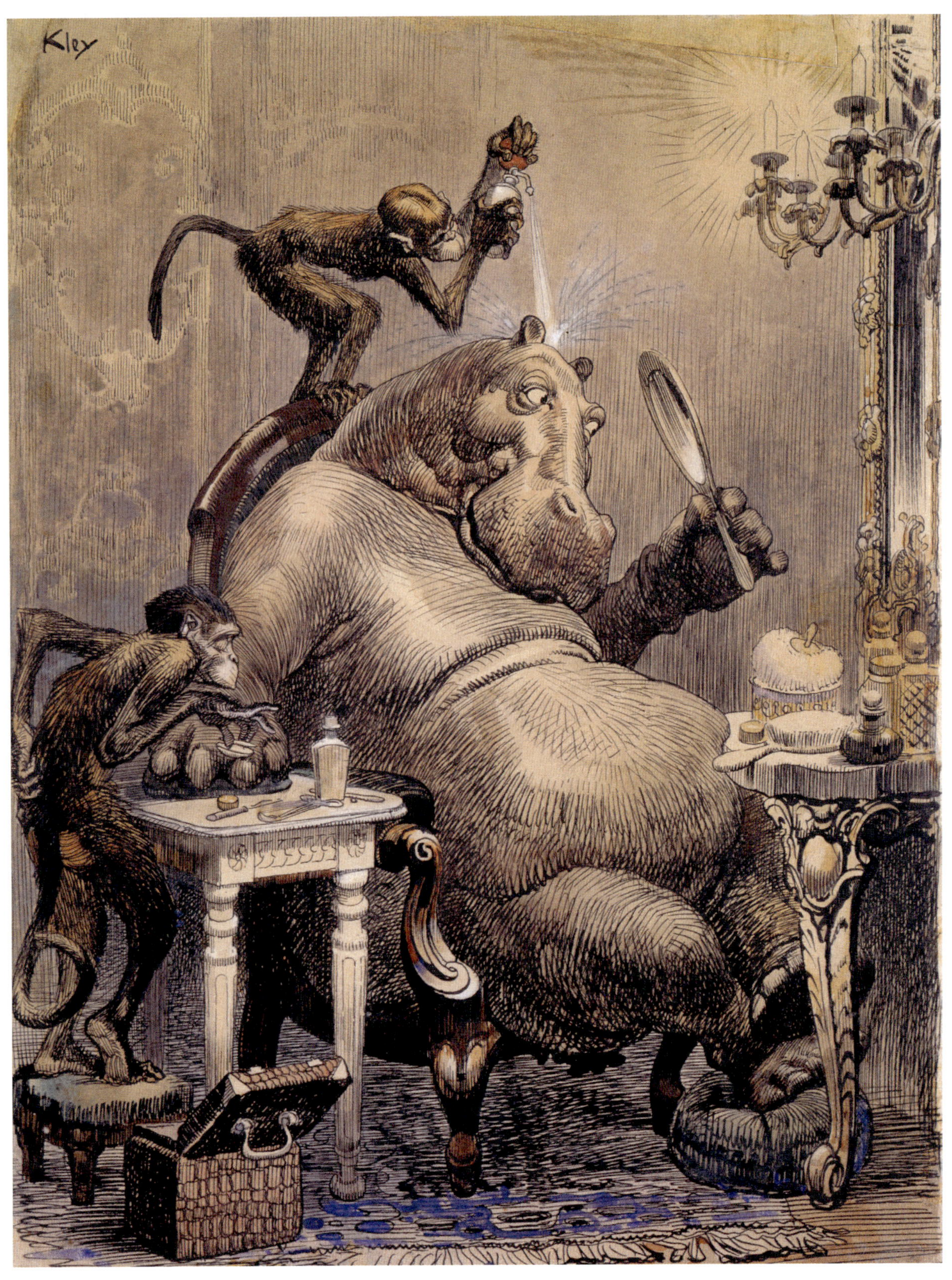
Kley

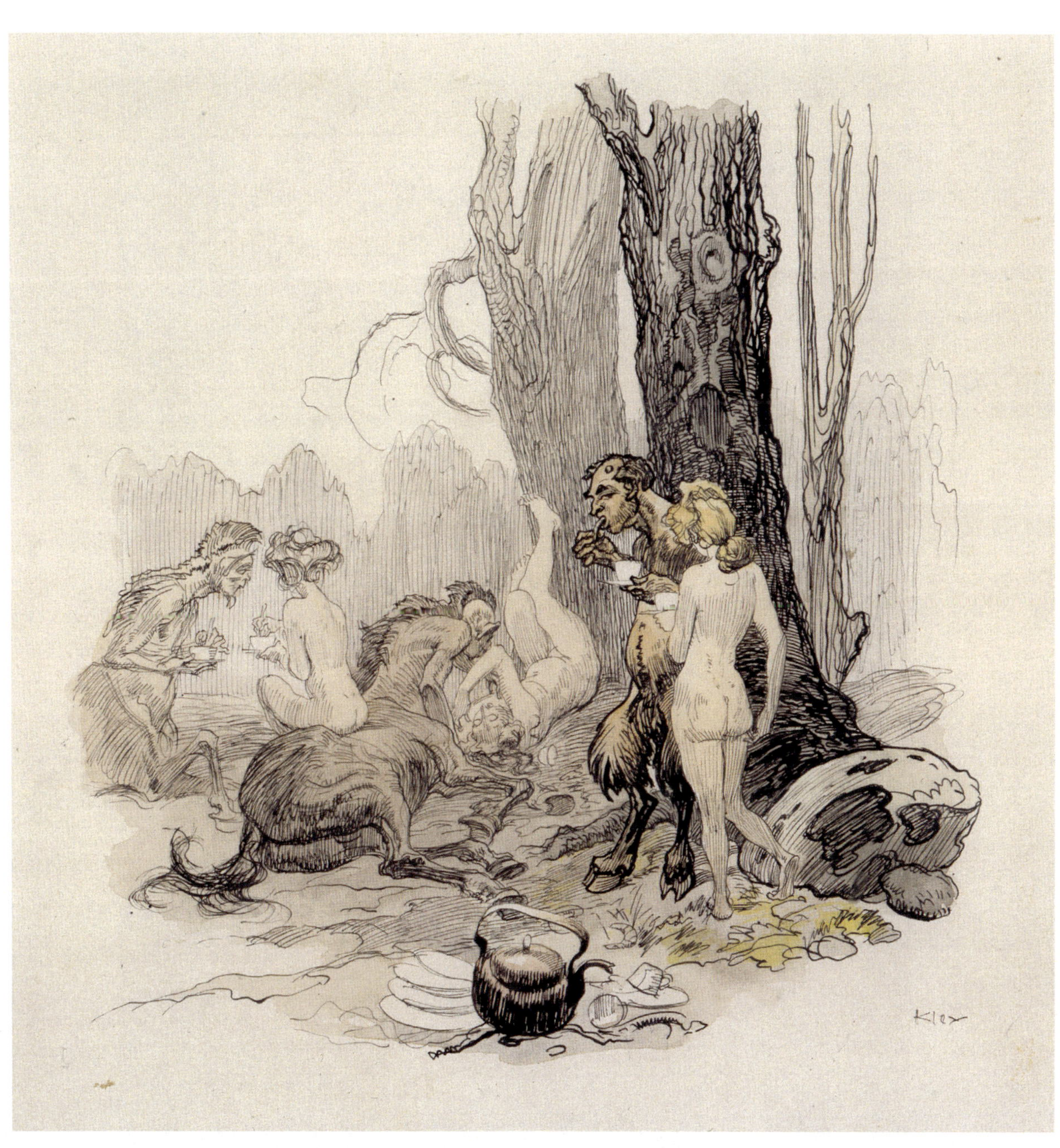
Kley

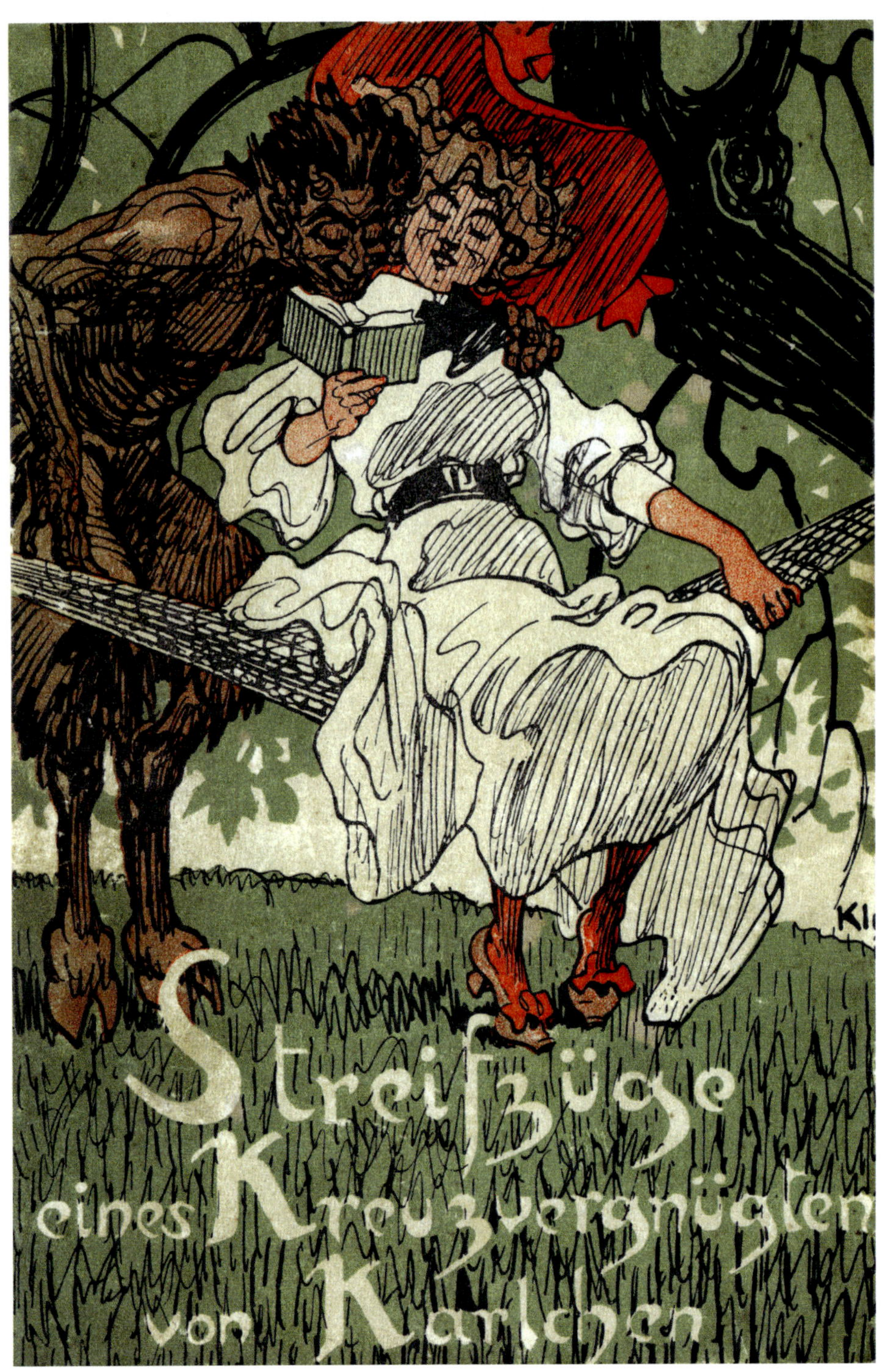

Roaming the City of Kreuzvergnügten
Streifzüge eines Kreuzvergnügten
Karlchen (Karl Ettlinger) • Munich: 1910
(see *Volume 1* for a series of pen-and-ink drawings from this book)

PAGES 41-50, SELECTIONS FROM

Reinke the Fox

Reinke der Fuchs

Wilhelm Fronemann • Stuttgart: 1930

(see *Volume 1* for a series of pen-and-ink drawings from this book)

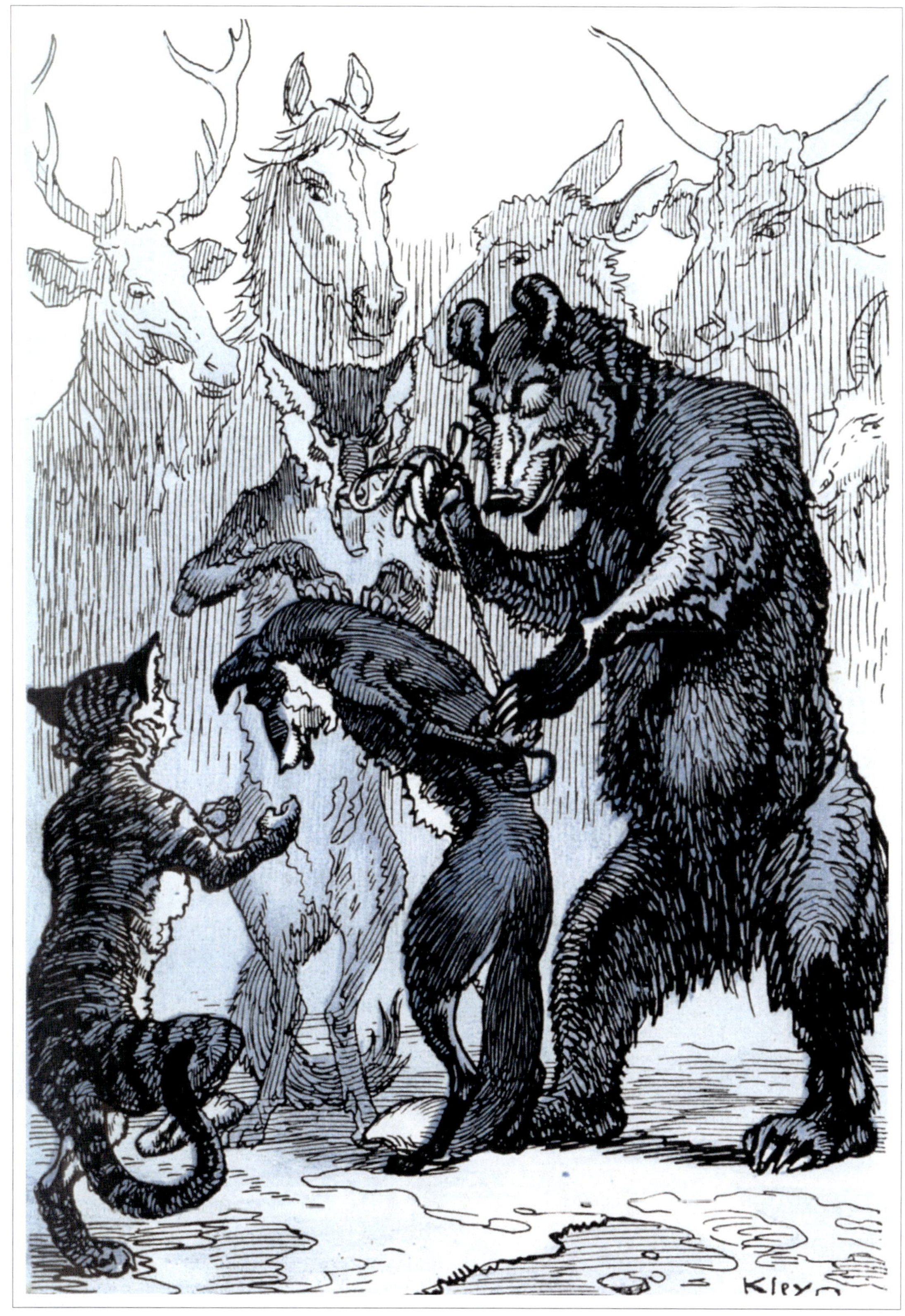

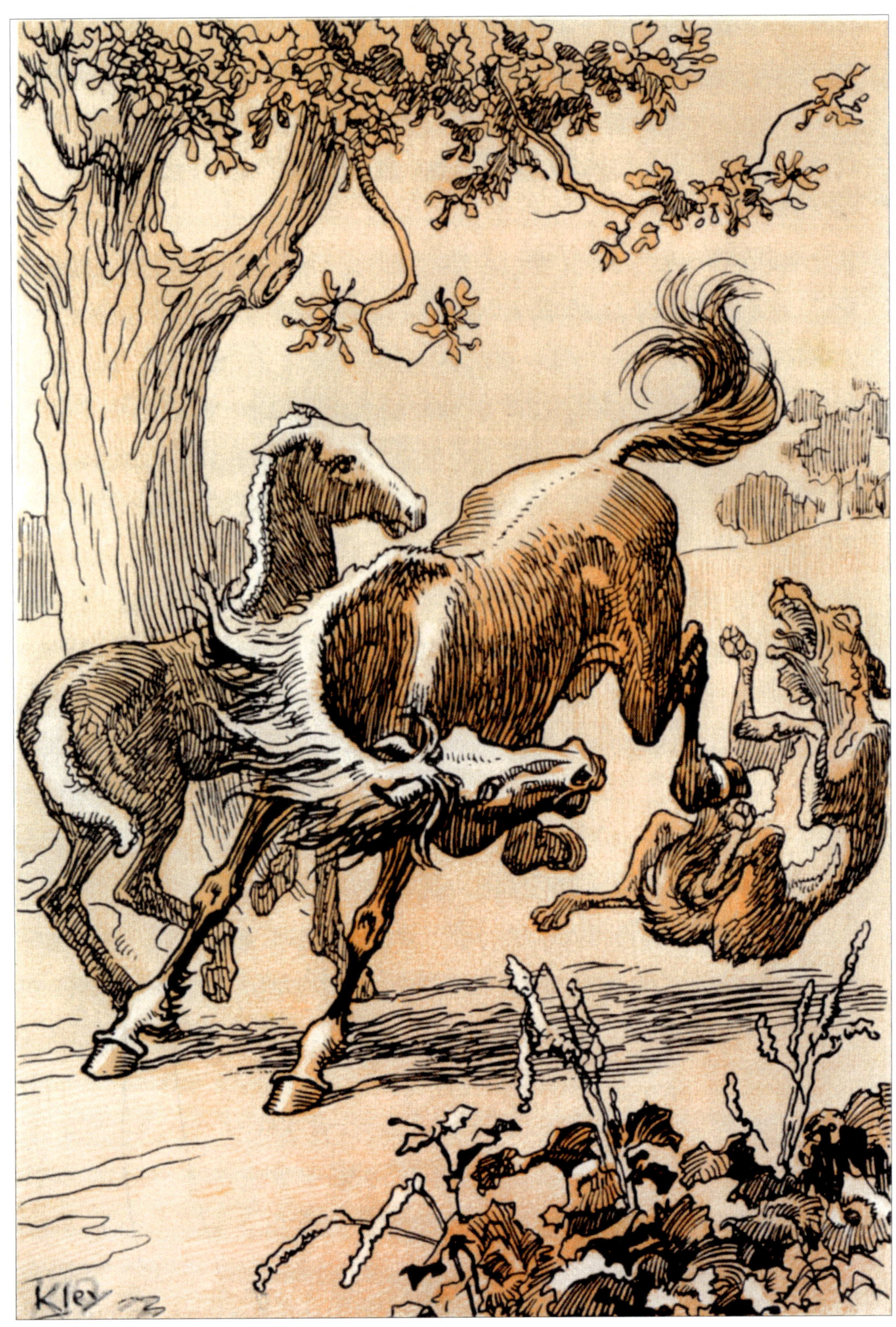
Kley

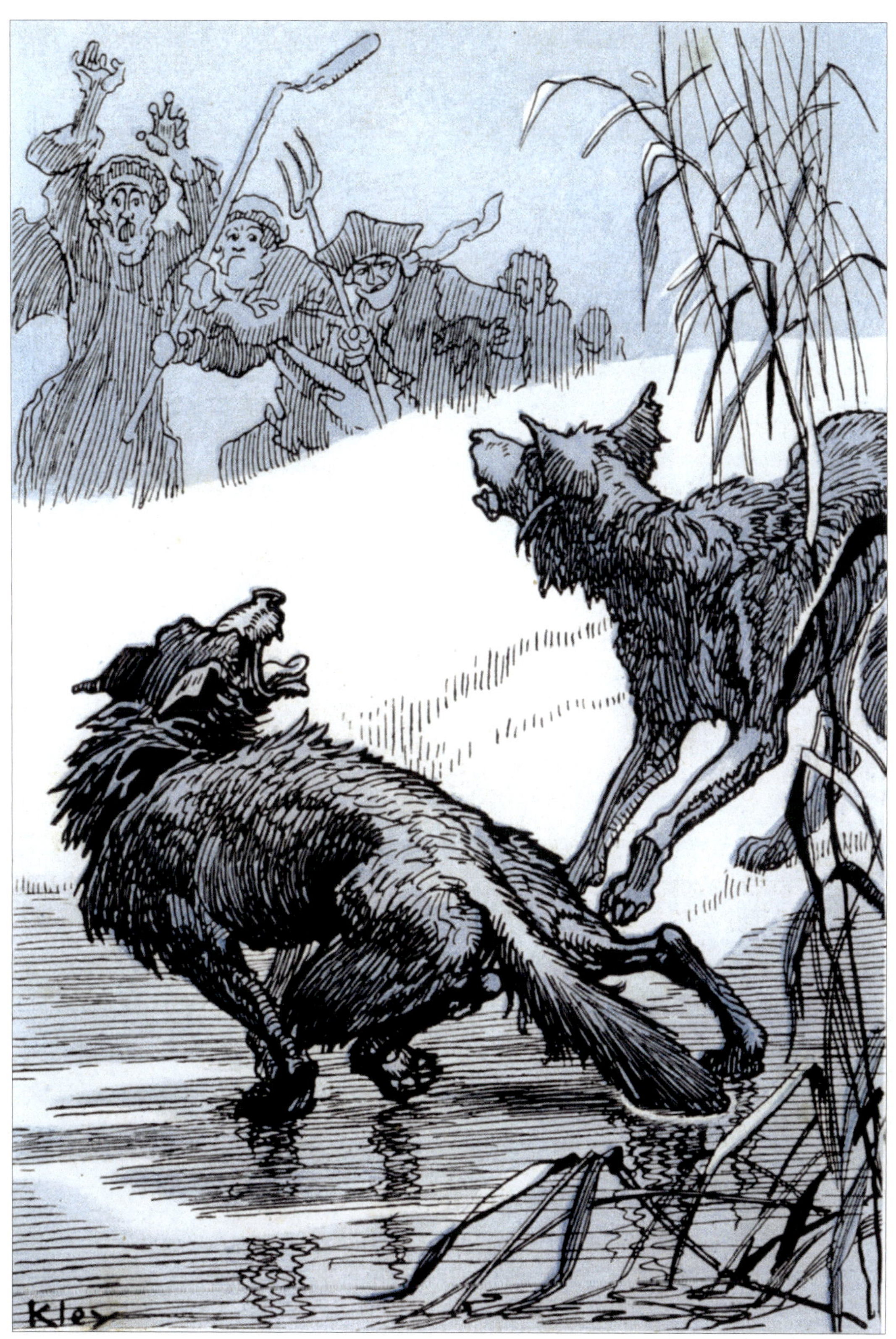
Kley

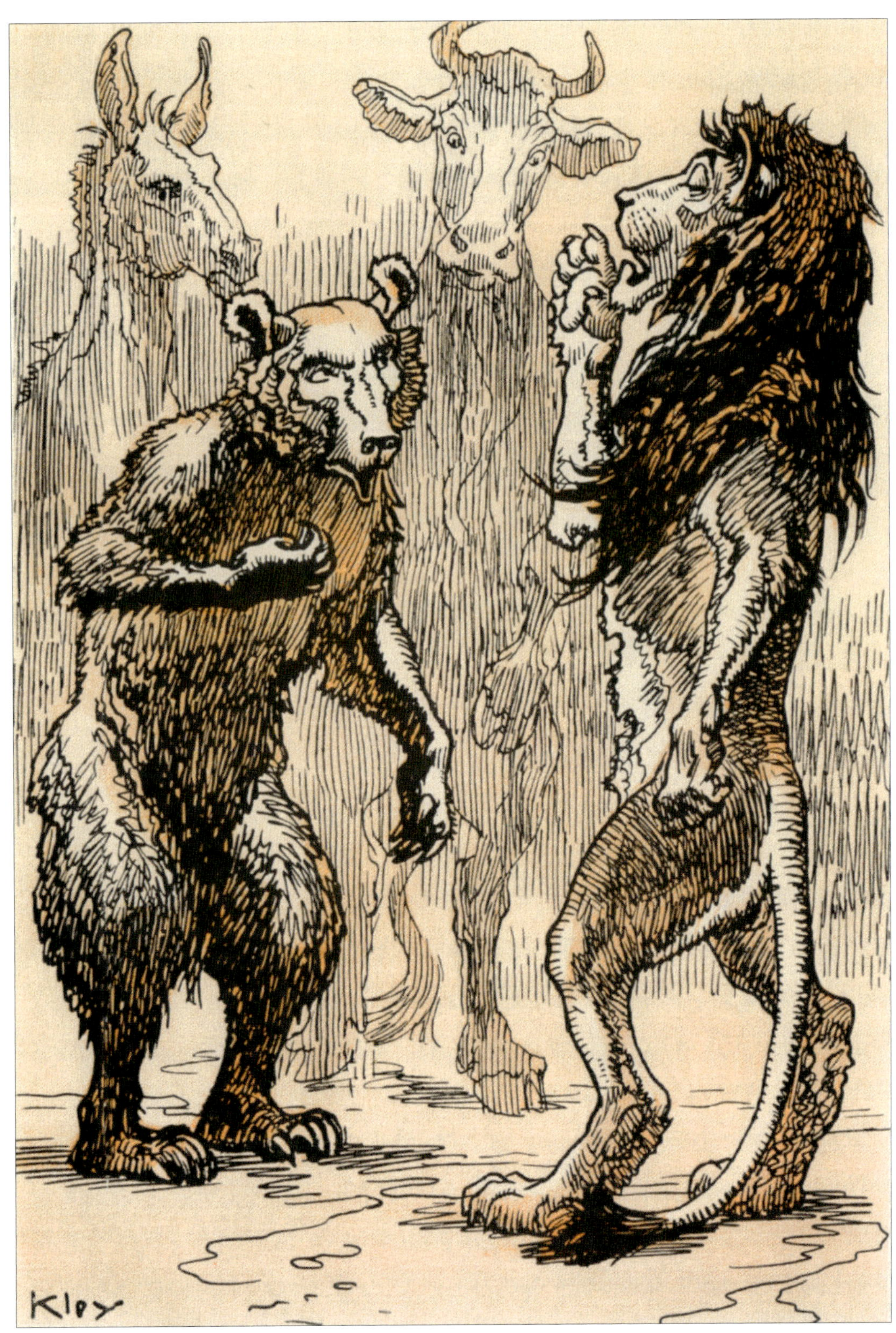
Kley

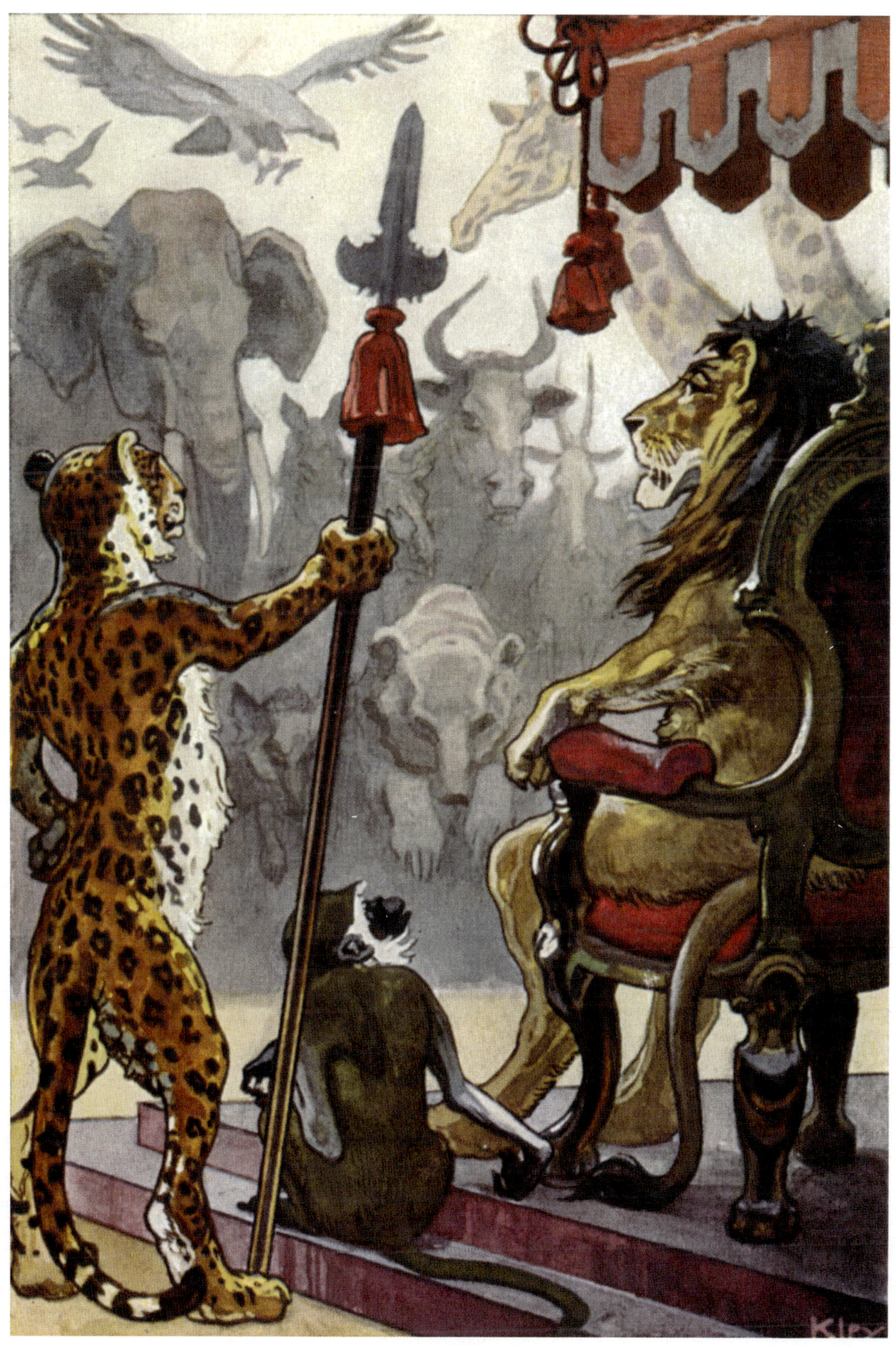
KLEY

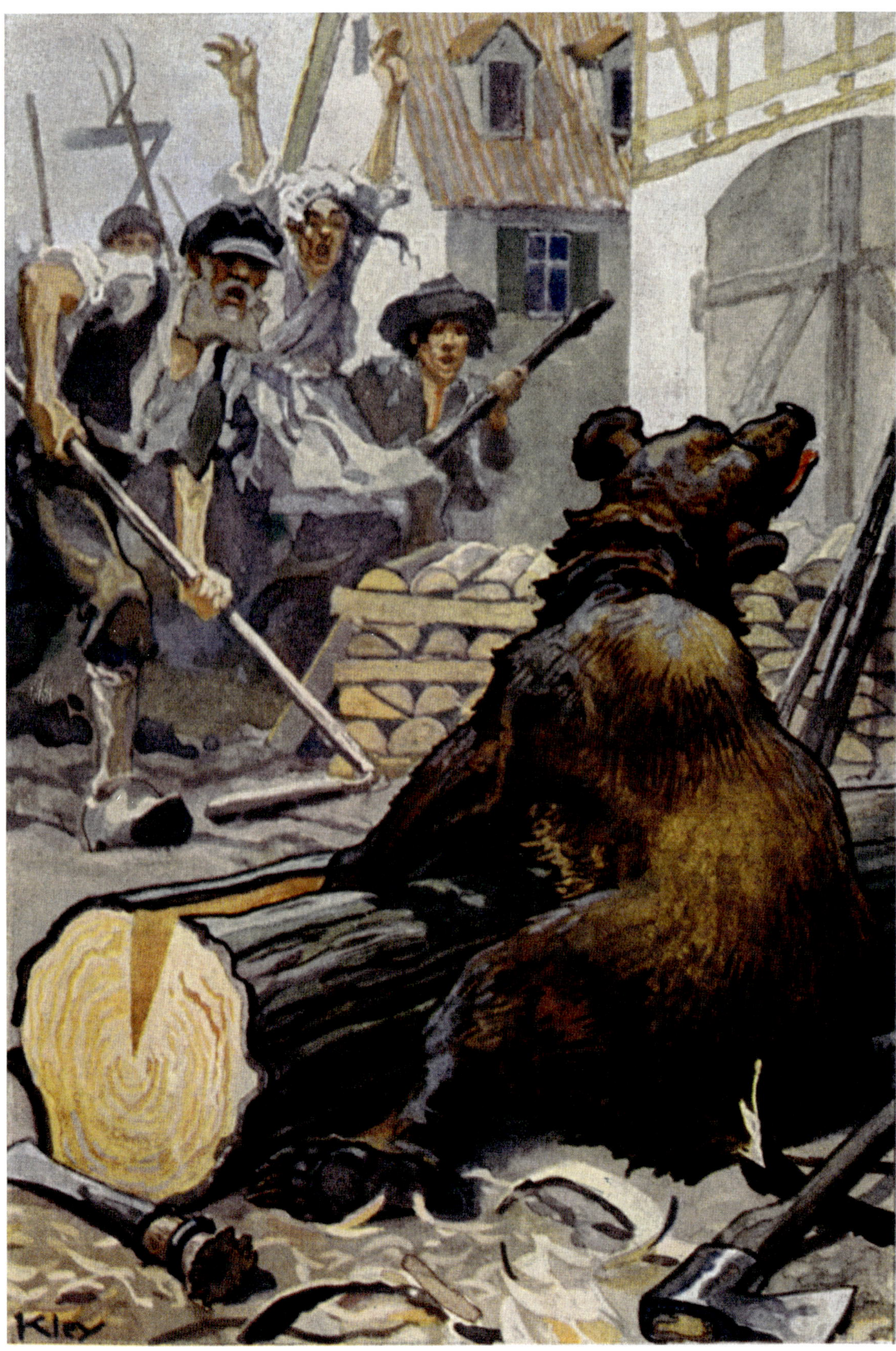
Kley

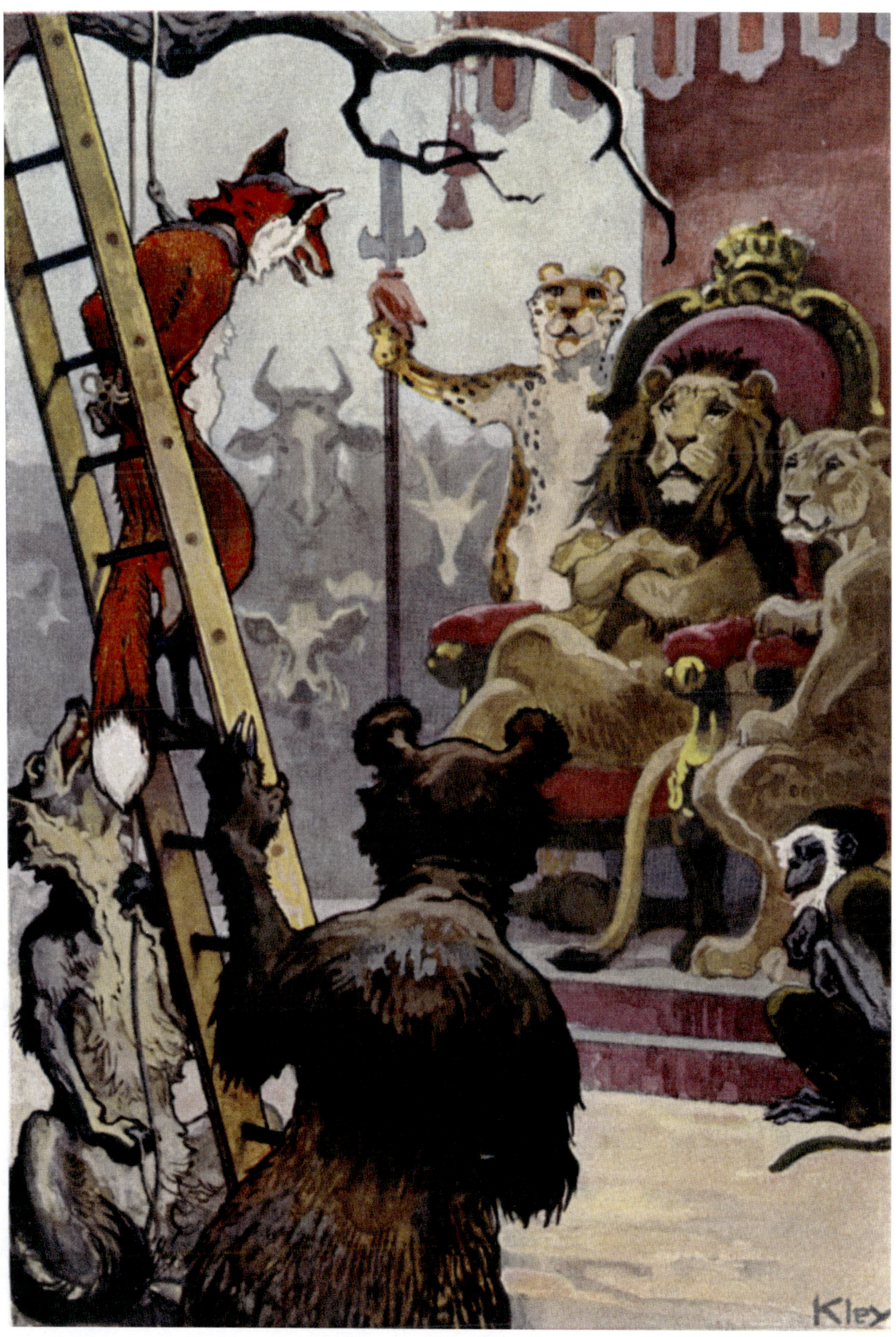
Kley

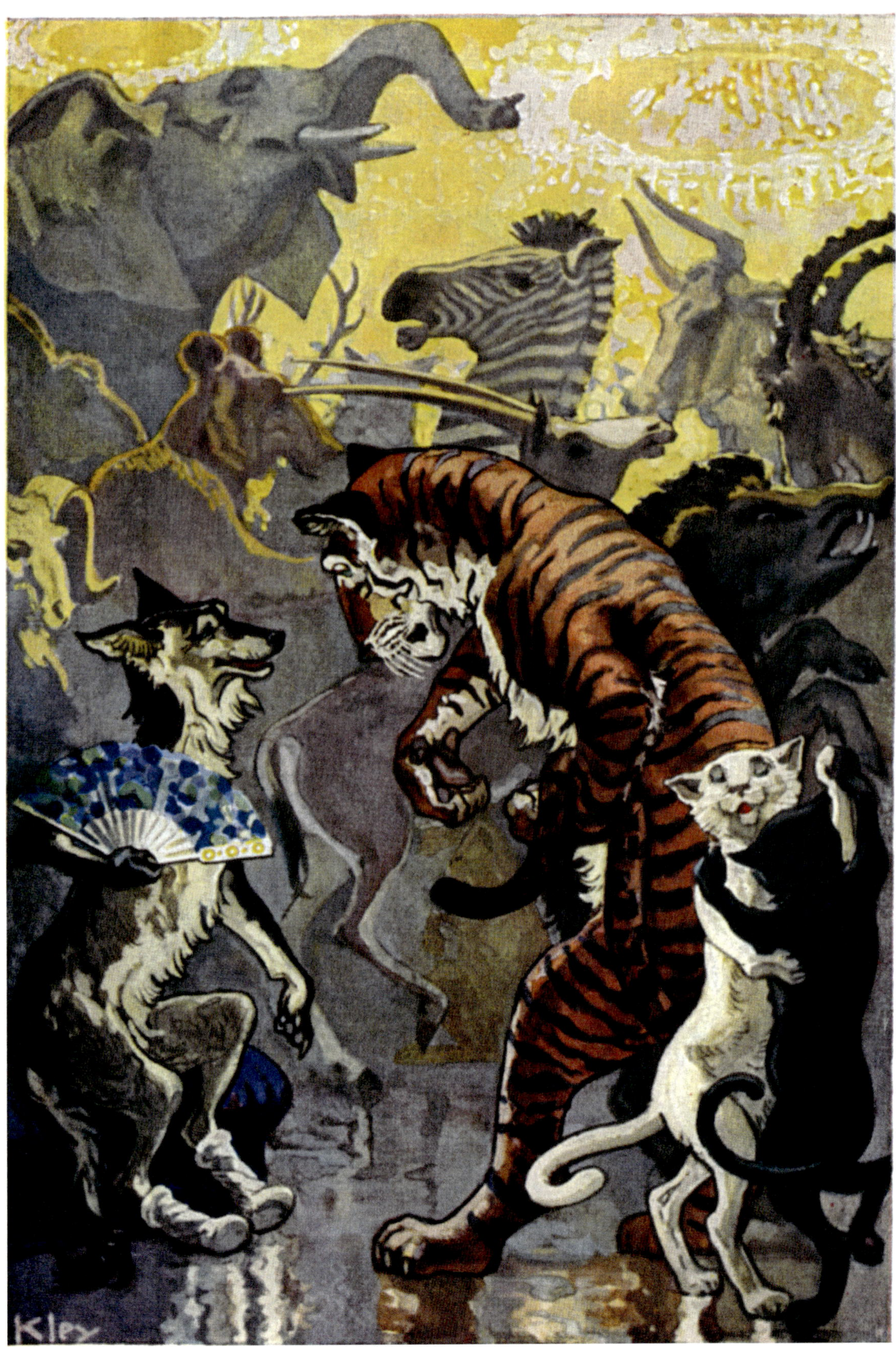
Kley

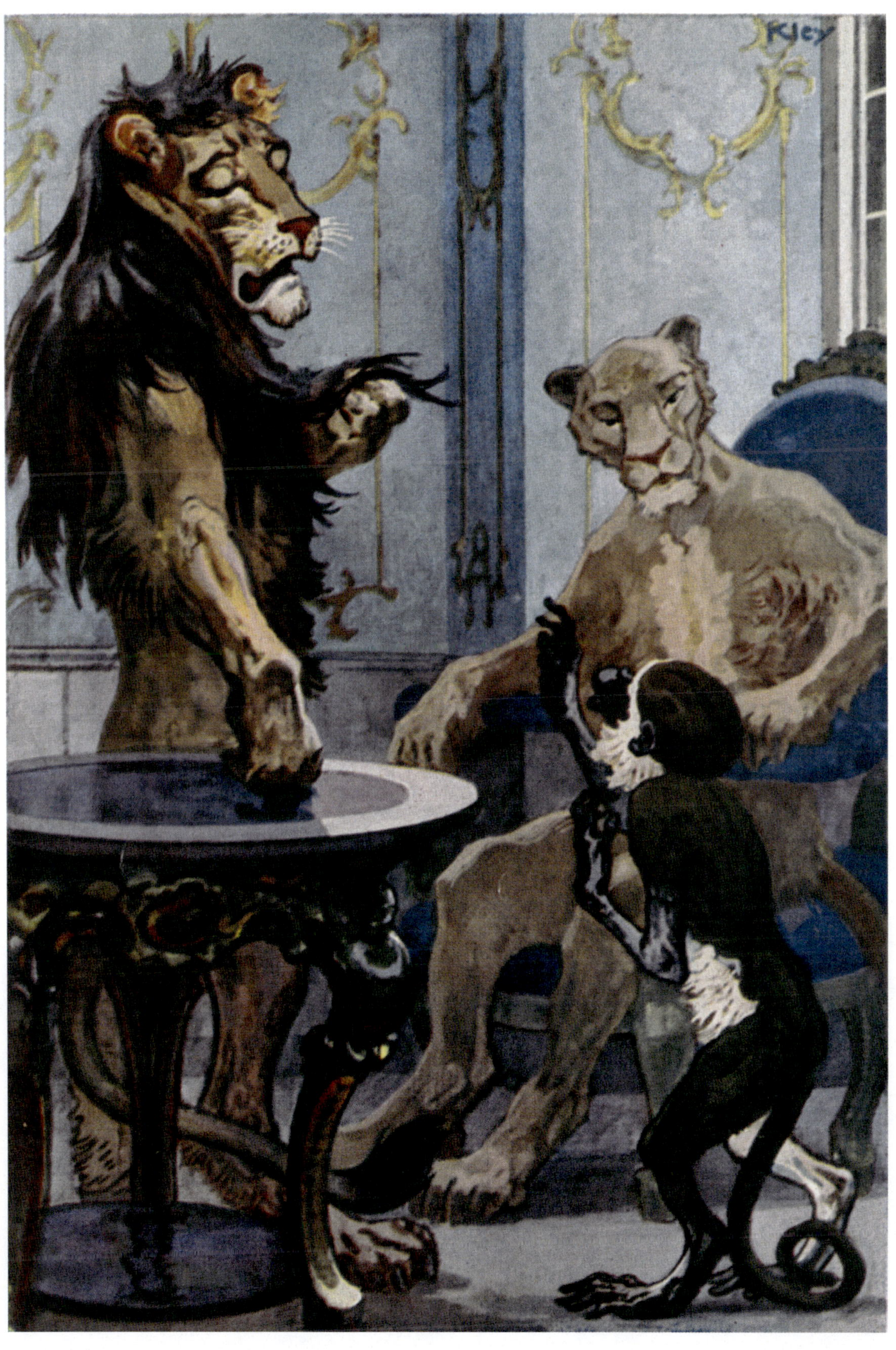
Kley

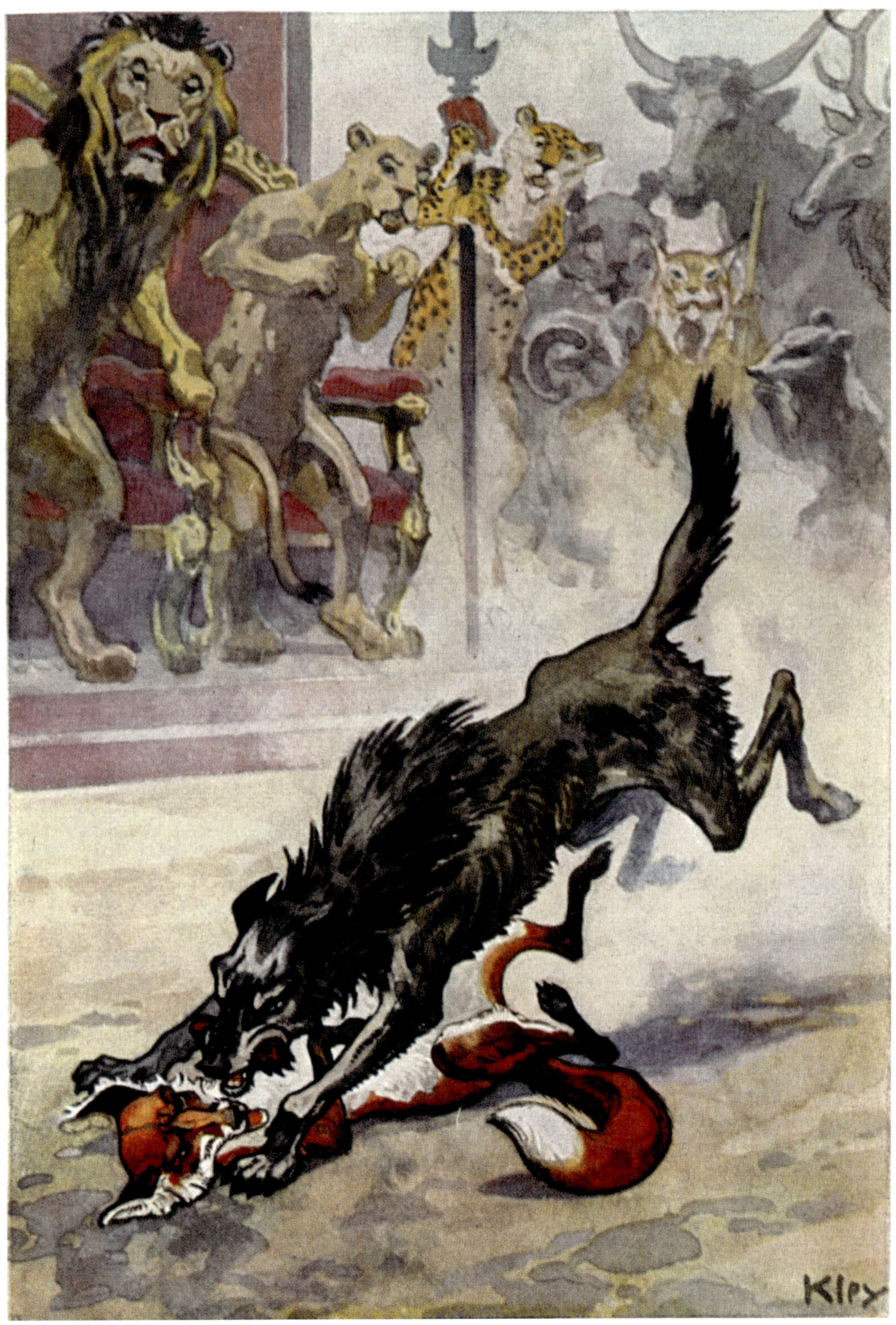
Kley

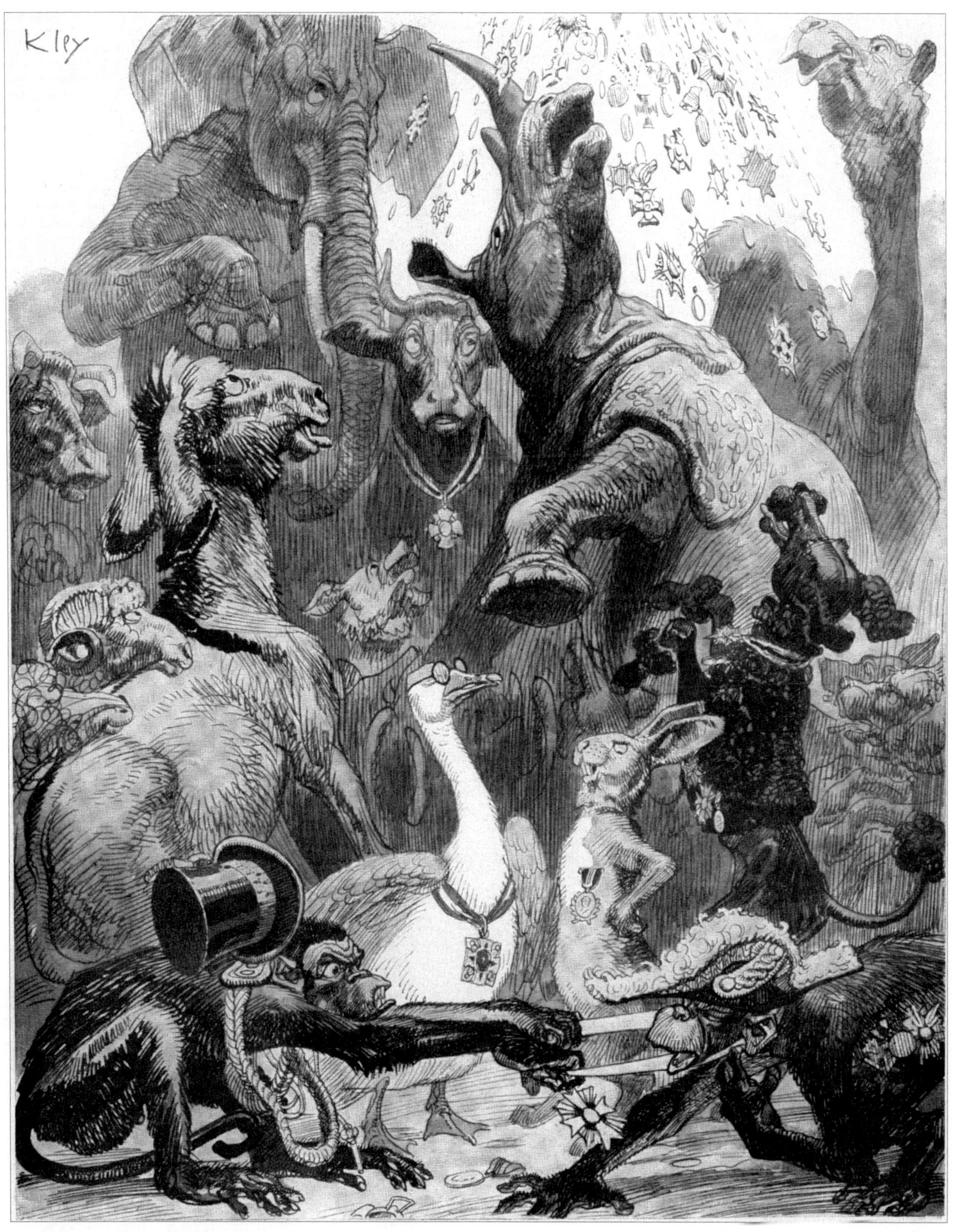

Rain of Medals

Ordensregen

Jugend (No. 53) • 1913

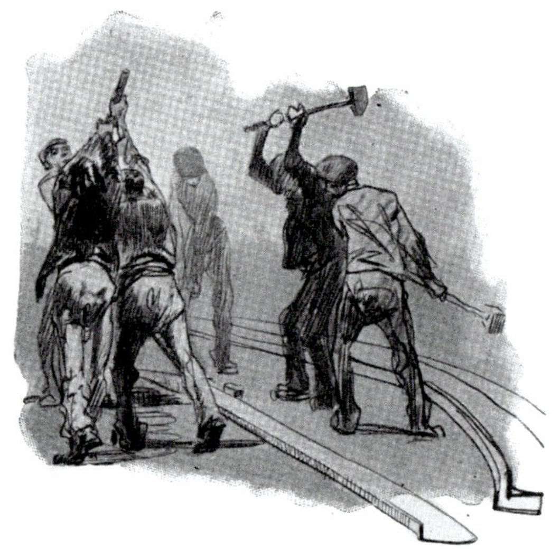

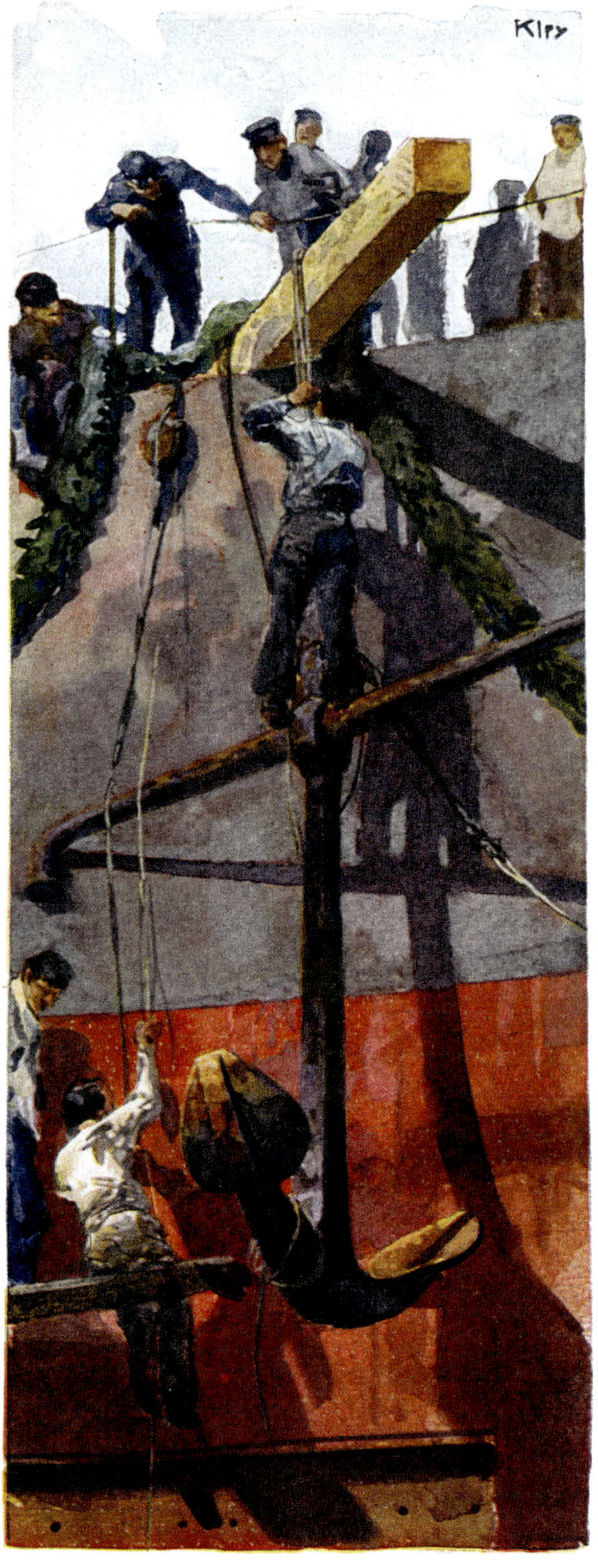

Before the Launch
Vor dem Stapellauf
Jugend (No. 40) • 1912

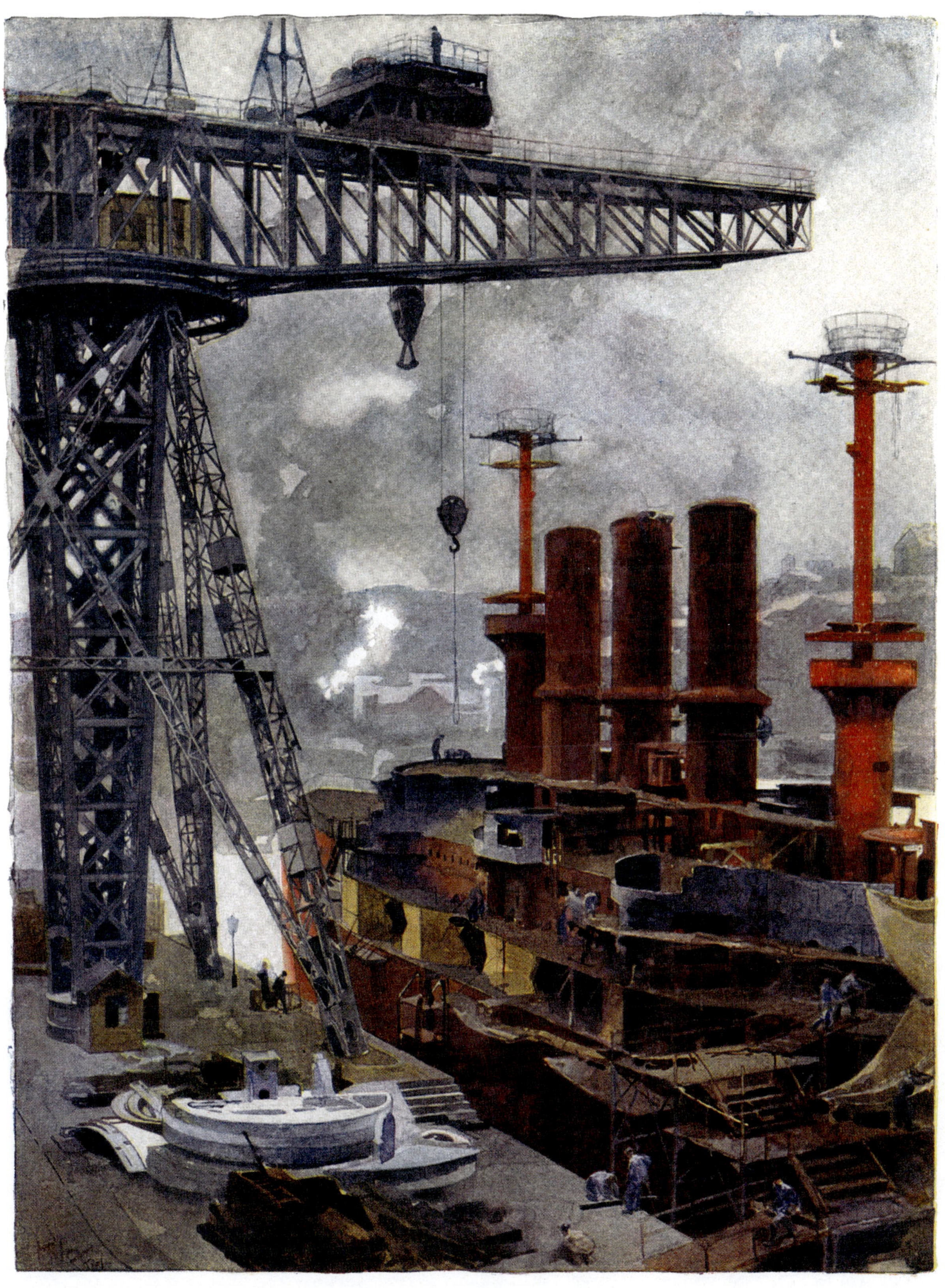

Battleship "Schleswig Holstein" in the Garmania shipyards
Linienschiff "Schleswig Holstein" auf der Germania-Werft
Jugend (No. 40) • 1912

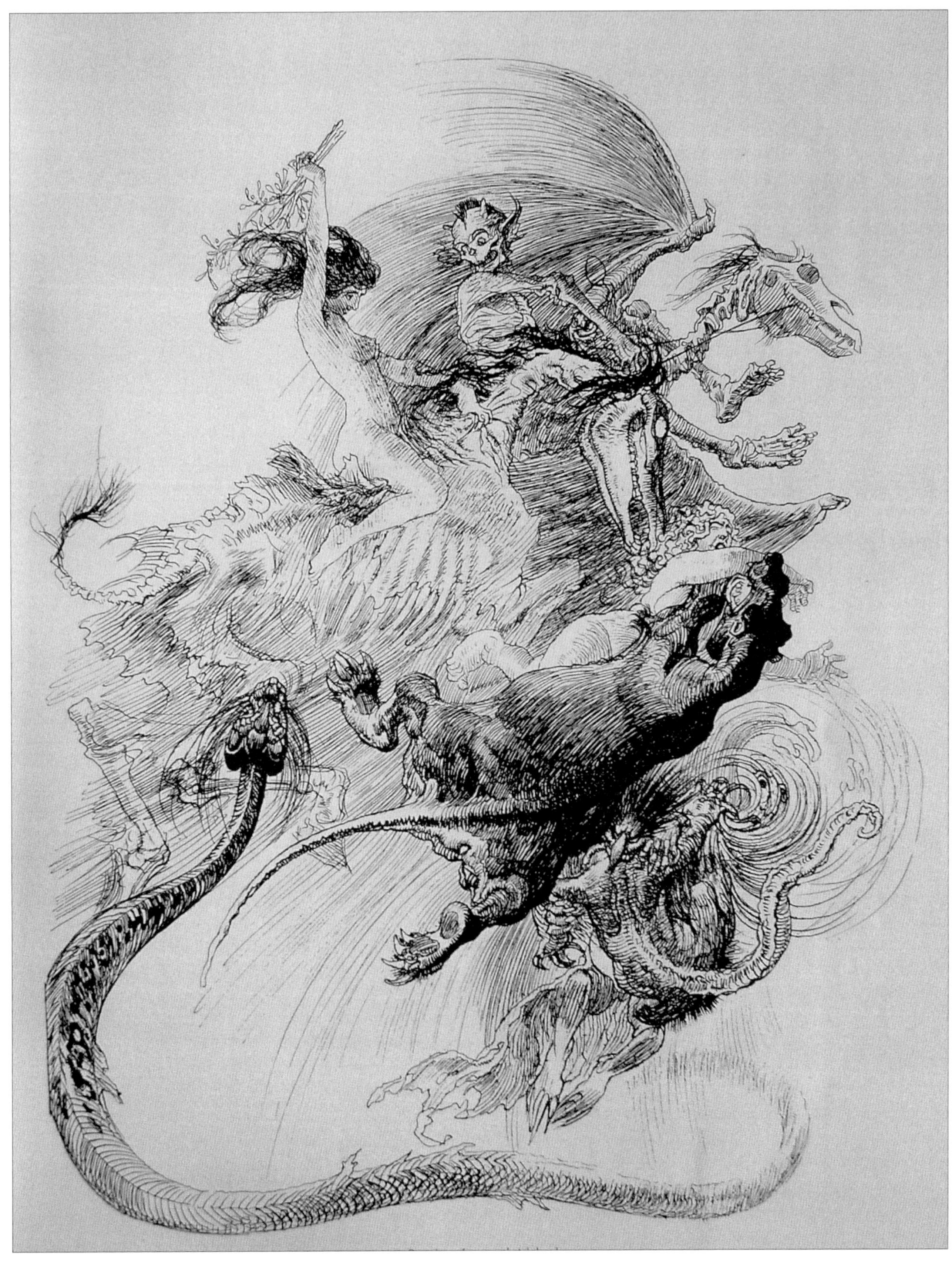

Illustration for *Faust*

Unpublished • 1923

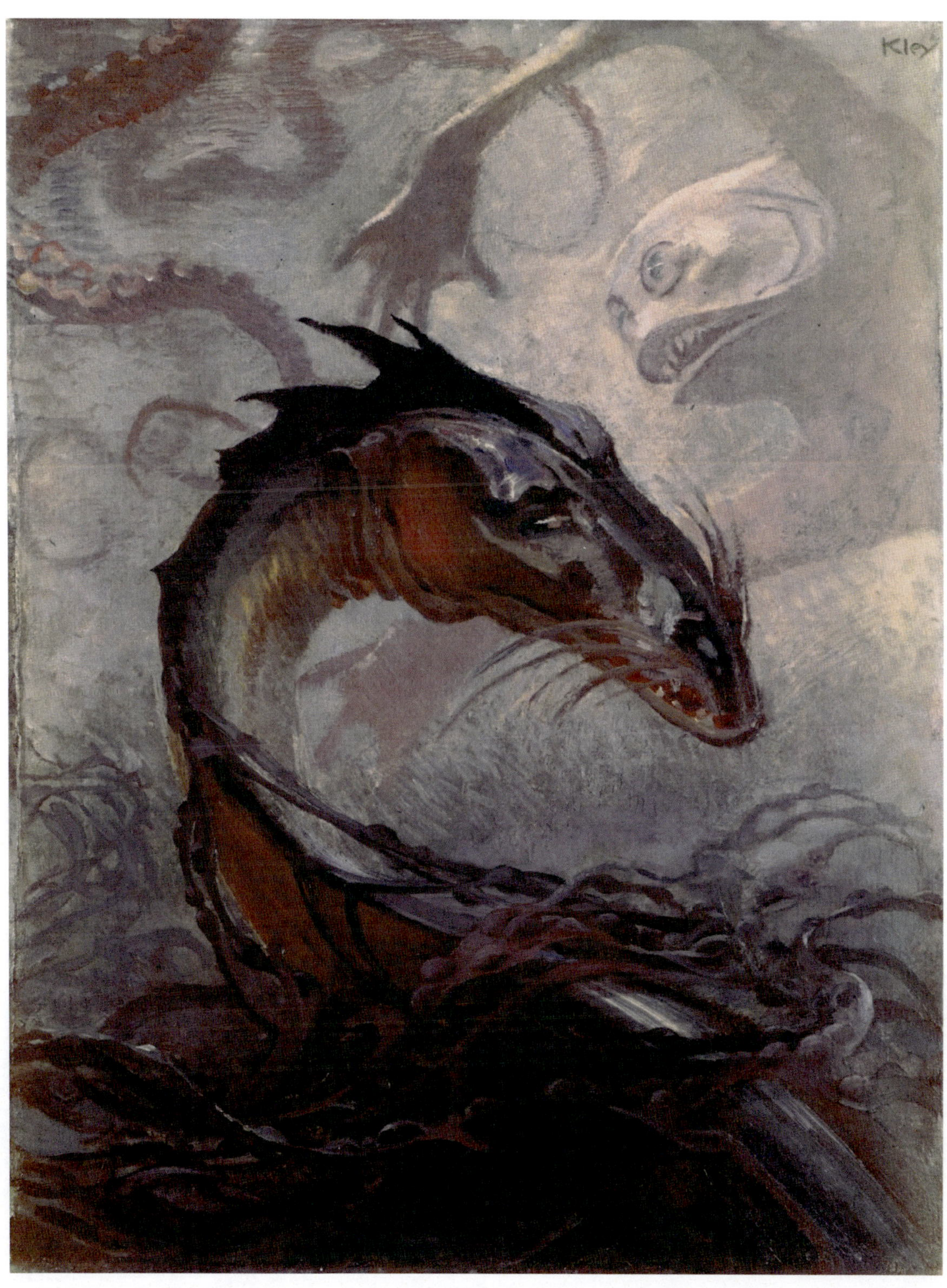
Kley

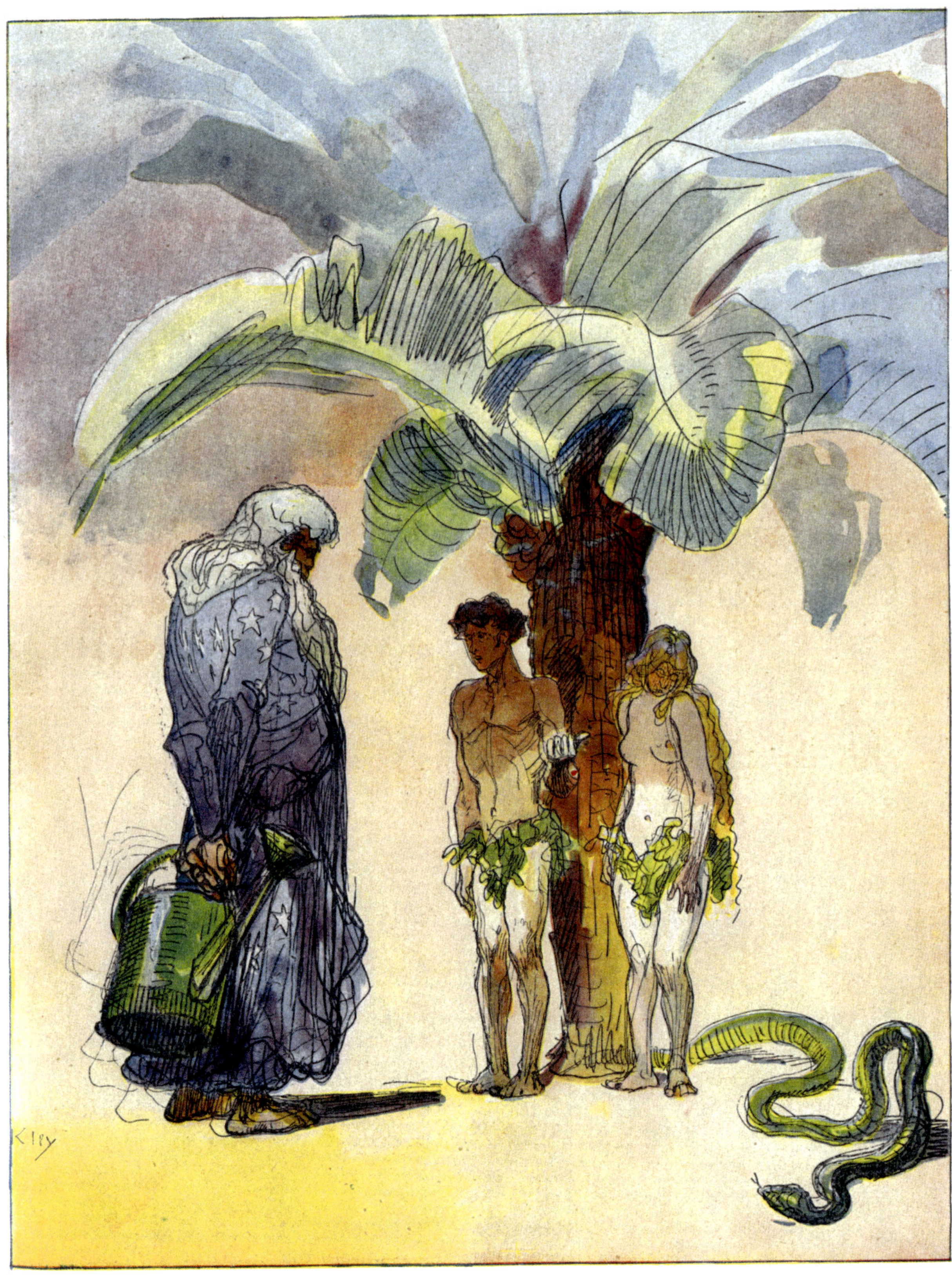

God and the Fall of Mankind
"I guess I'm just too trusting! My competition in Rome would have had you swear the Oath Against Modernism!"
Der liebe Gott und der Sündenfall
"Ich bin halt zu vertrauensselig! Meine Konkurrenz in Rom hätt' Euch einfach den Modernisten-Eid schwören lassen!"
Jugend (No. 3) • 1911

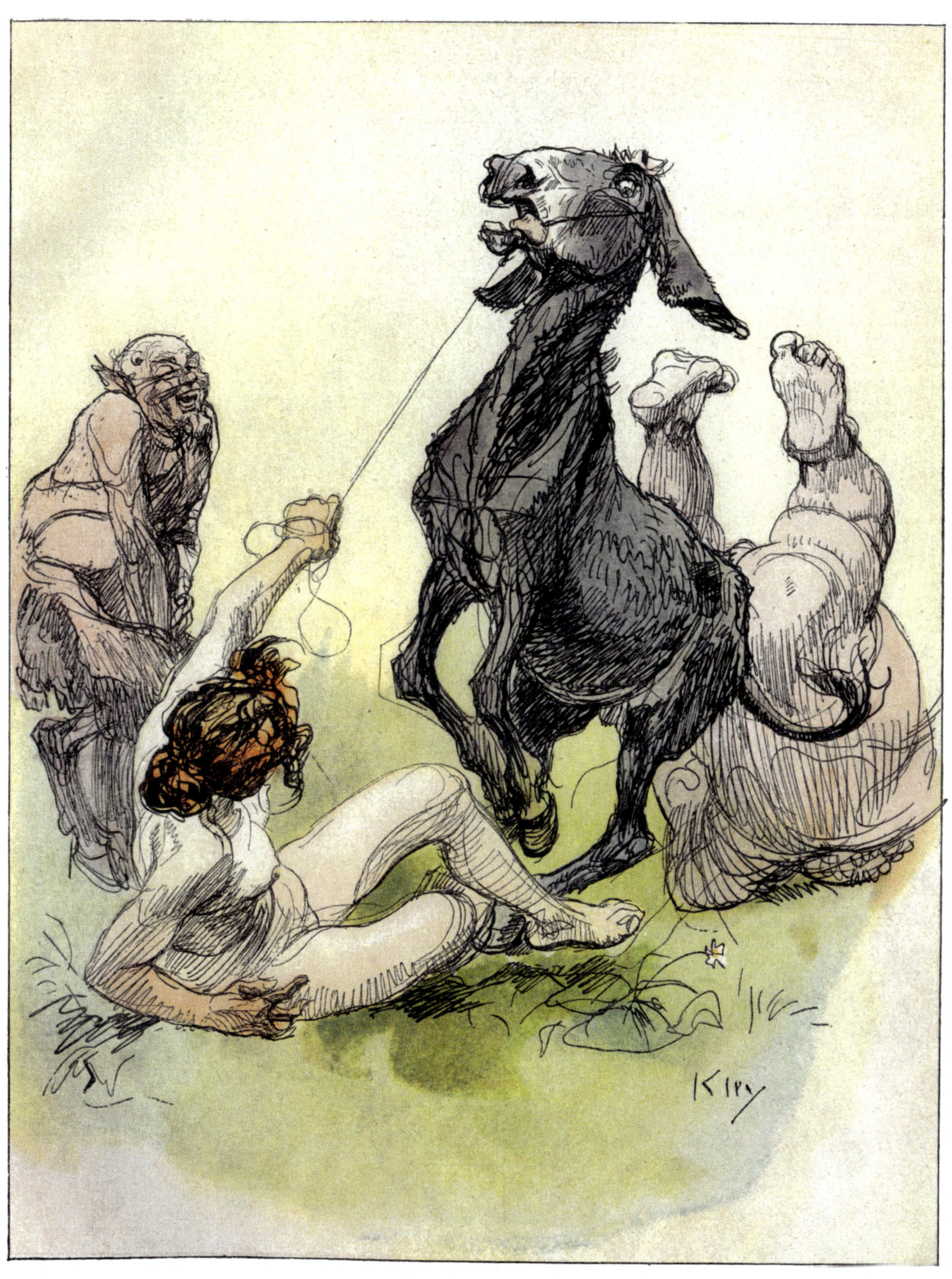

The Satyr's Donkey
Der Esel des Silen
Jugend (No. 45) • 1911

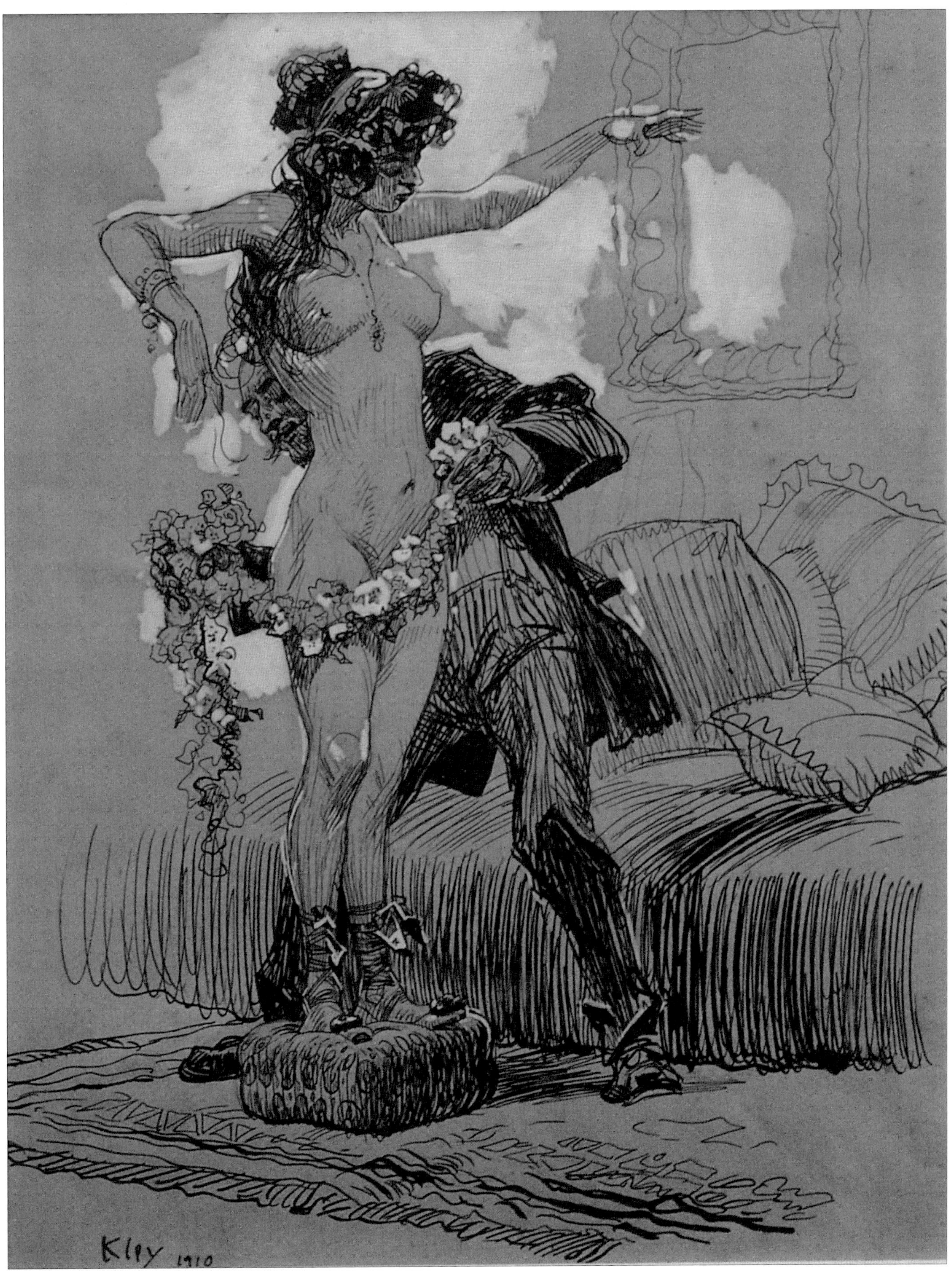
Kley 1910

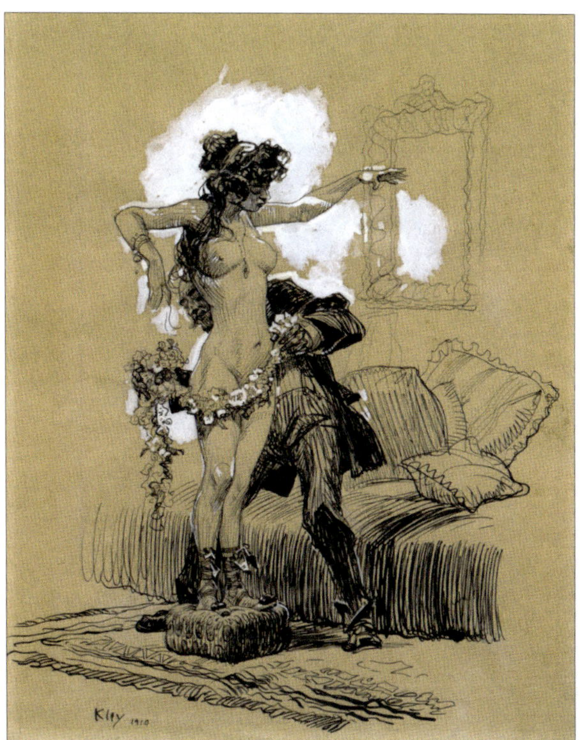

Decorate Your Home!
Schmücke dein heim!

Jugend (No. 53) • 1910

The figures in this drawing are likenesses of Kley and his first wife, Theophanie.
(left and detail on opposite page)

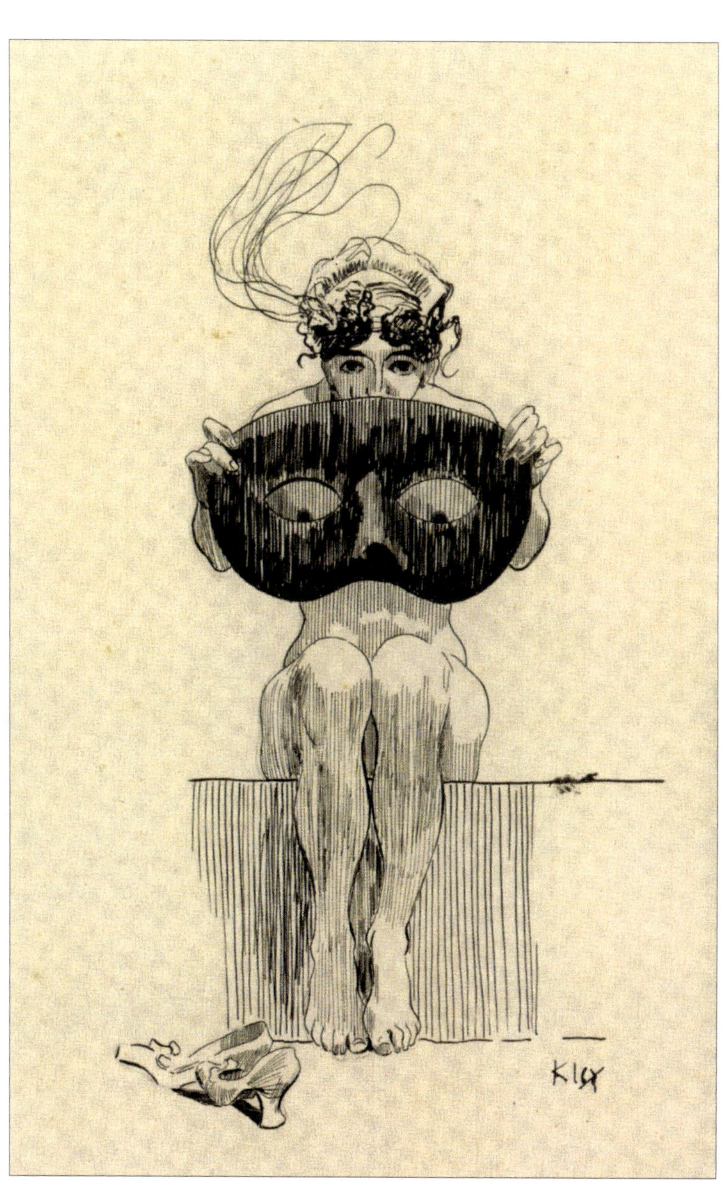

In Private
Unter Vier Augen
approx. 1912

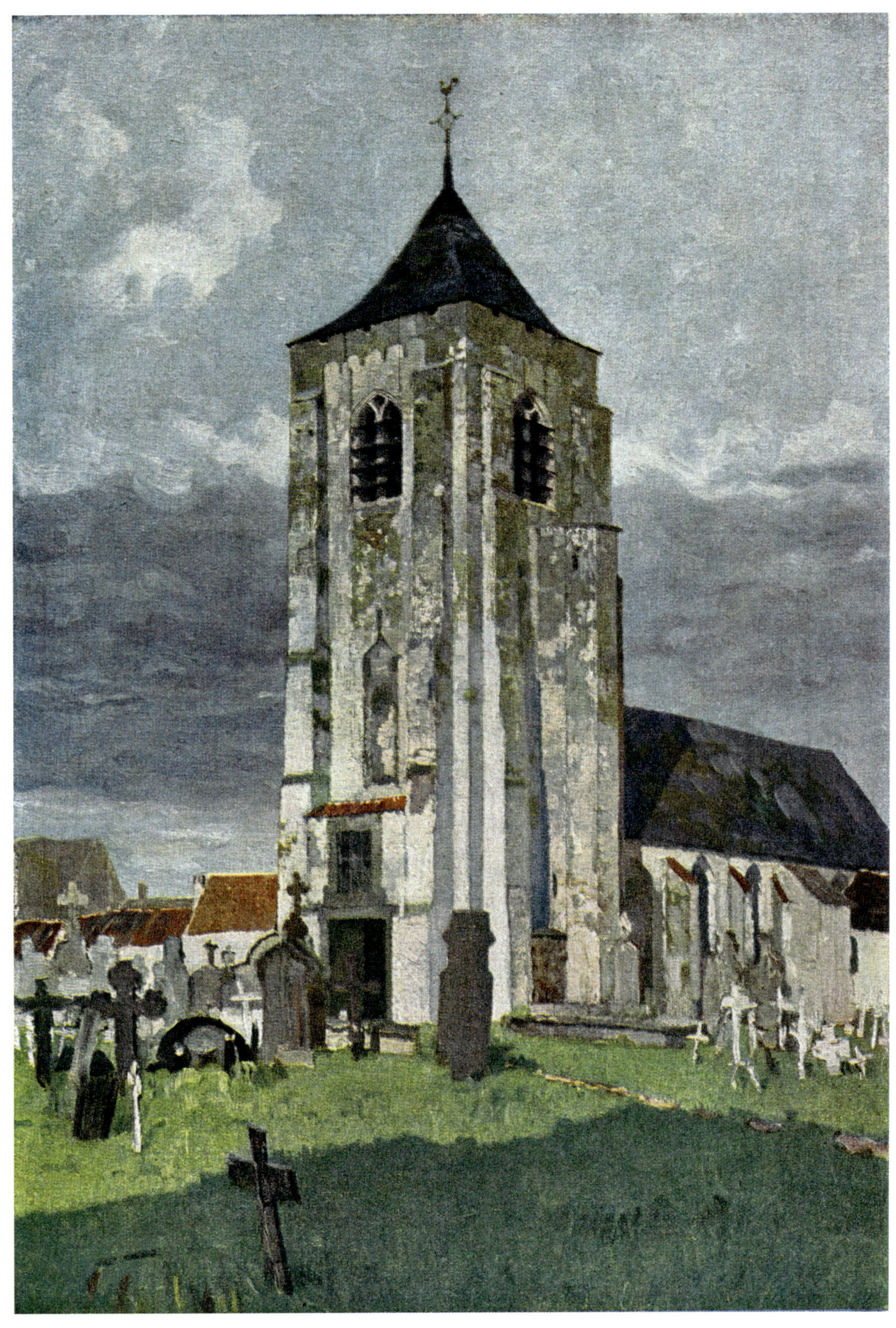

Maria Kerke in Ostend
Maria Kerke bei Ostende
Jugend • 1910

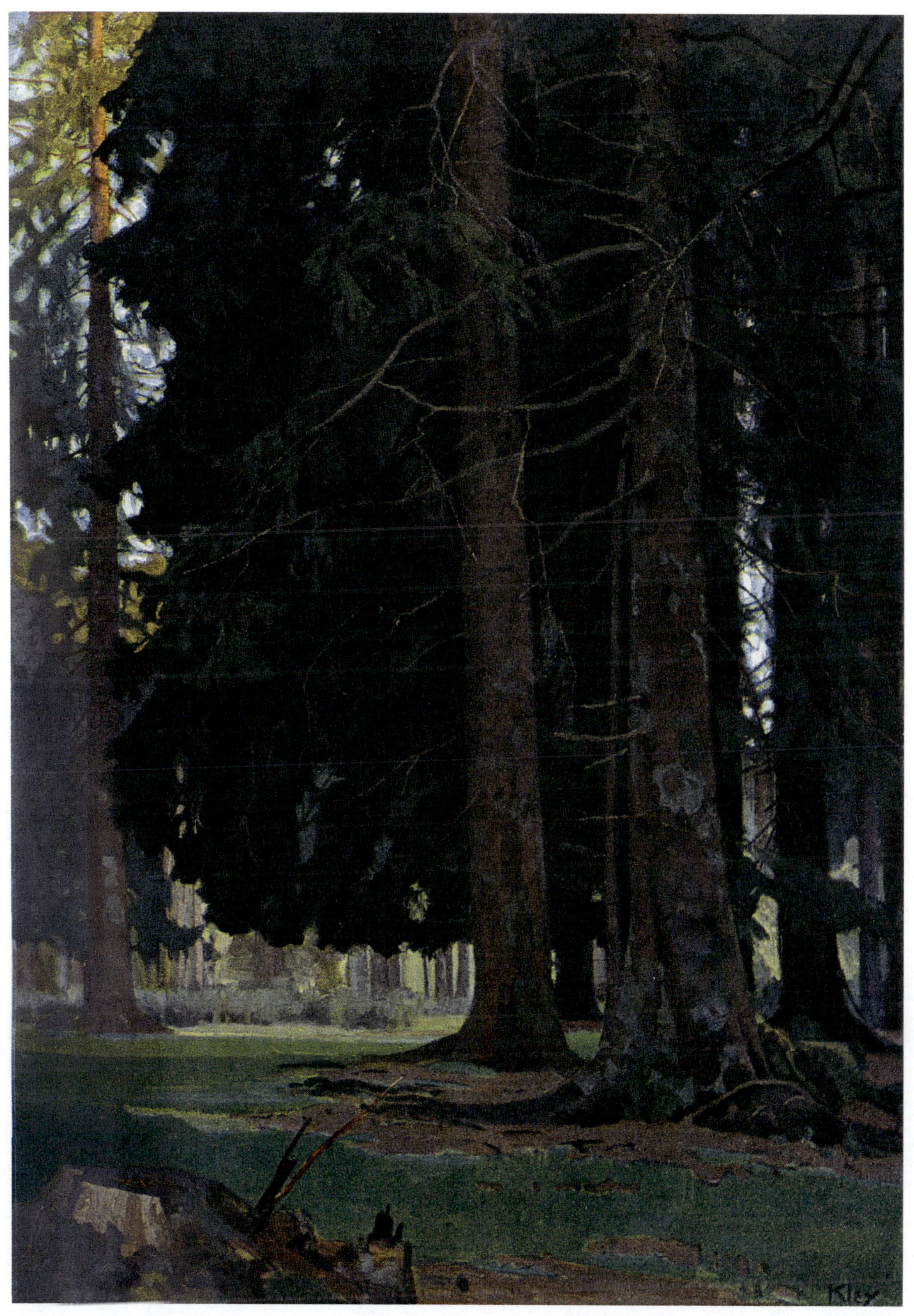

The Black Forest
Jugend • 1910

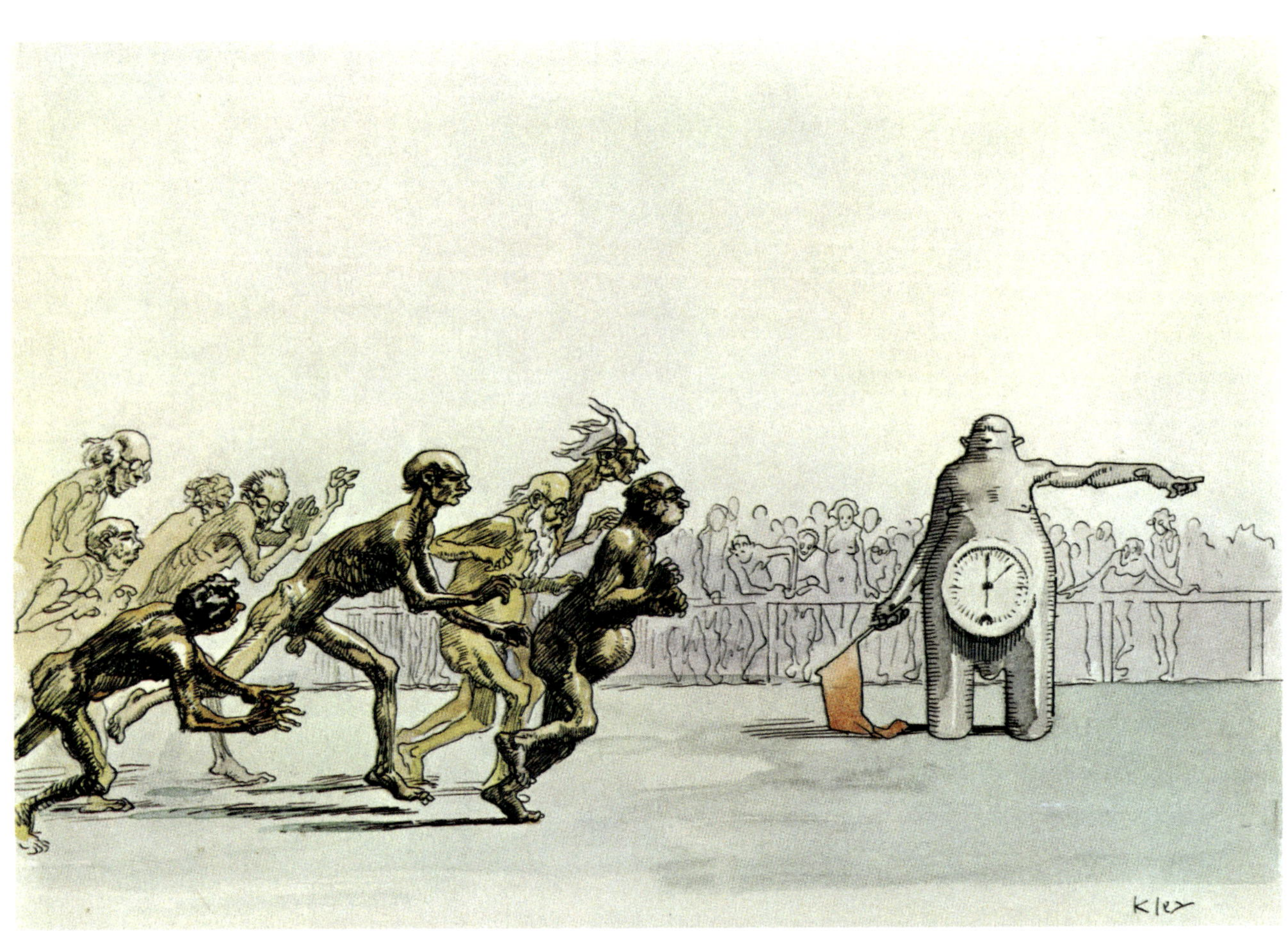
Kley

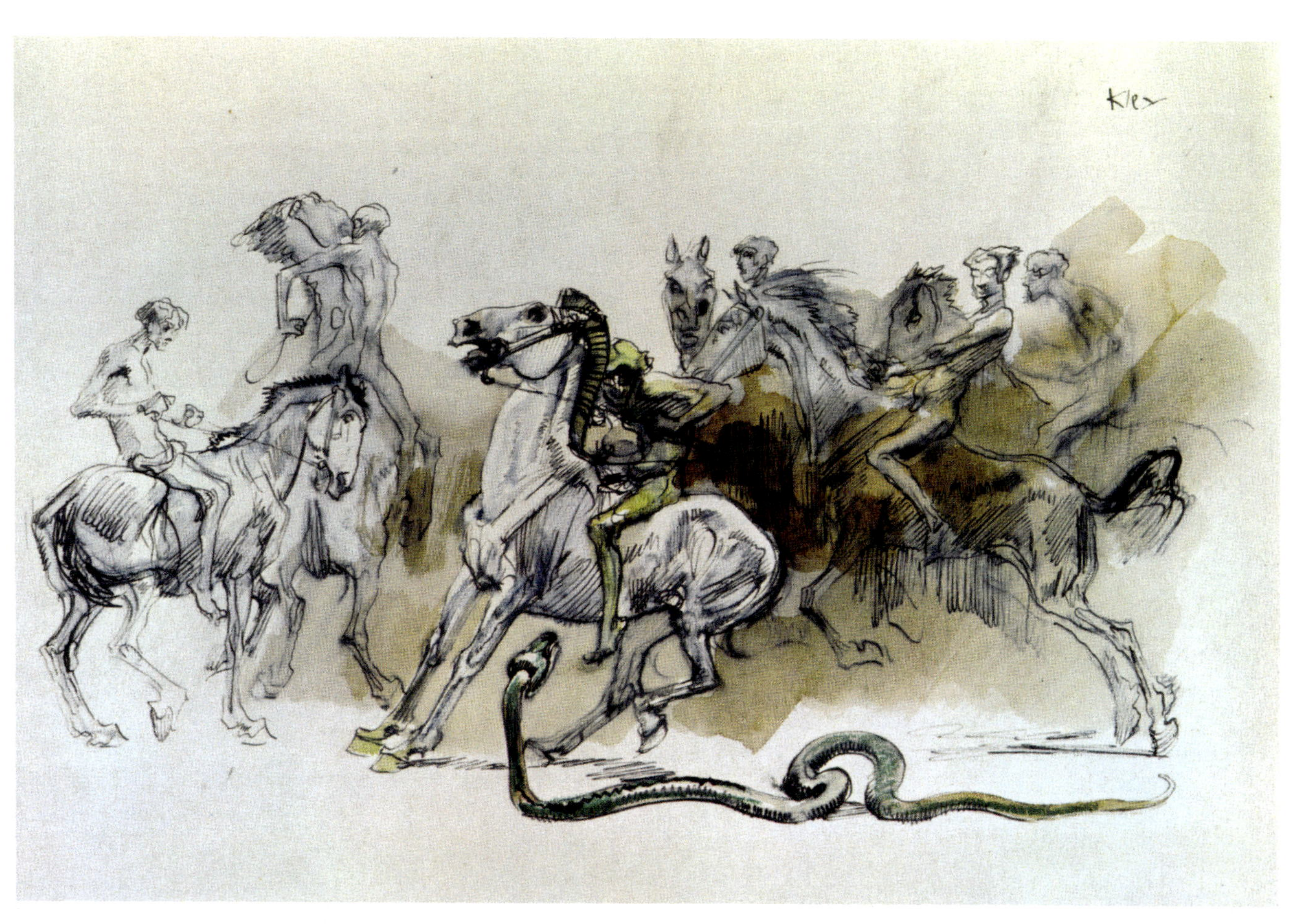

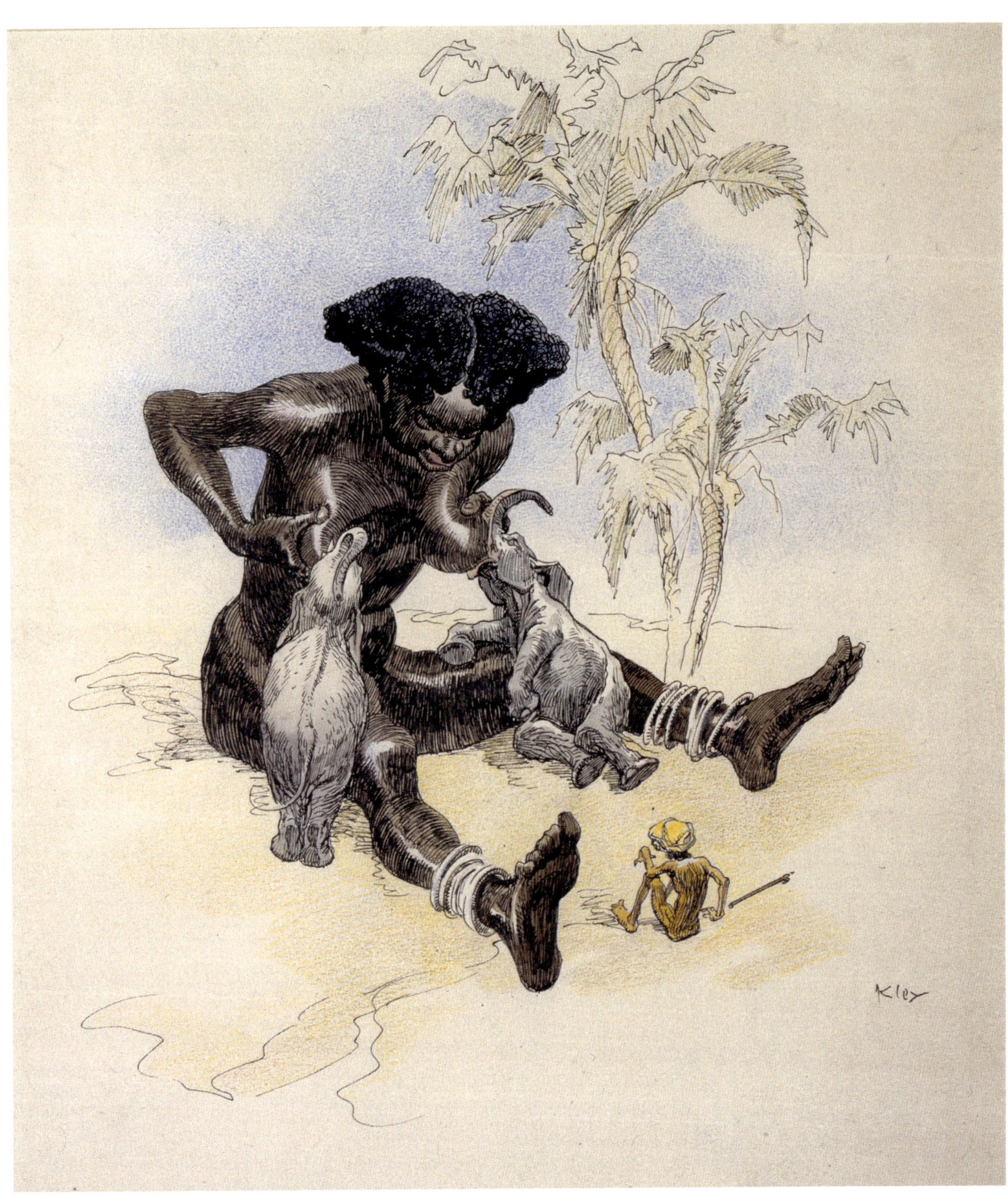
Kley

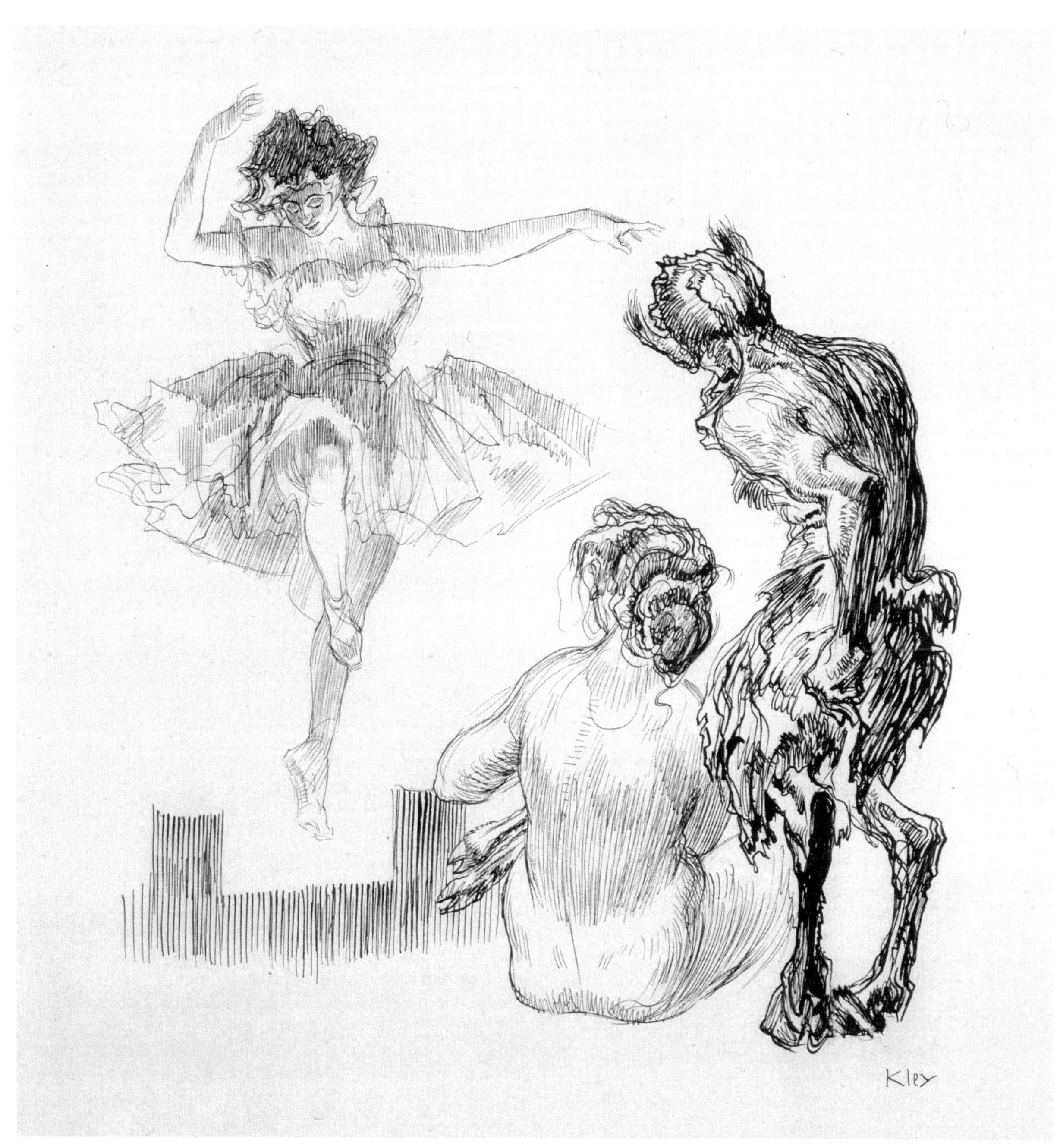
Kley

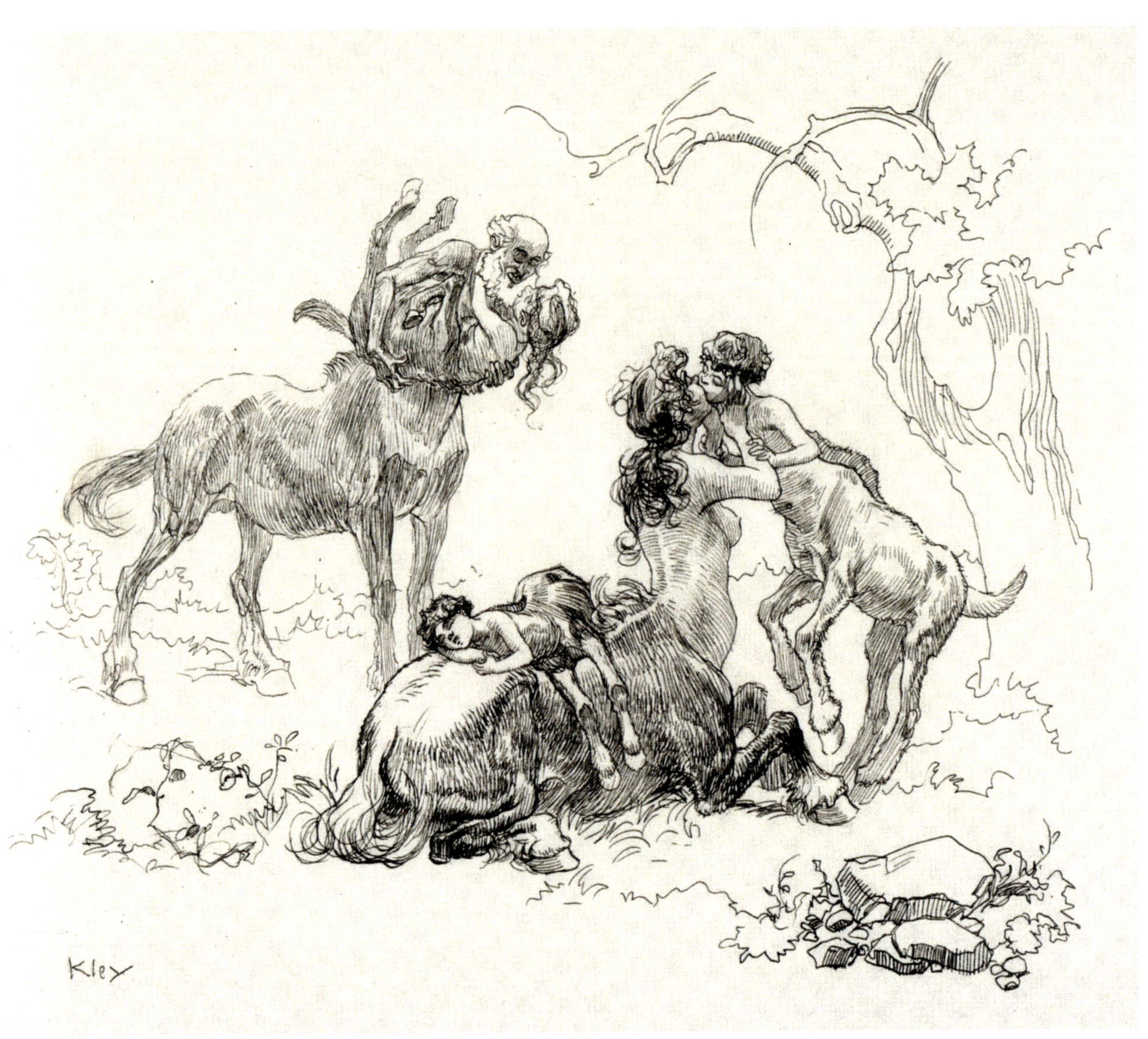

The Centaur Family

Approximately 1910

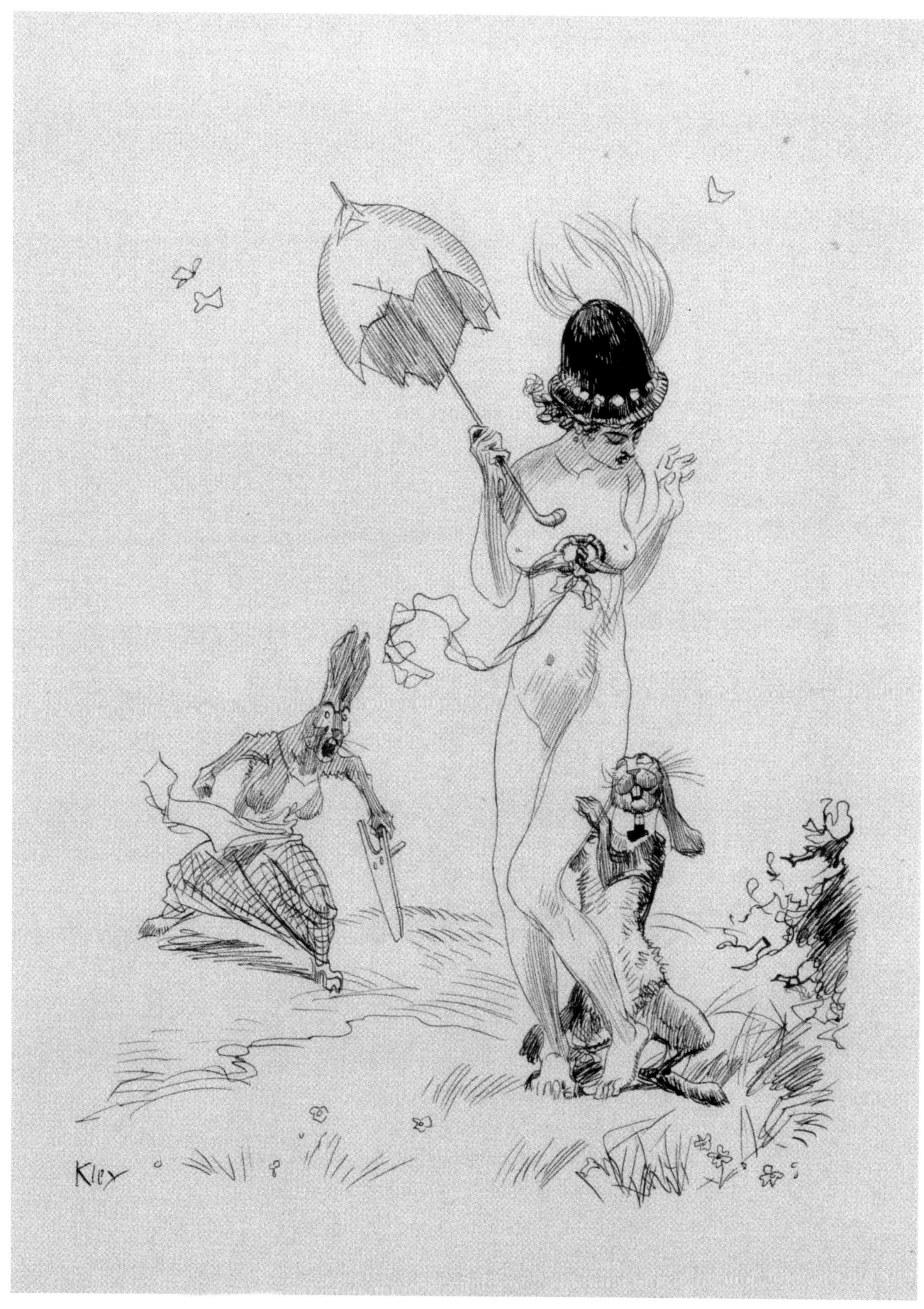

The Bunny
Der Osterhase
1912

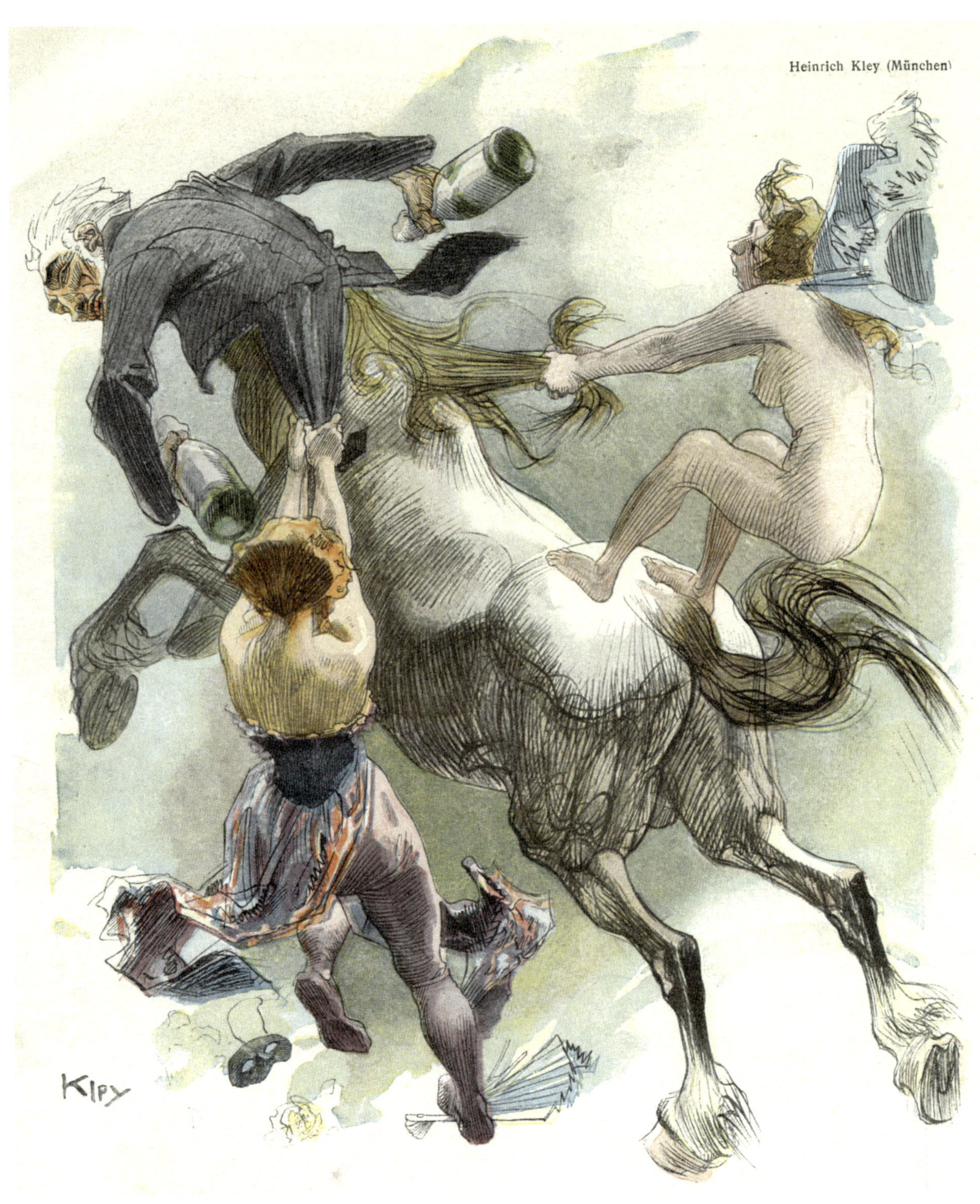

The Champagne Centaur
Der Sekt-Centaur
Jugend (No. 6) • 1914

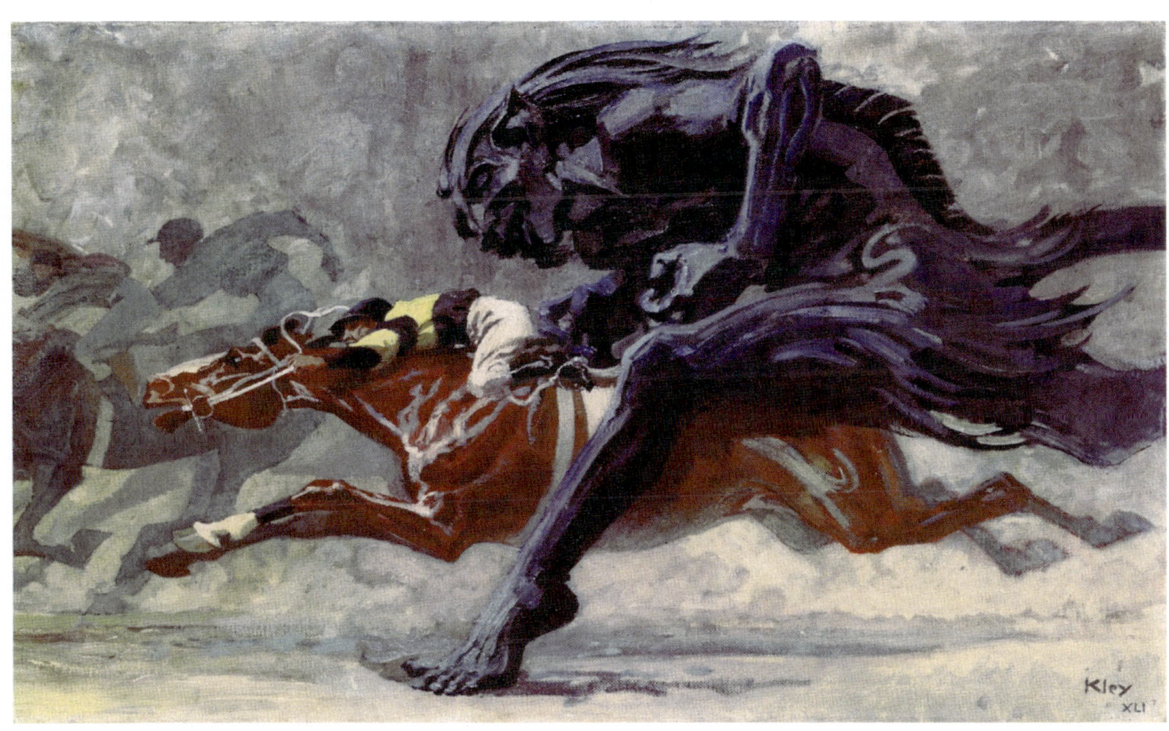
Kley
XLI

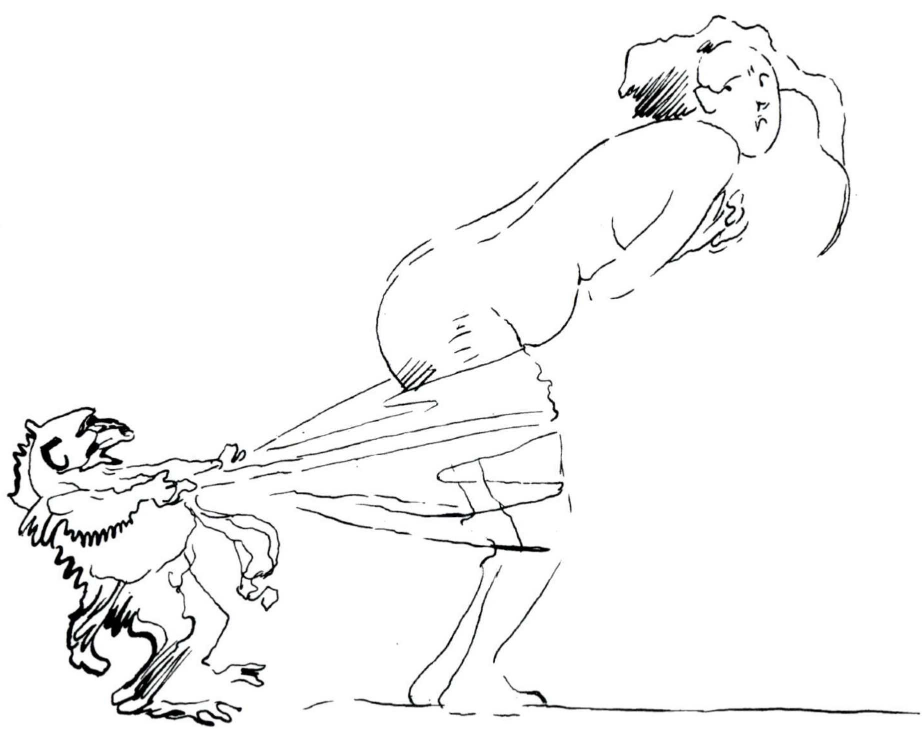

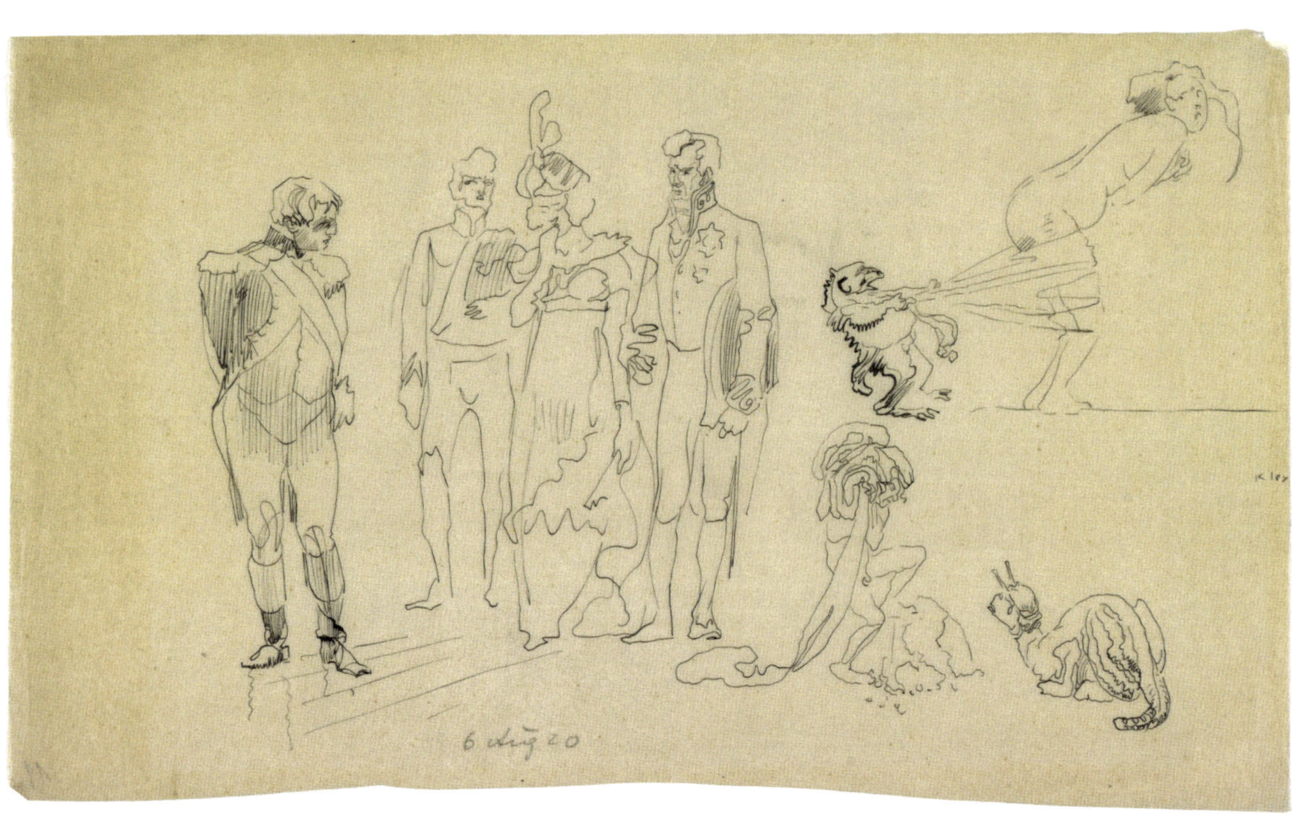

The largest drawing on the above sheet was a preliminary sketch
for an illustration that eventually appeared in *From the War Years 1806–1813* (see *Volume 1*, p. 68).

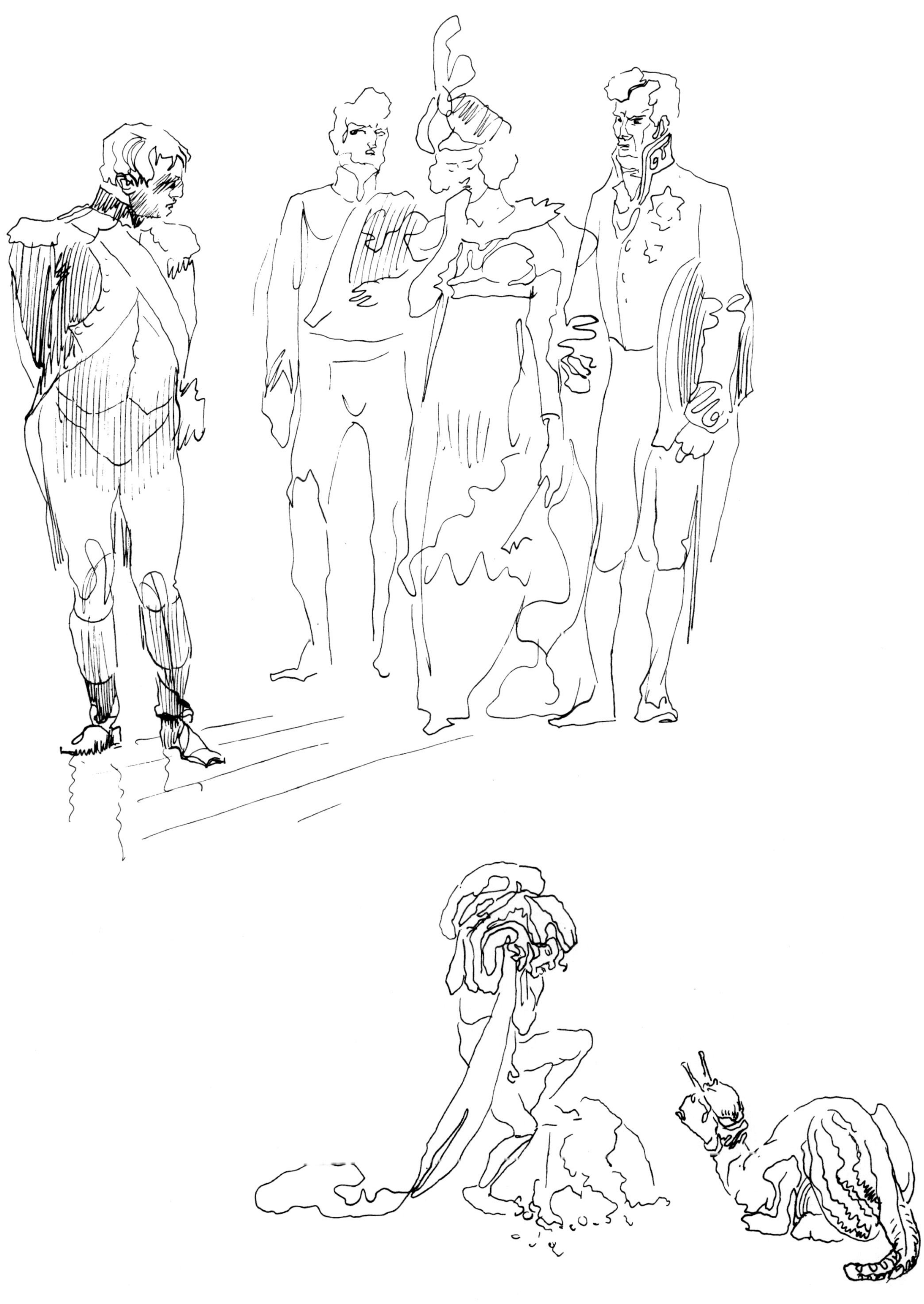

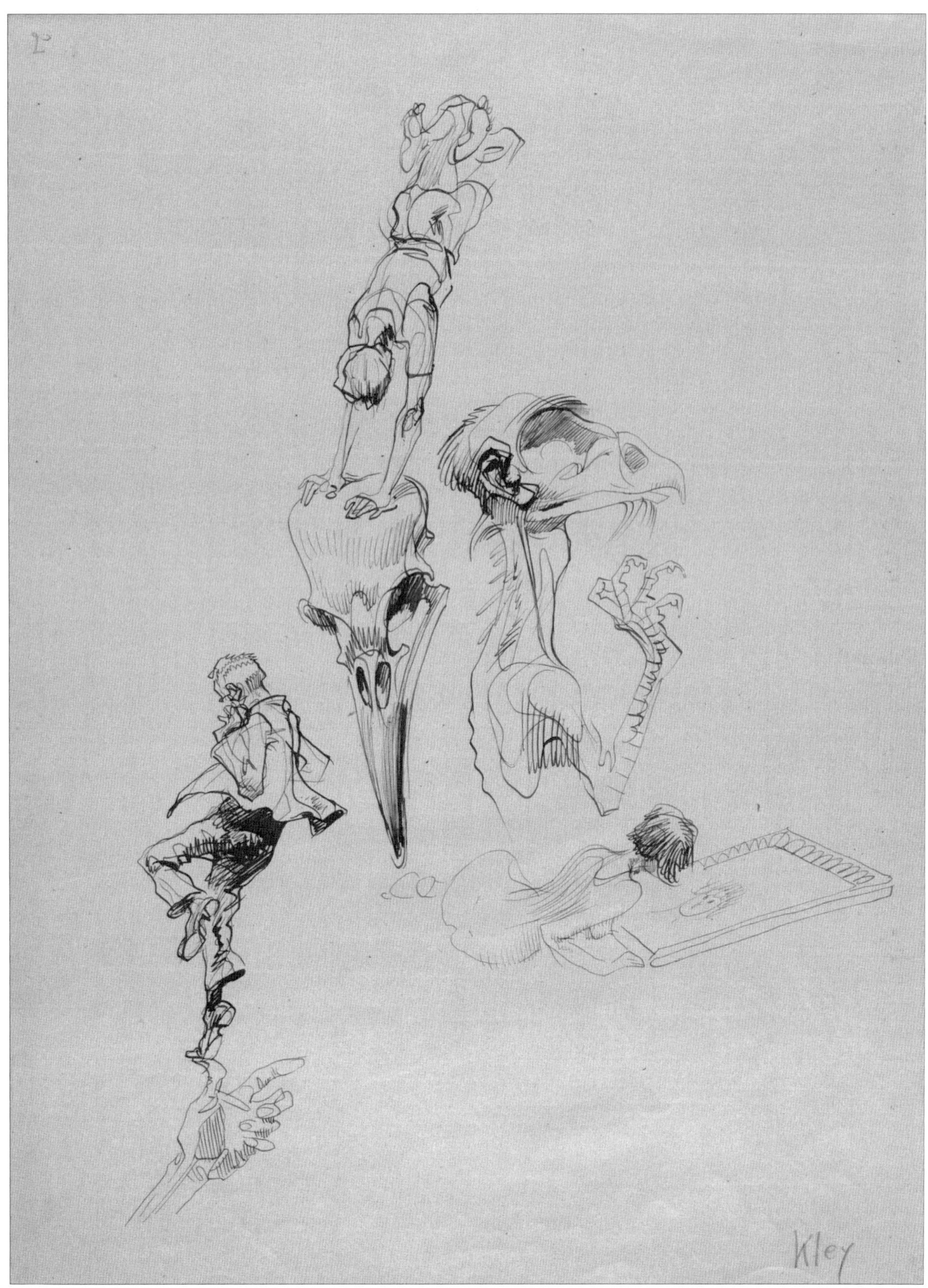

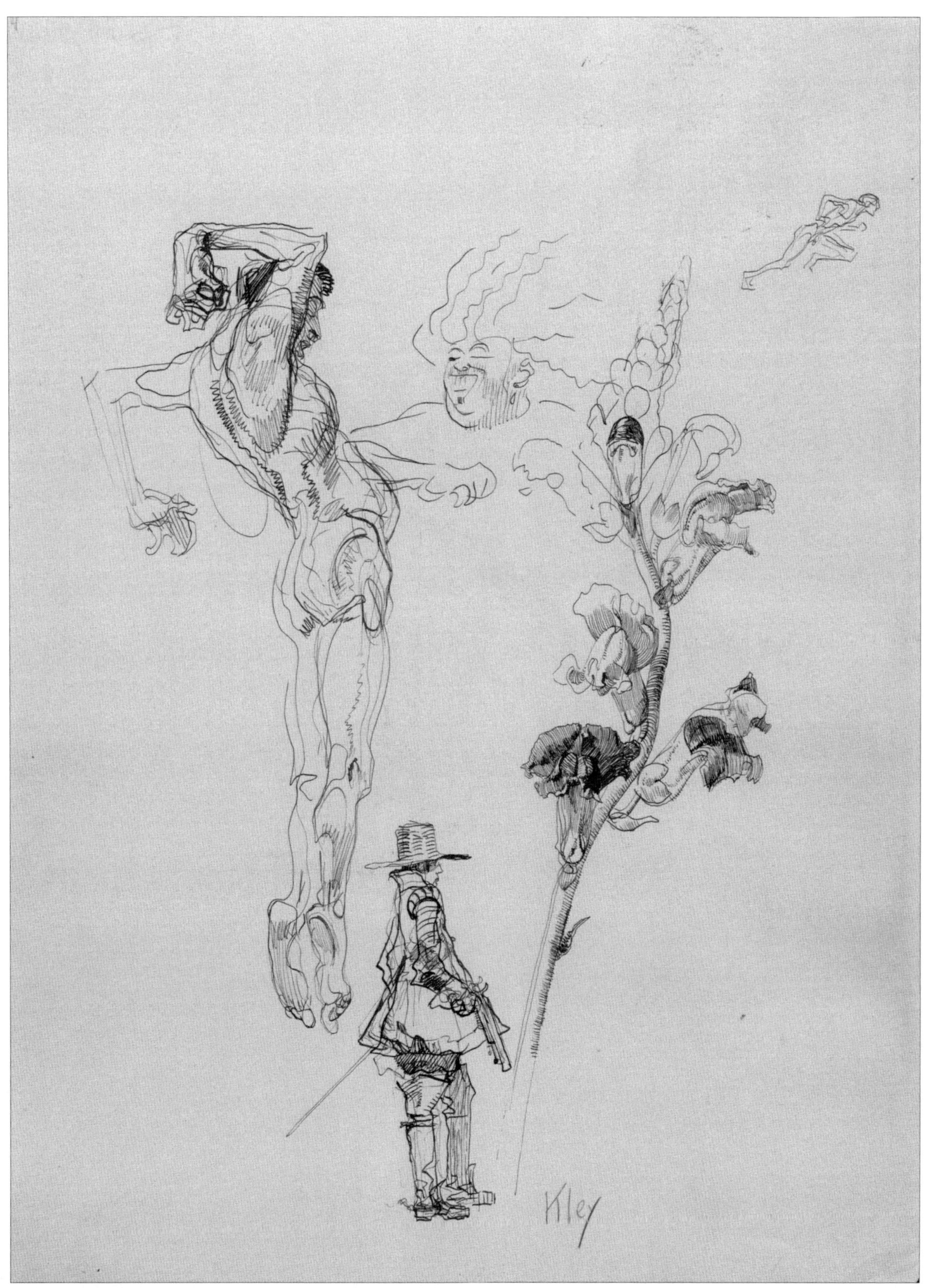
Kley

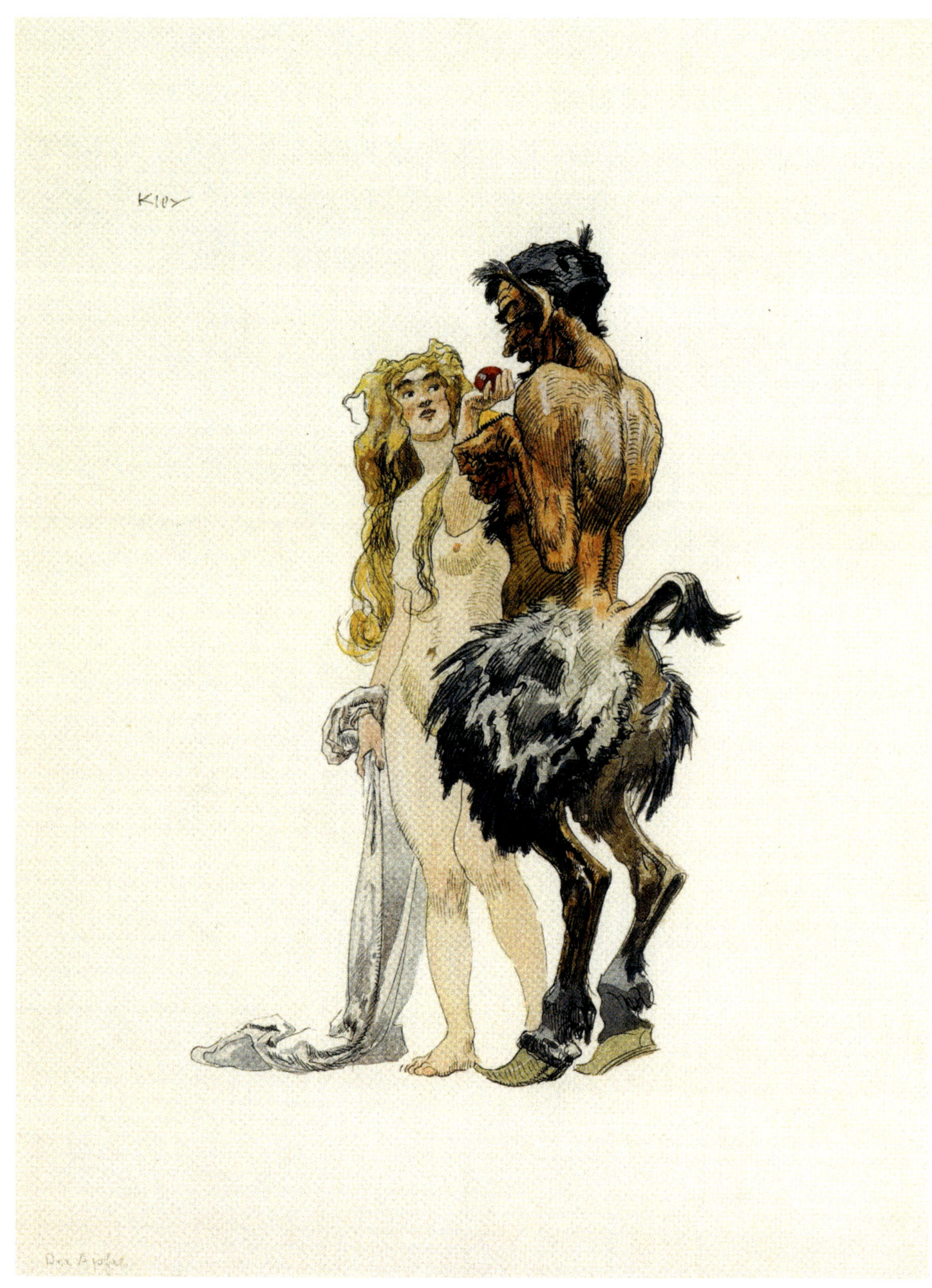

The Apple
Der Apfel
Approximately 1910

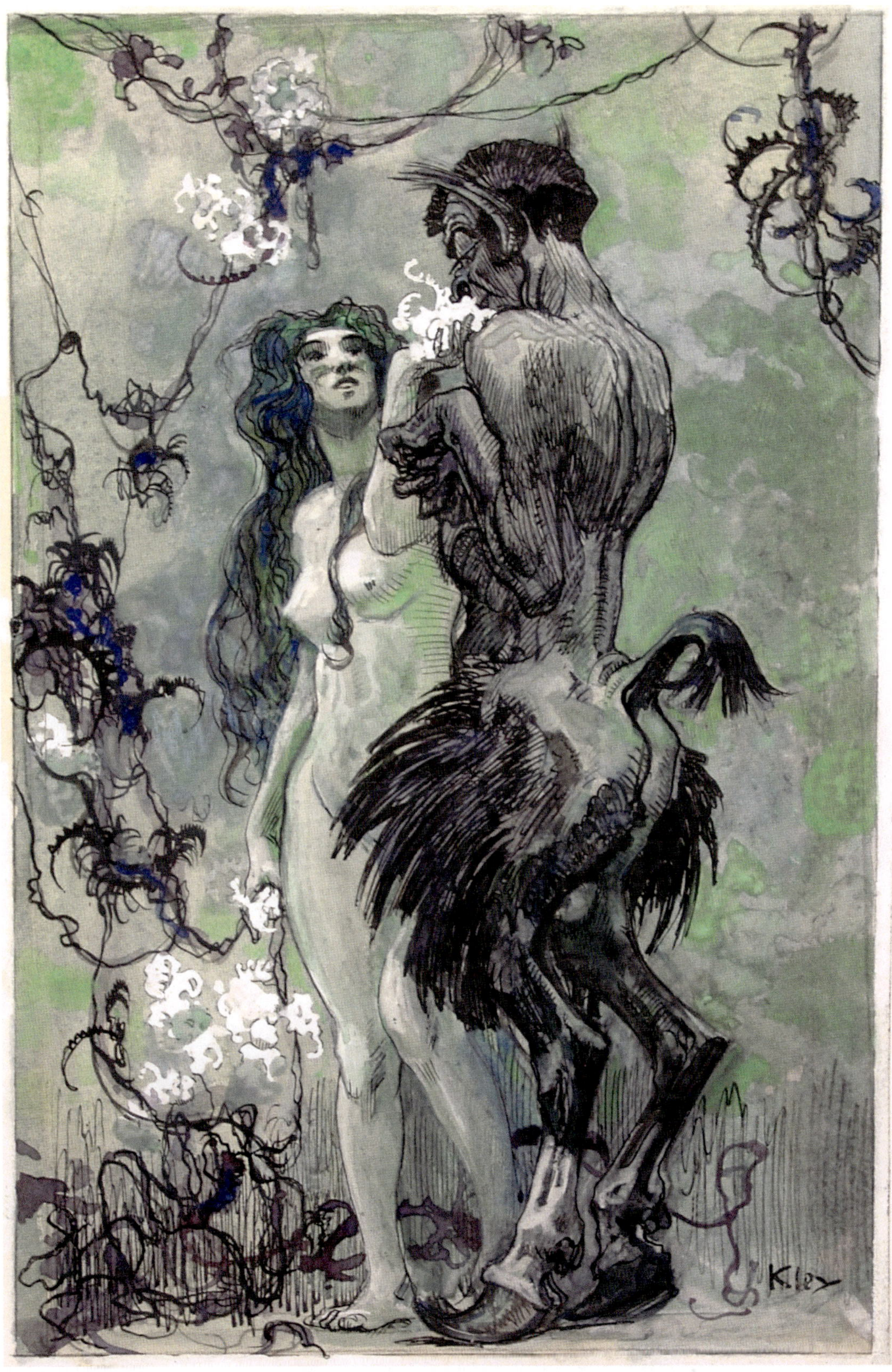
Kley

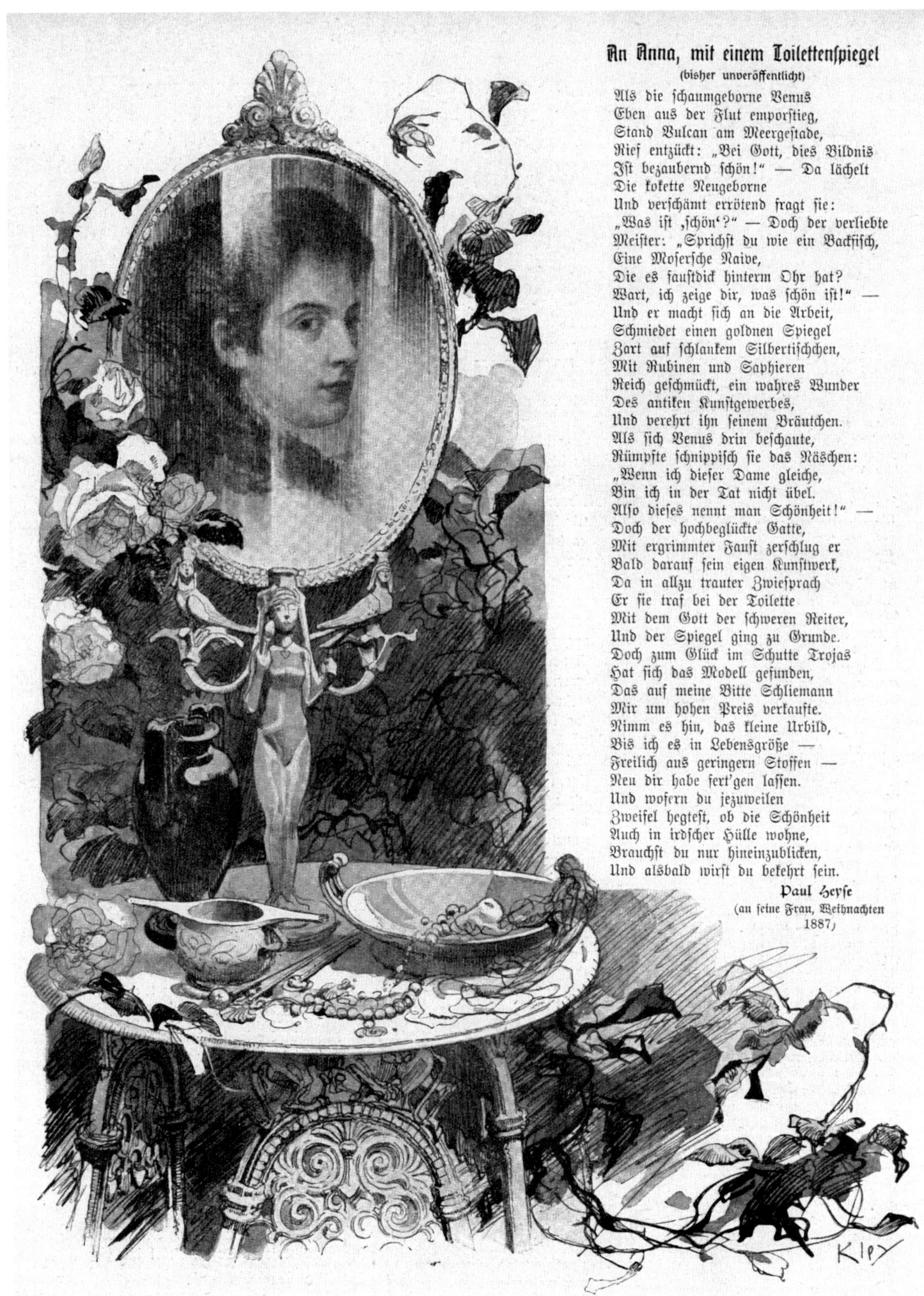

An Anna, mit einem Toilettenspiegel

(bisher unveröffentlicht)

Als die schaumgeborne Venus
Eben aus der Flut emporstieg,
Stand Vulcan am Meergestade,
Rief entzückt: „Bei Gott, dies Bildnis
Ist bezaubernd schön!“ — Da lächelt
Die kokette Neugeborne
Und verschämt errötend fragt sie:
„Was ist ‚schön‘?“ — Doch der verliebte
Meister: „Sprichst du wie ein Backfisch,
Eine Mosersche Naive,
Die es faustdick hinterm Ohr hat?
Wart, ich zeige dir, was schön ist!“ —
Und er macht sich an die Arbeit,
Schmiedet einen goldnen Spiegel
Zart auf schlankem Silbertischchen,
Mit Rubinen und Saphieren
Reich geschmückt, ein wahres Wunder
Des antiken Kunstgewerbes,
Und verehrt ihn seinem Bräutchen.
Als sich Venus drin beschaute,
Rümpfte schnippisch sie das Näschen:
„Wenn ich dieser Dame gleiche,
Bin ich in der Tat nicht übel.
Also dieses nennt man Schönheit!“ —
Doch der hochbeglückte Gatte,
Mit ergrimmter Faust zerschlug er
Bald darauf sein eigen Kunstwerk,
Da in allzu trauter Zwiesprach
Er sie traf bei der Toilette
Mit dem Gott der schweren Reiter,
Und der Spiegel ging zu Grunde.
Doch zum Glück im Schutte Trojas
Hat sich das Modell gefunden,
Das auf meine Bitte Schliemann
Mir um hohen Preis verkaufte.
Nimm es hin, das kleine Urbild,
Bis ich es in Lebensgröße —
Freilich aus geringern Stoffen —
Neu dir habe fert'gen lassen.
Und wofern du jezuweilen
Zweifel hegtest, ob die Schönheit
Auch in irdscher Hülle wohne,
Brauchst du nur hineinzublicken,
Und alsbald wirst du bekehrt sein.

Paul Heyse
(an seine Frau, Weihnachten 1887)

To Anna, in the vanity mirror
An Anna, mit einem toilettenspiegel
Jugend • 1910

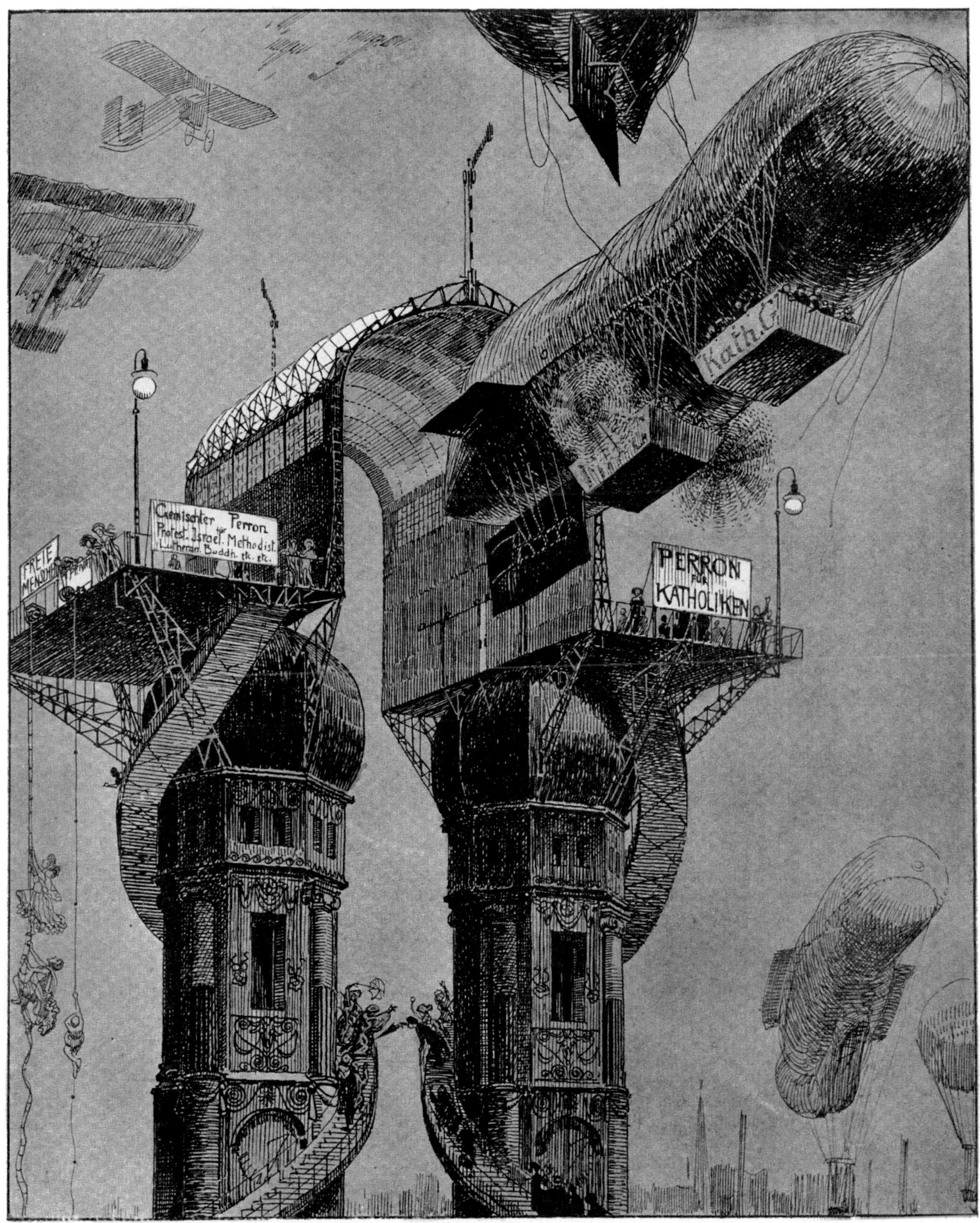

Airship Traffic between Isarathens and Oberammergau

Accompanied by the people's Dionysian applause, the first Parseval-Drachen airship left for its Icarus flight into the blue ocean of clouds. The gondolas, which were divided by denomination, proved very popular. The only thing that disgruntled a few black sheep was that the vehicle was filled with equalizing gas.

Jugend • 1910

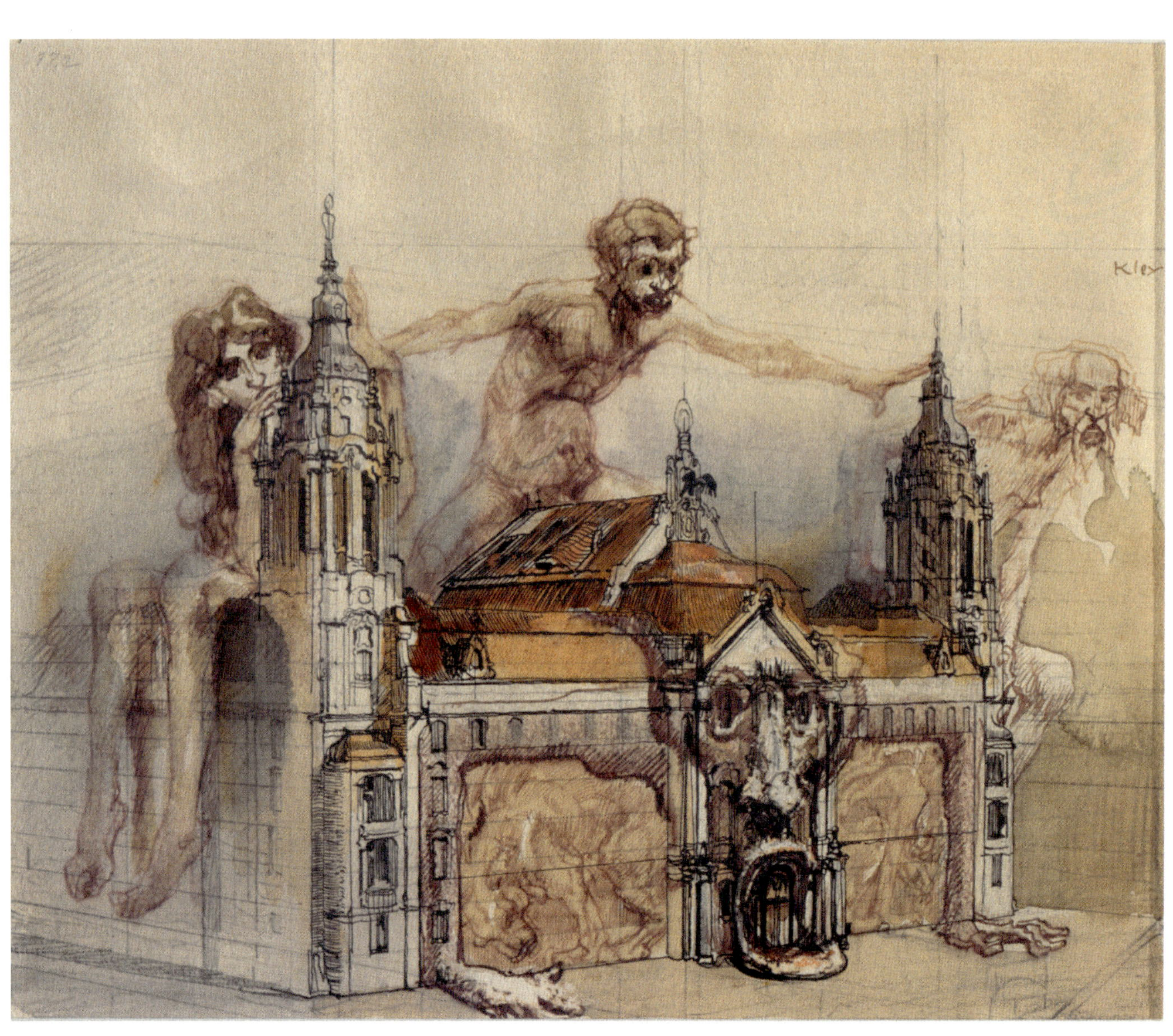
Kley

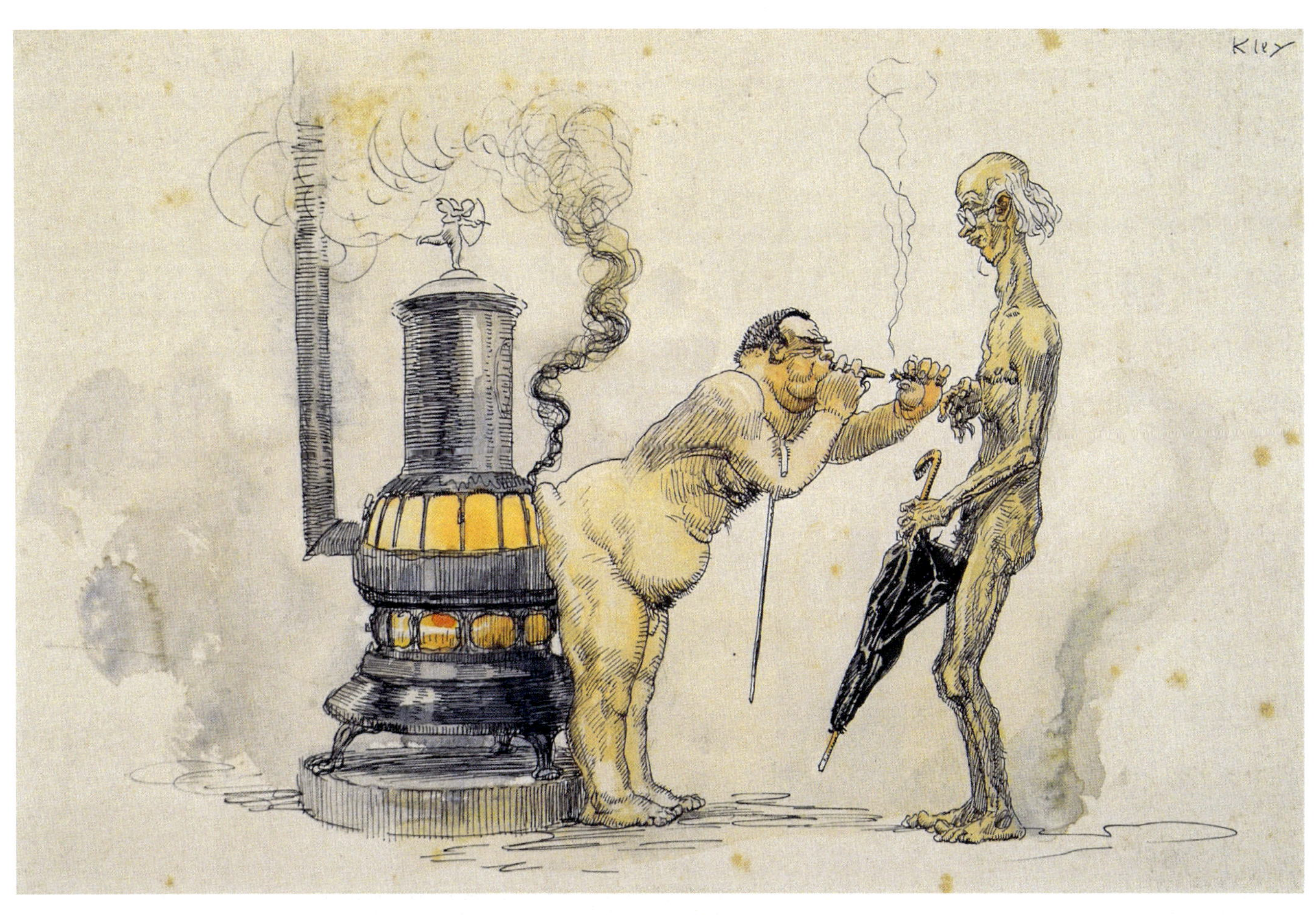
Kley

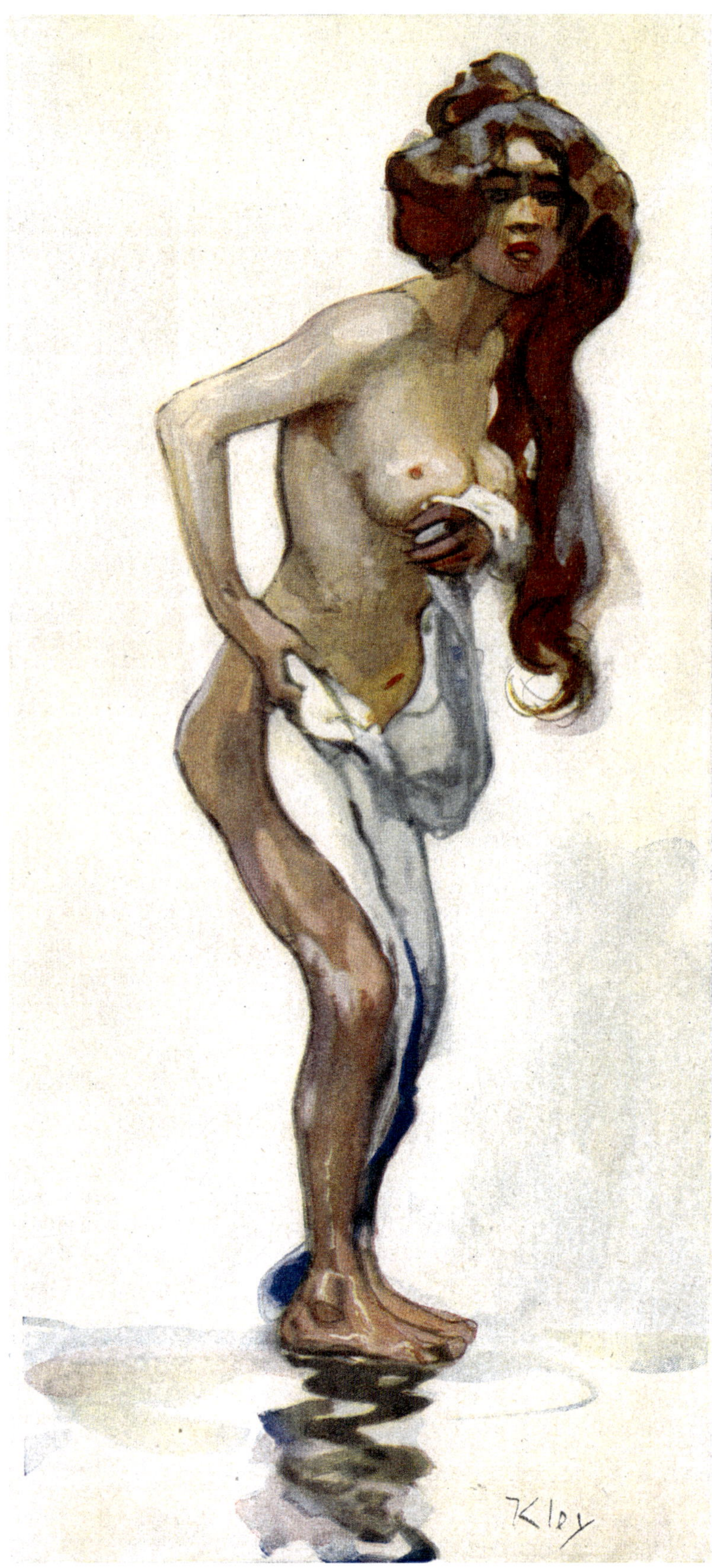

The Loreley
"I wish I knew how to get to St. Goarshausen—I broke my comb!"
Die Loreley
"Wenn ich nur wüsst', wie ich nach St. Goarshausen käm': mein Kamm ist mir gebrochen!"
Jugend • 1911

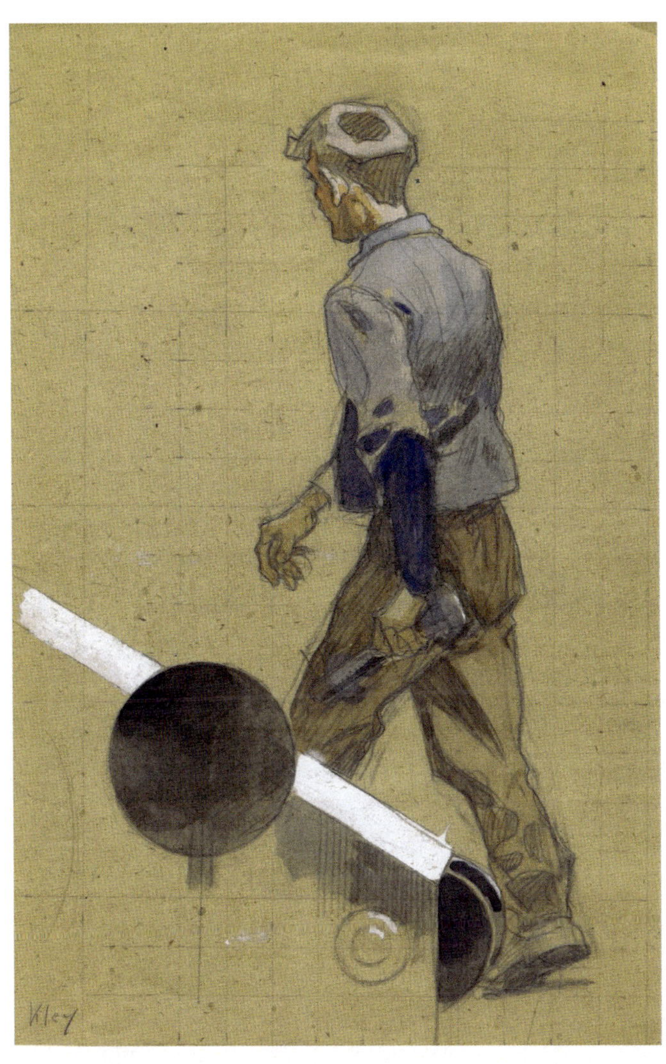
Kley

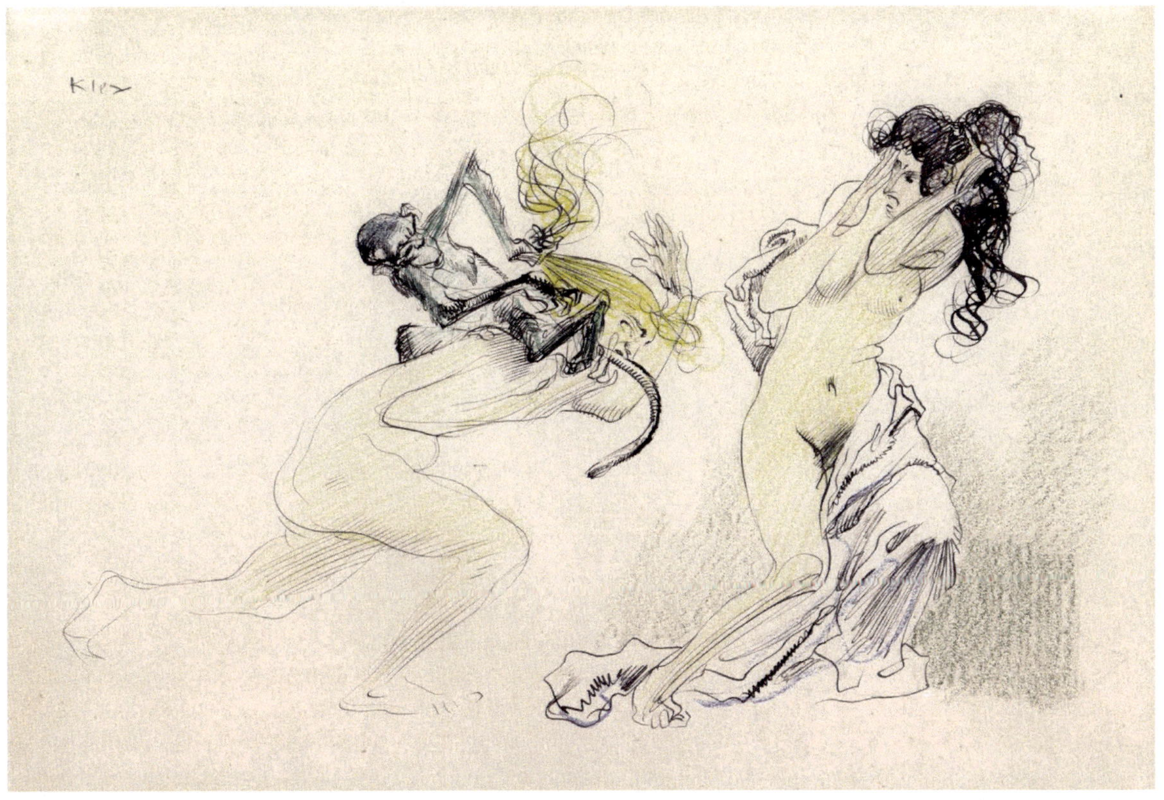
Kley

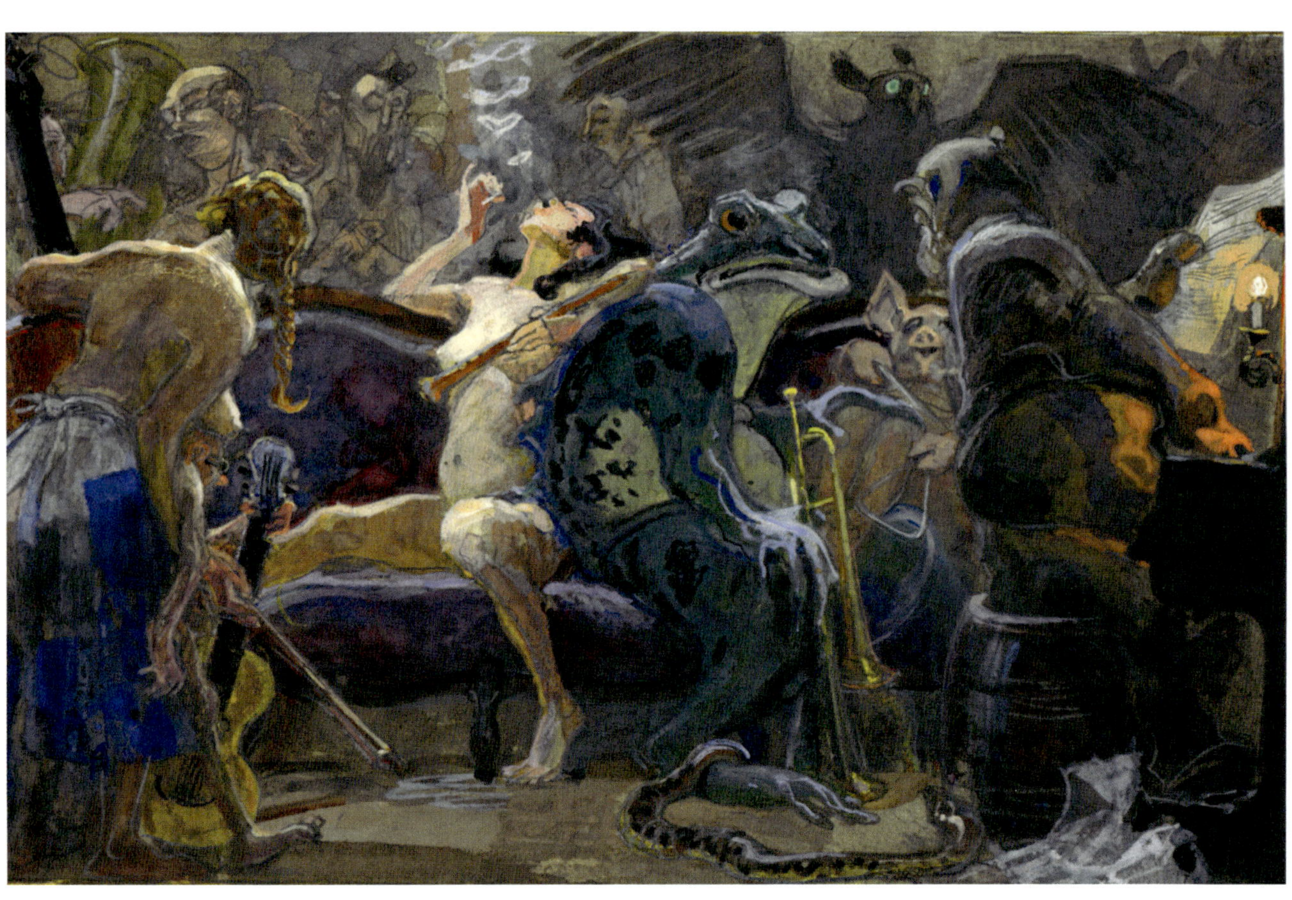

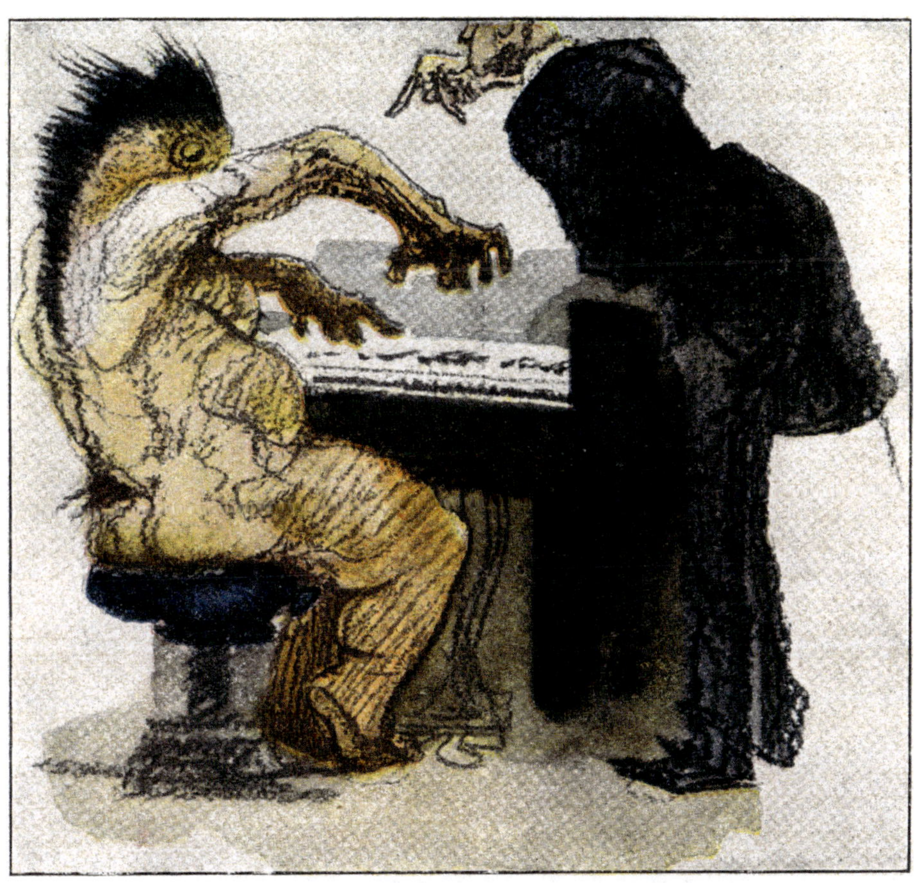

Rudimentary Exercises
Anfangsgründe
Jugend • 1911

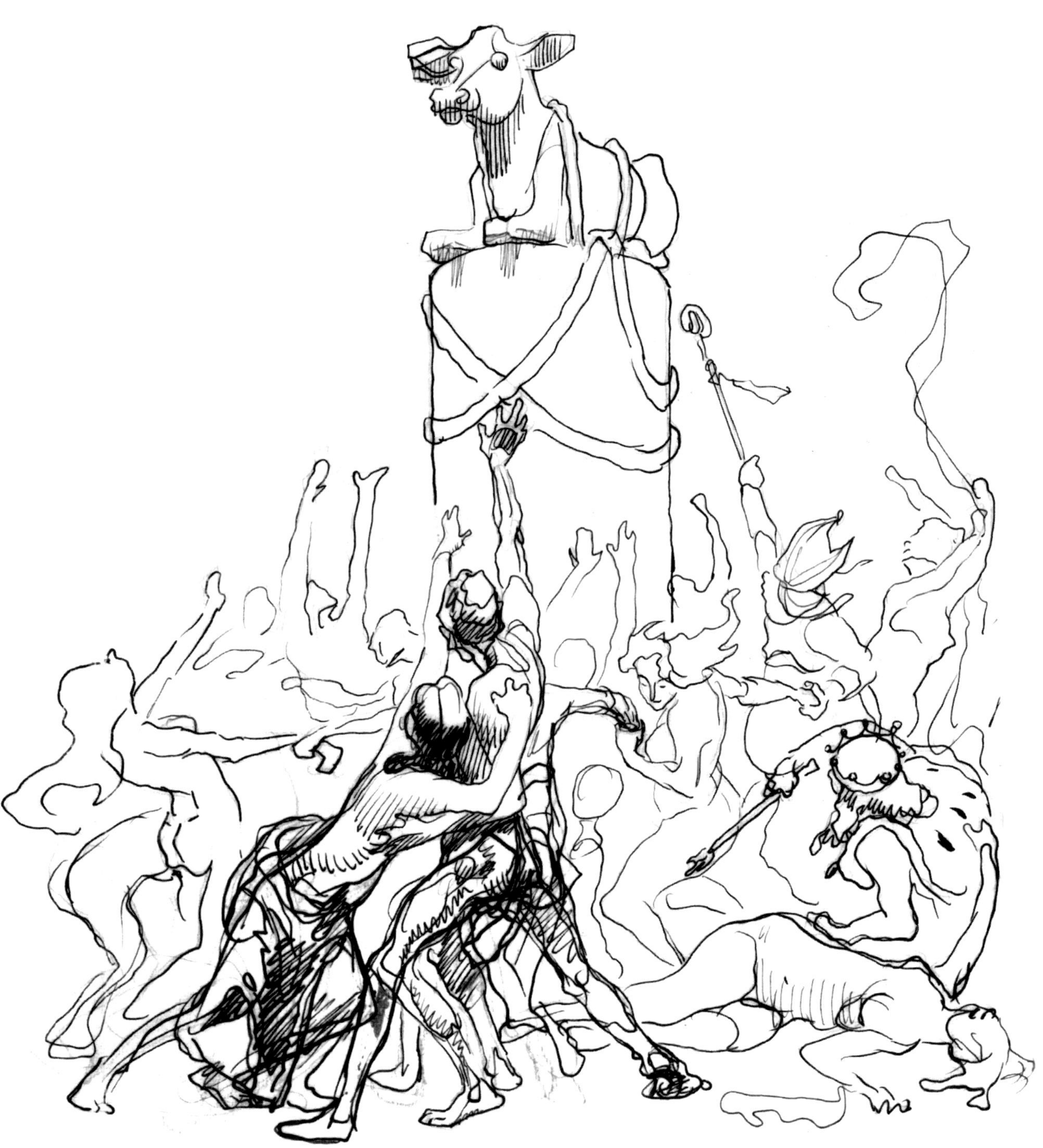

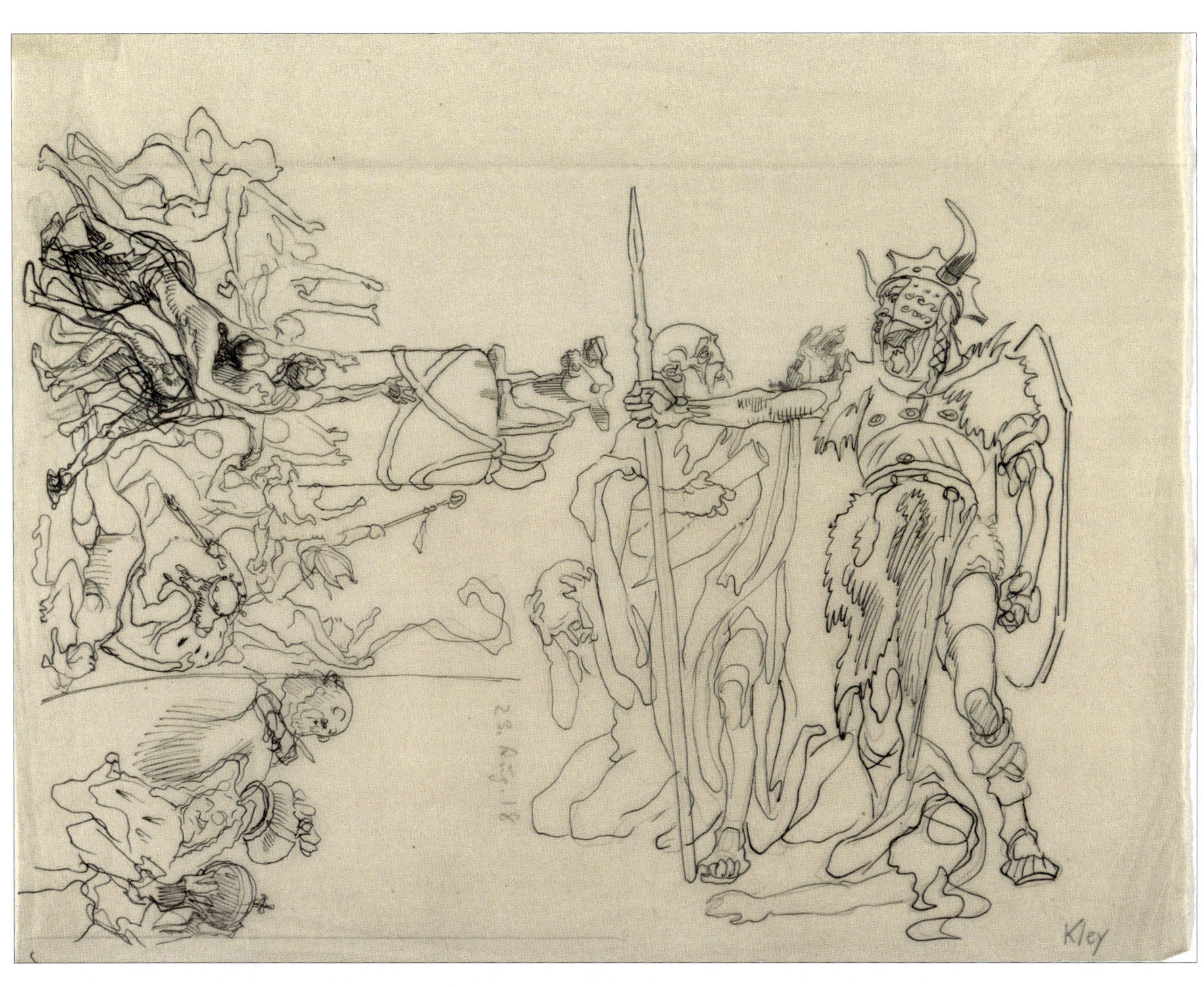
Kley

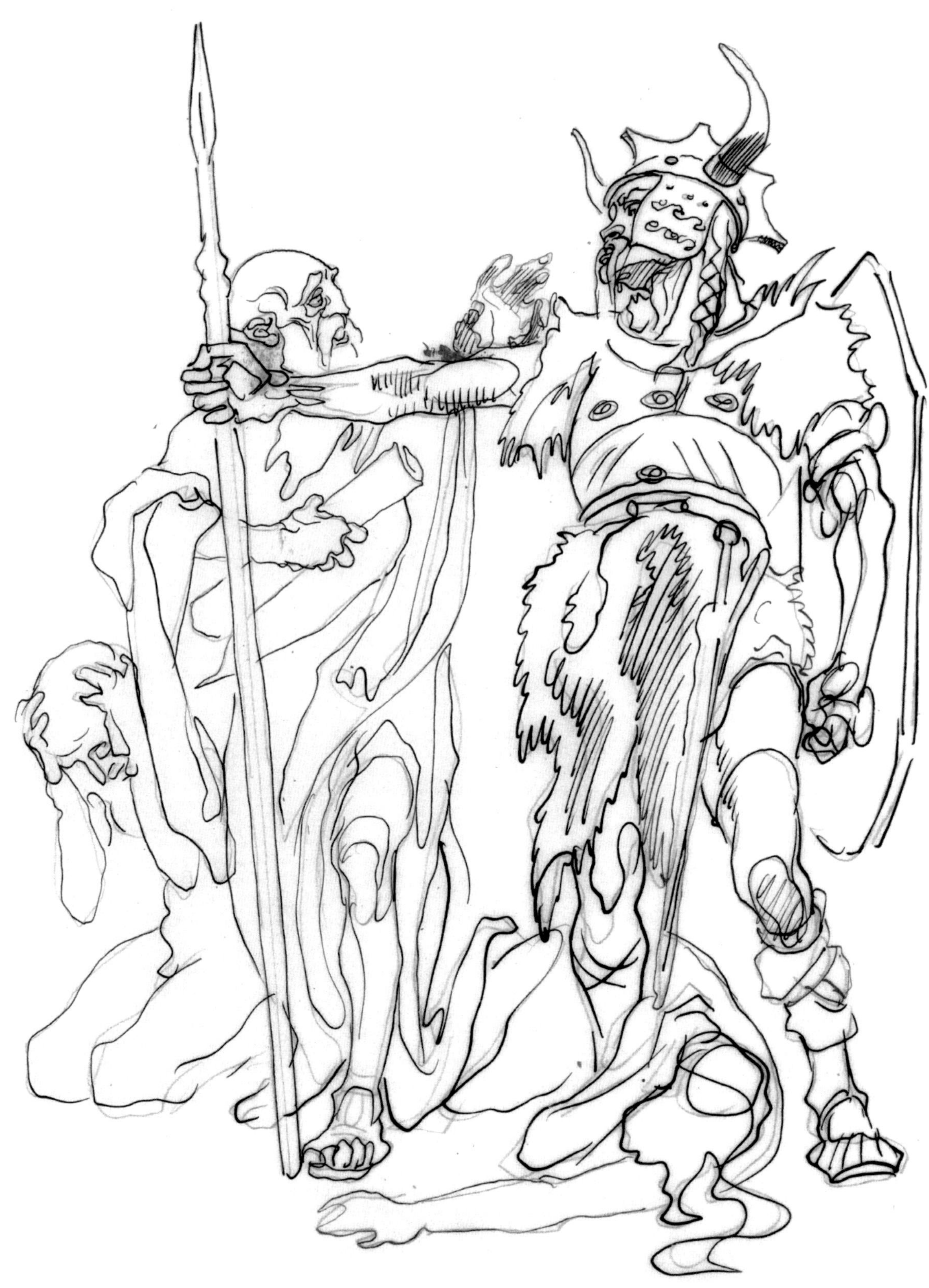

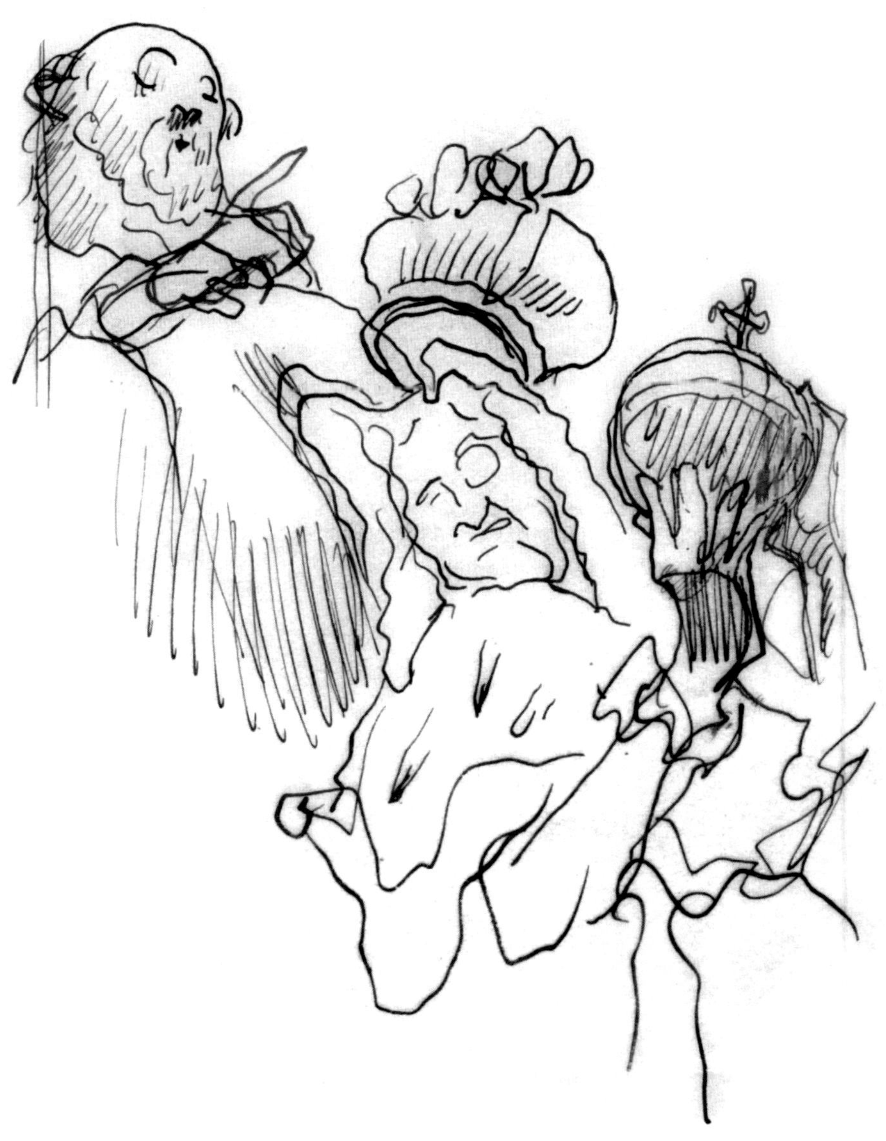

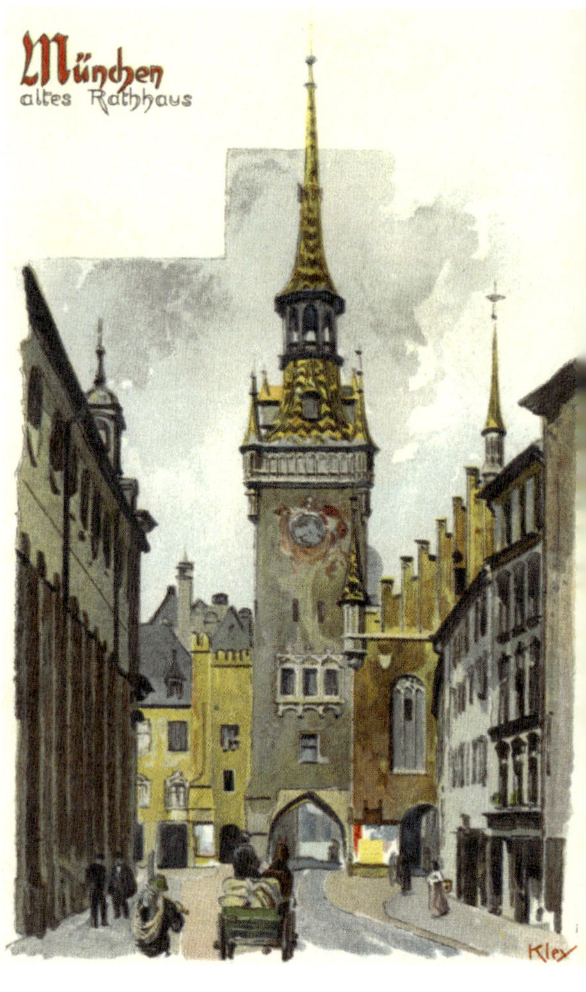

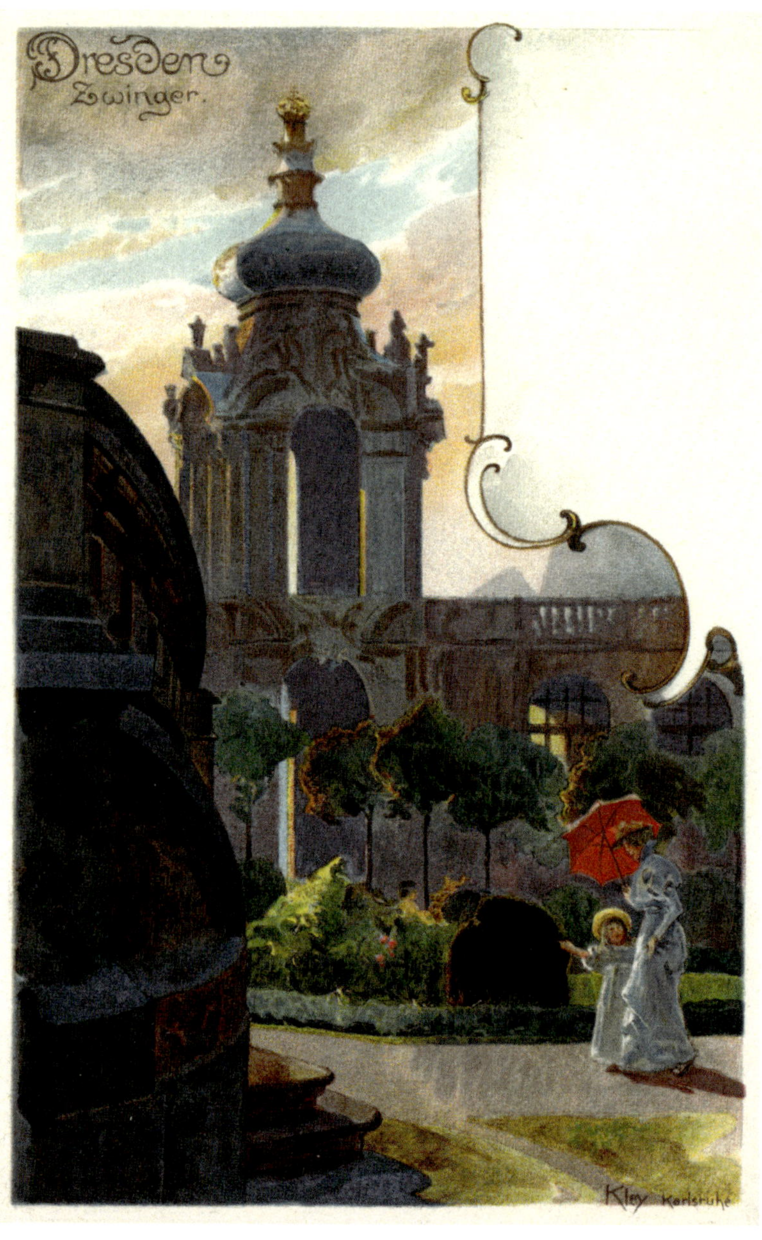

Some examples of the dozens of postcards Kley painted of local landmarks and buildings throughout Germany.

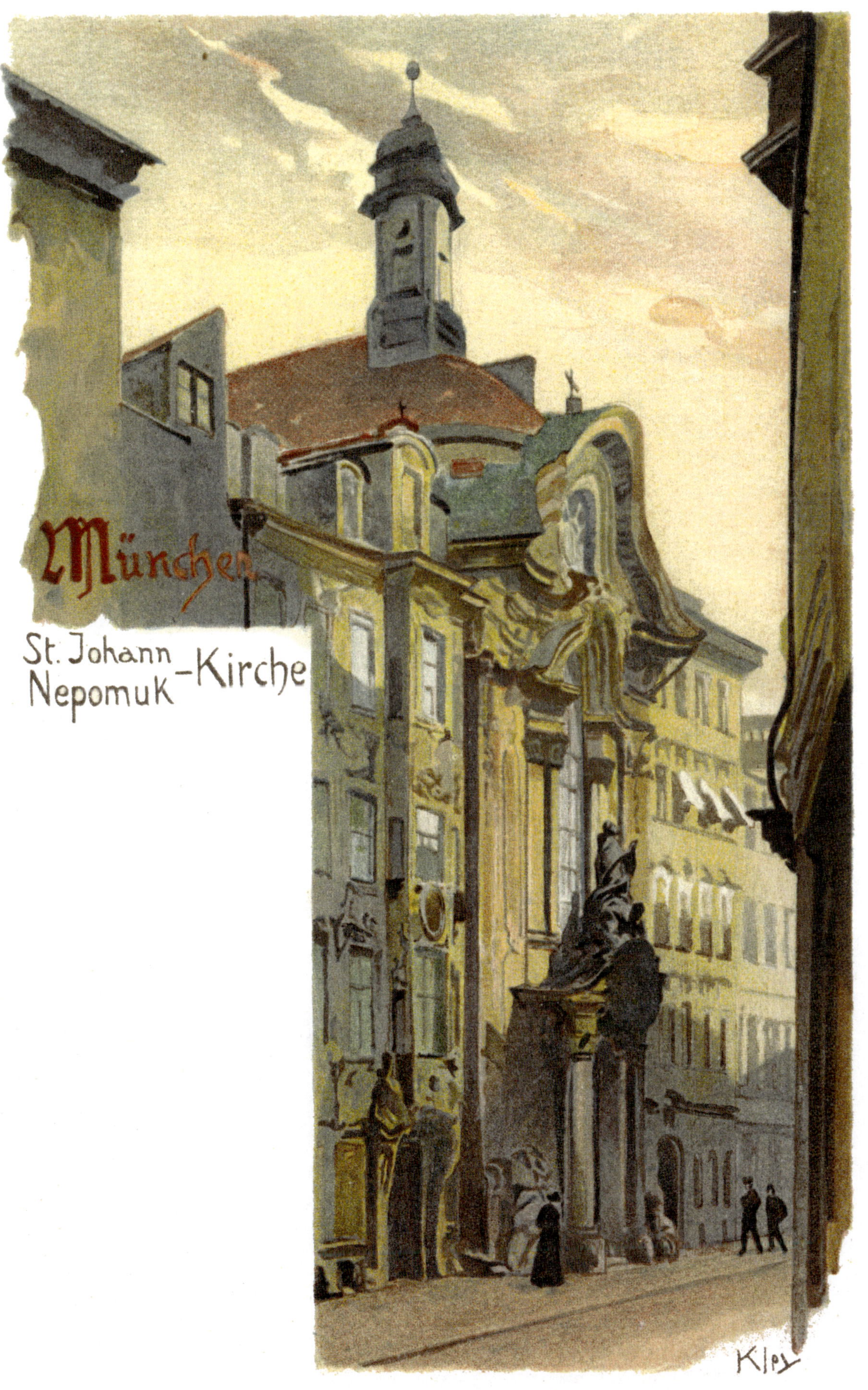
München
St. Johann Nepomuk-Kirche
Kley

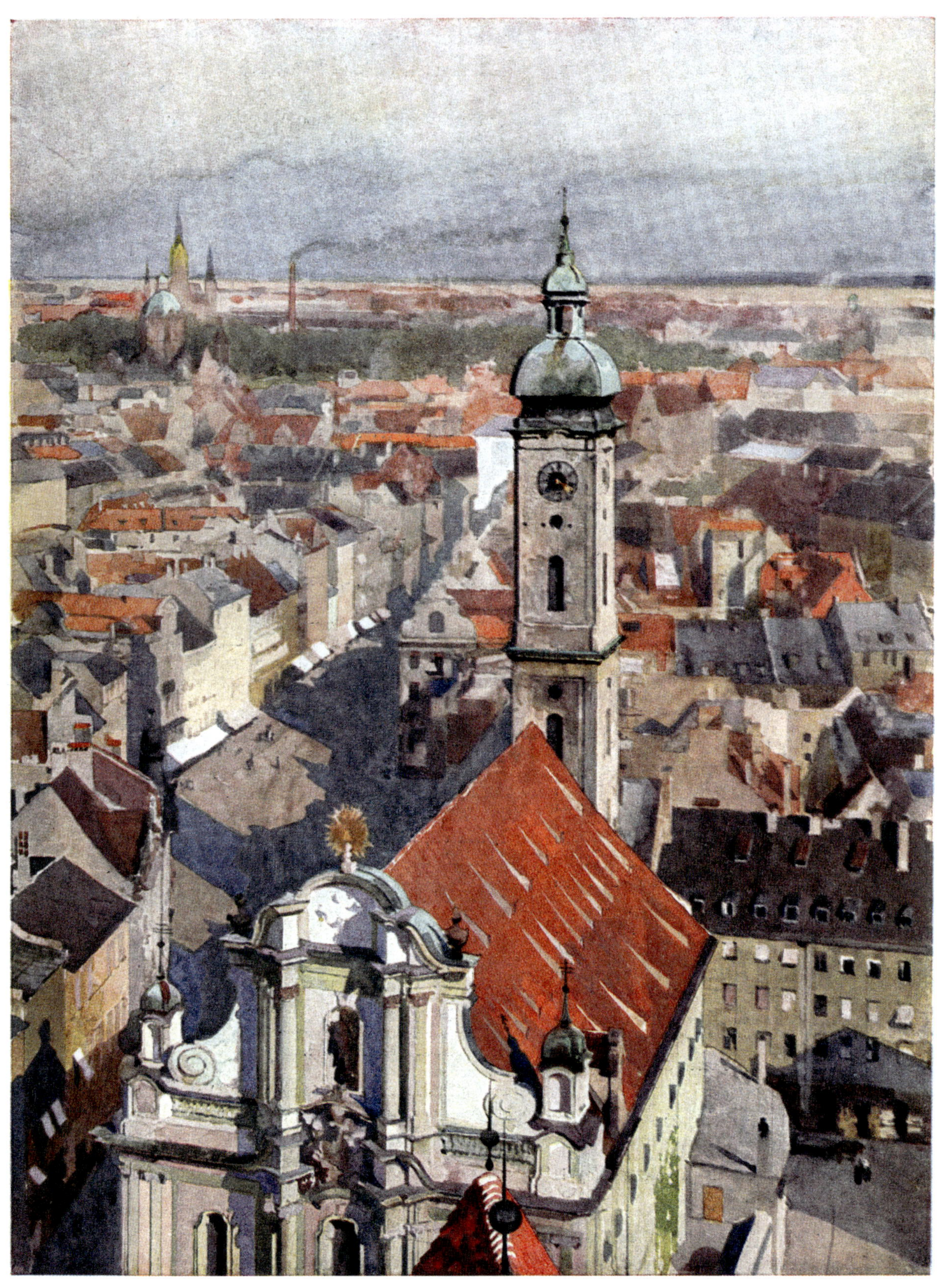

Munich from St. Peter's Church
München vom alten peter
Jugend • 1913

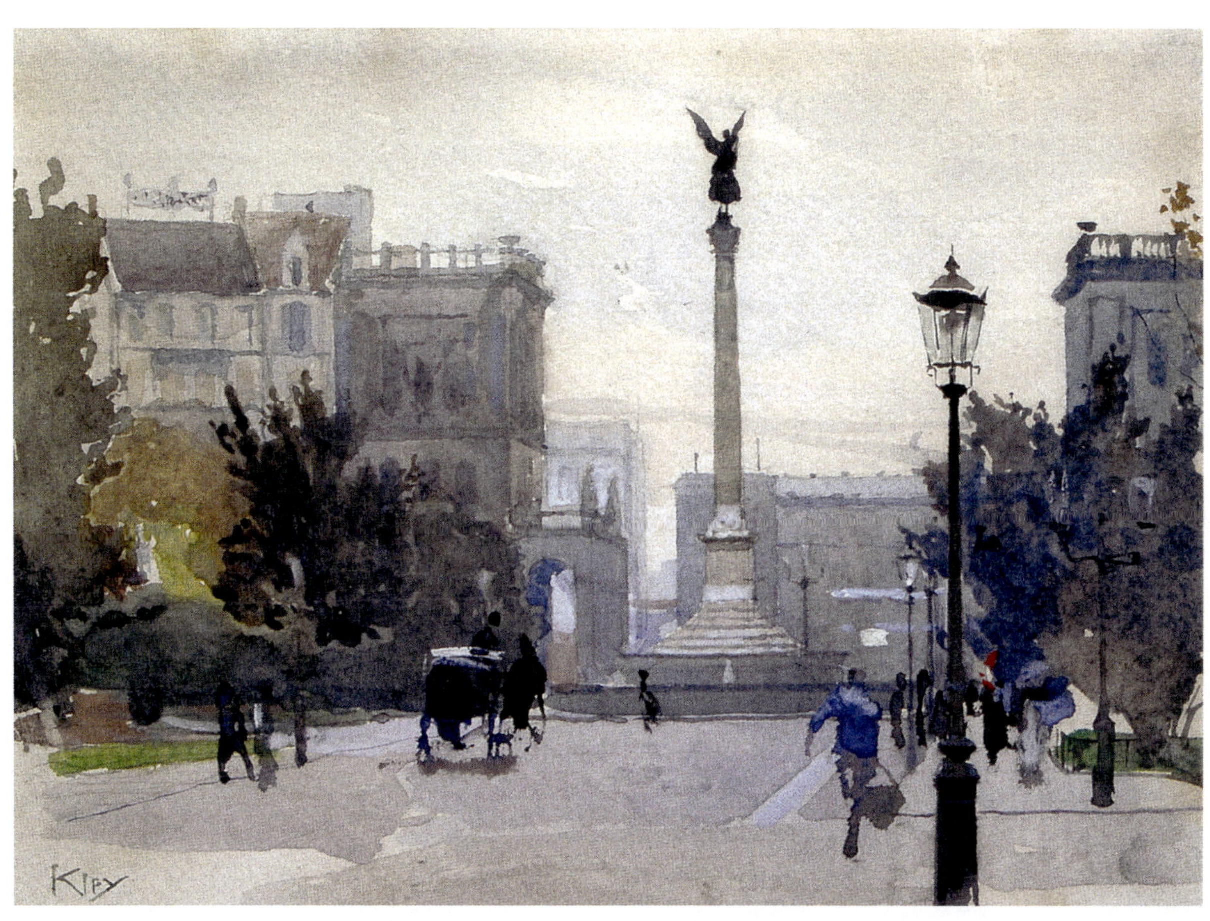
Kley

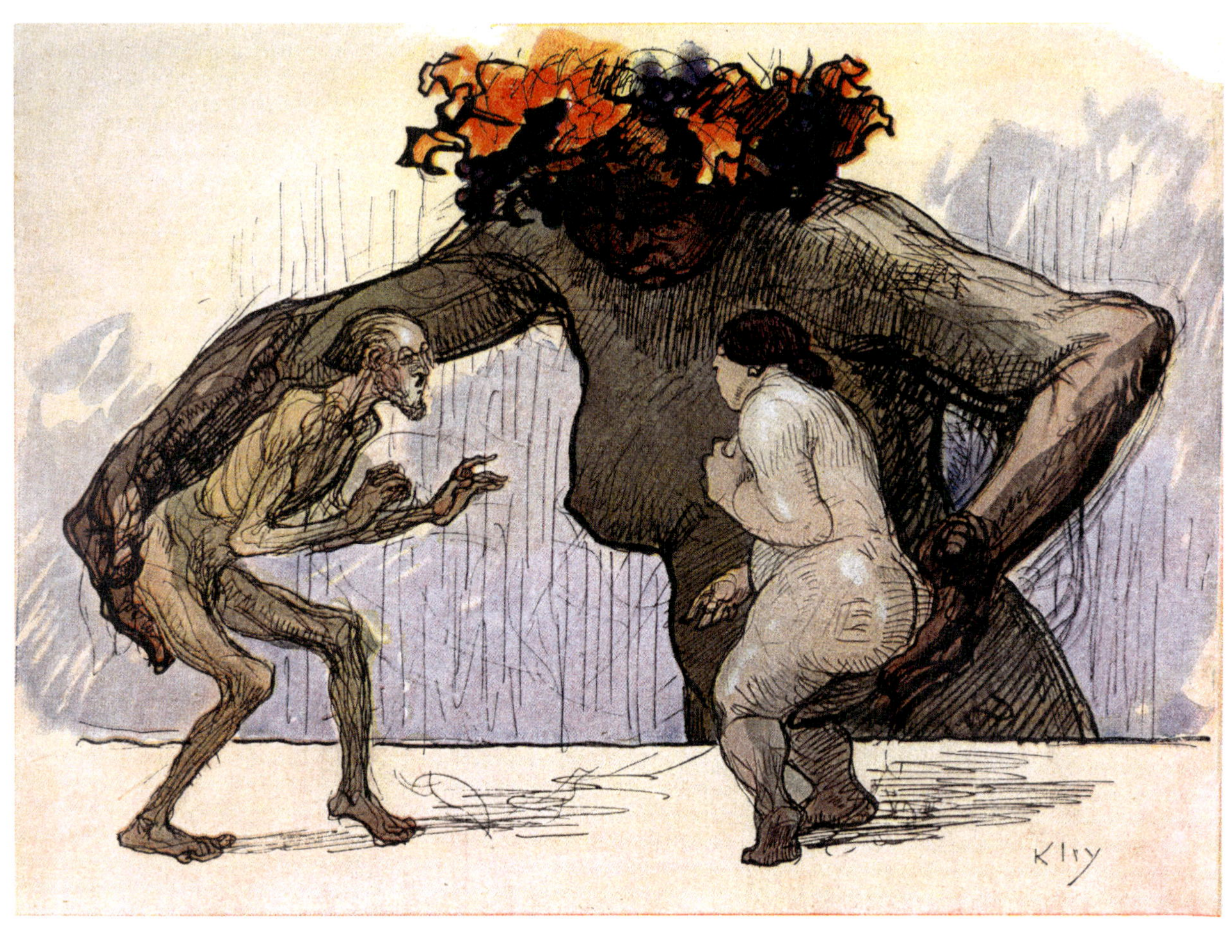

When People Are Ready for Love
Wenn die Menschen reif zur Liebe werden
Jugend • 1910

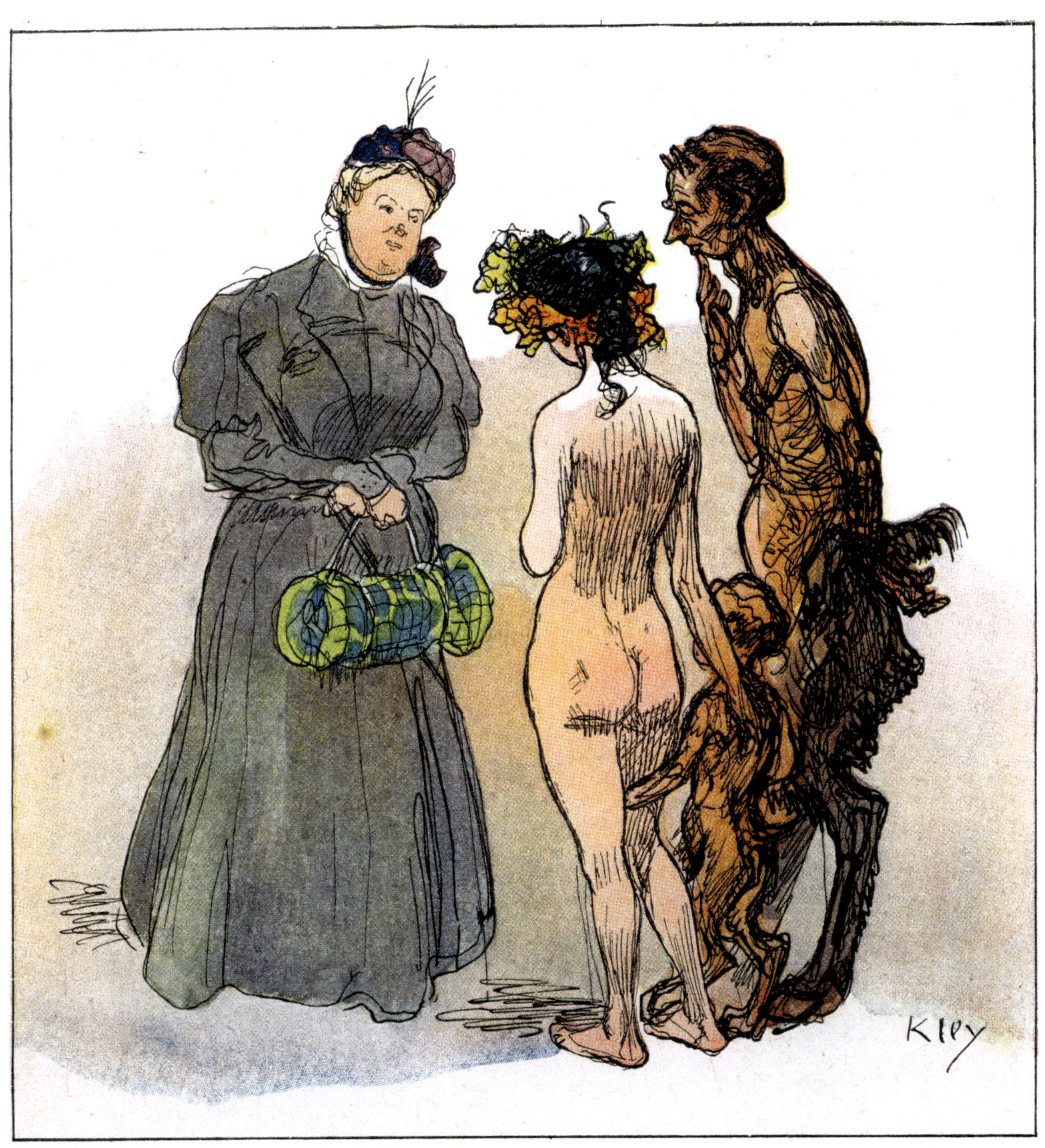

Tourism
"Sure, you can get a forest cave for ten obols, ma'am!
With acorns and spring water, it's five obols more!"
Fremdenverkehr
"Sie können schon eine Waldhöhle zu zehn Obolen haben, gnädige Frau! Mit Eicheln und Quellwasser fünf Obolen mehr!"

Jugend • 1910

The "obol" was an antique coin dating back to ancient Greece.

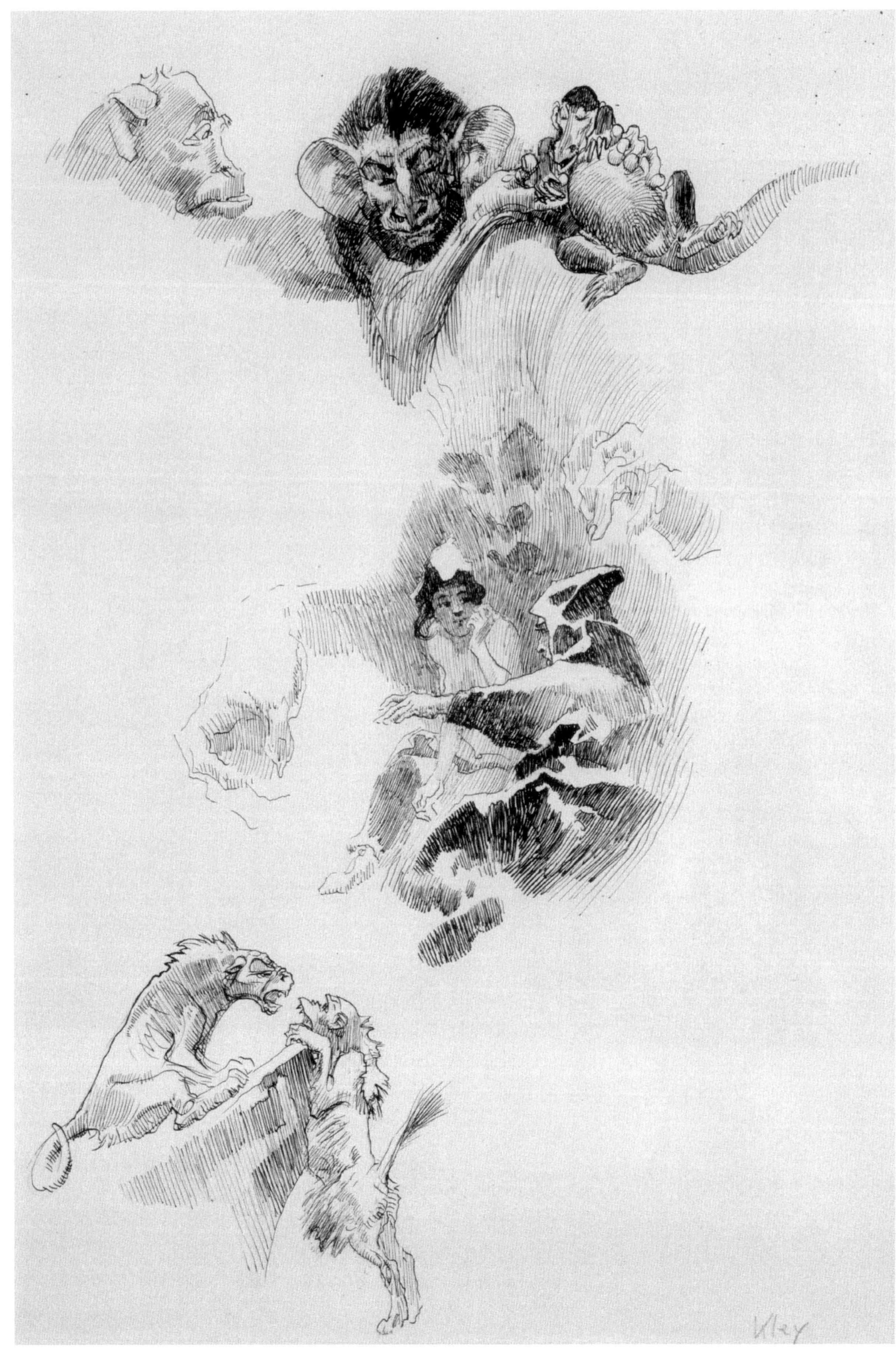
Kley

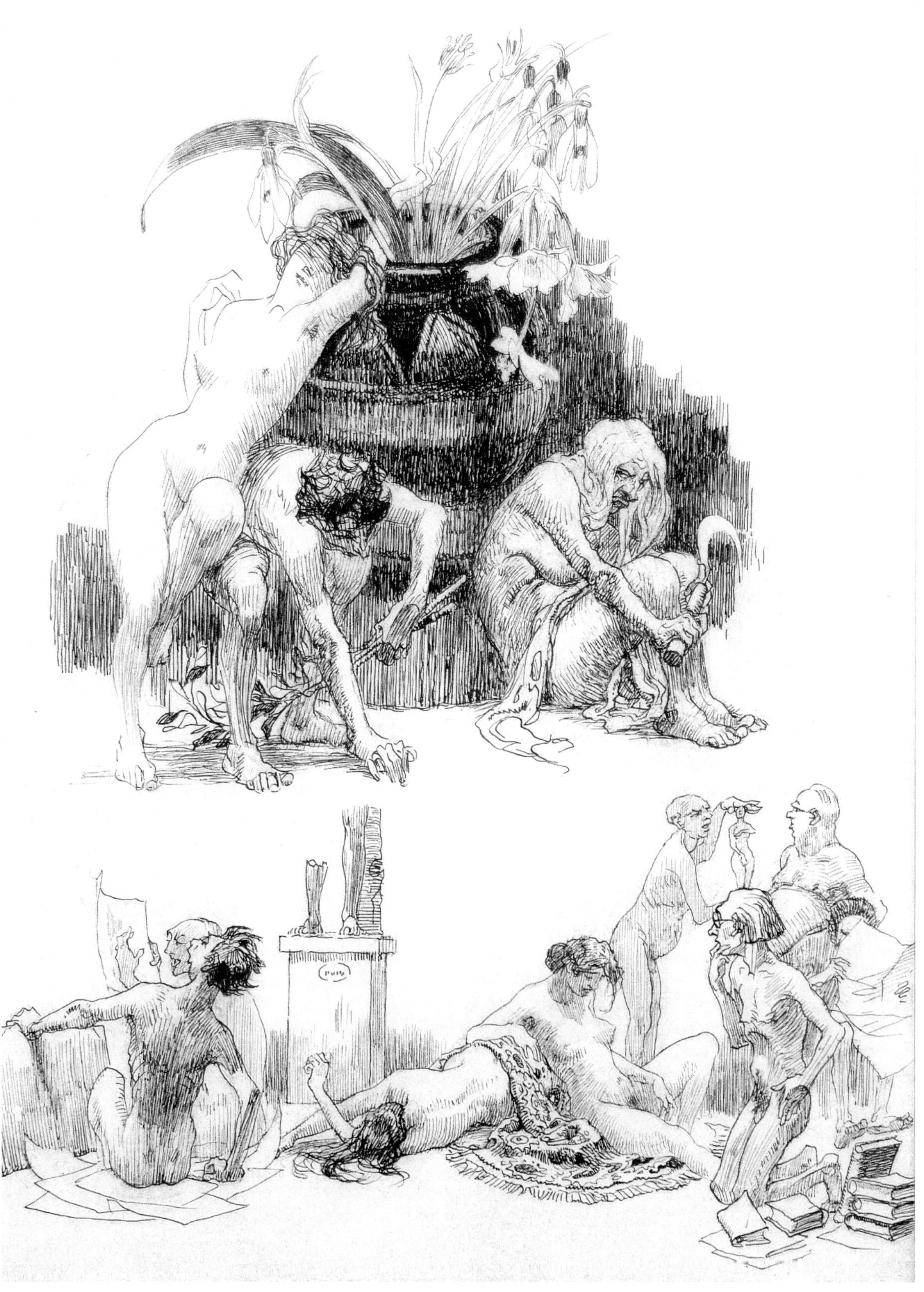

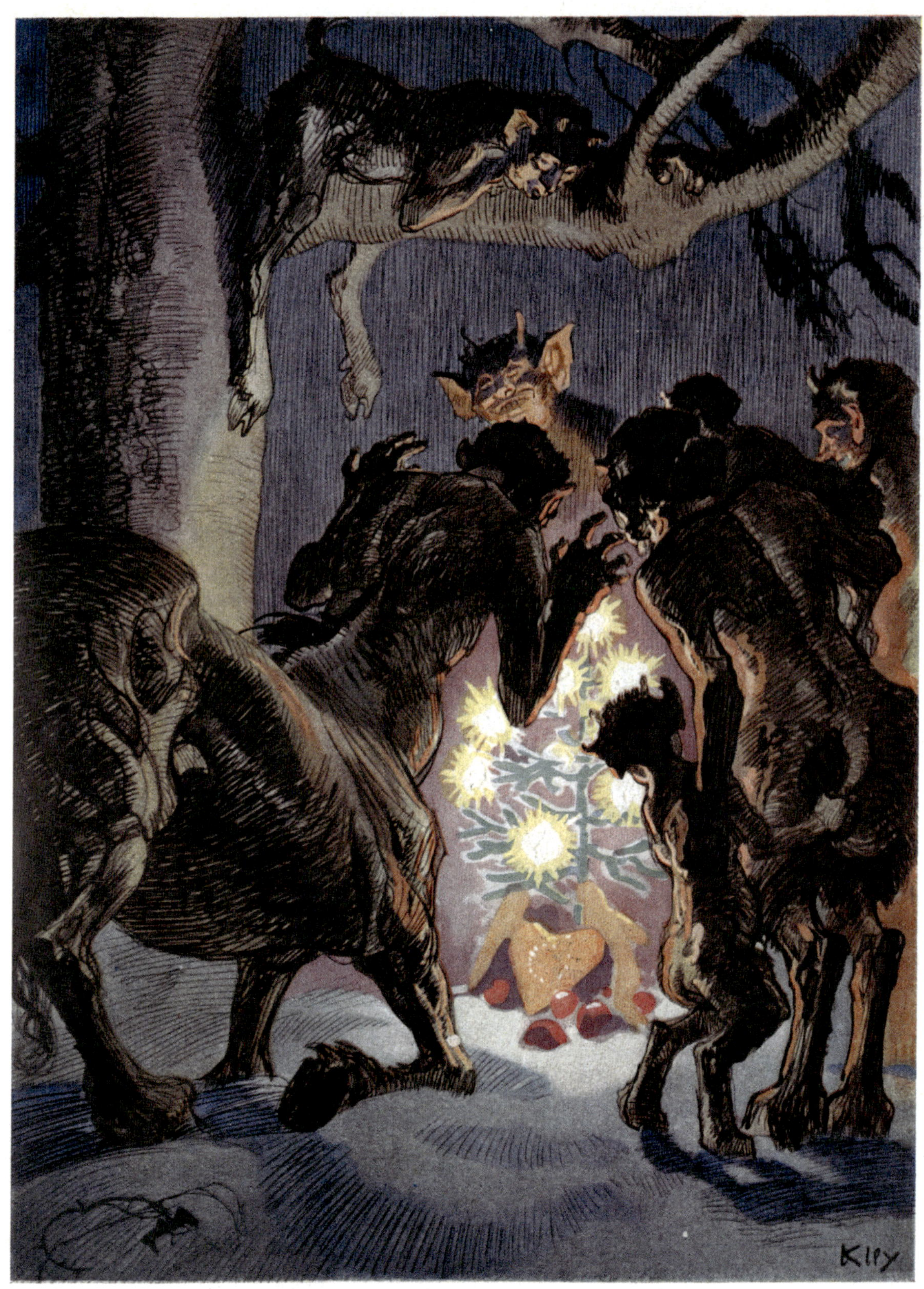

The Discovery in the Wintery Forest
Der Fund im Winterwalde
Jugend • 1912

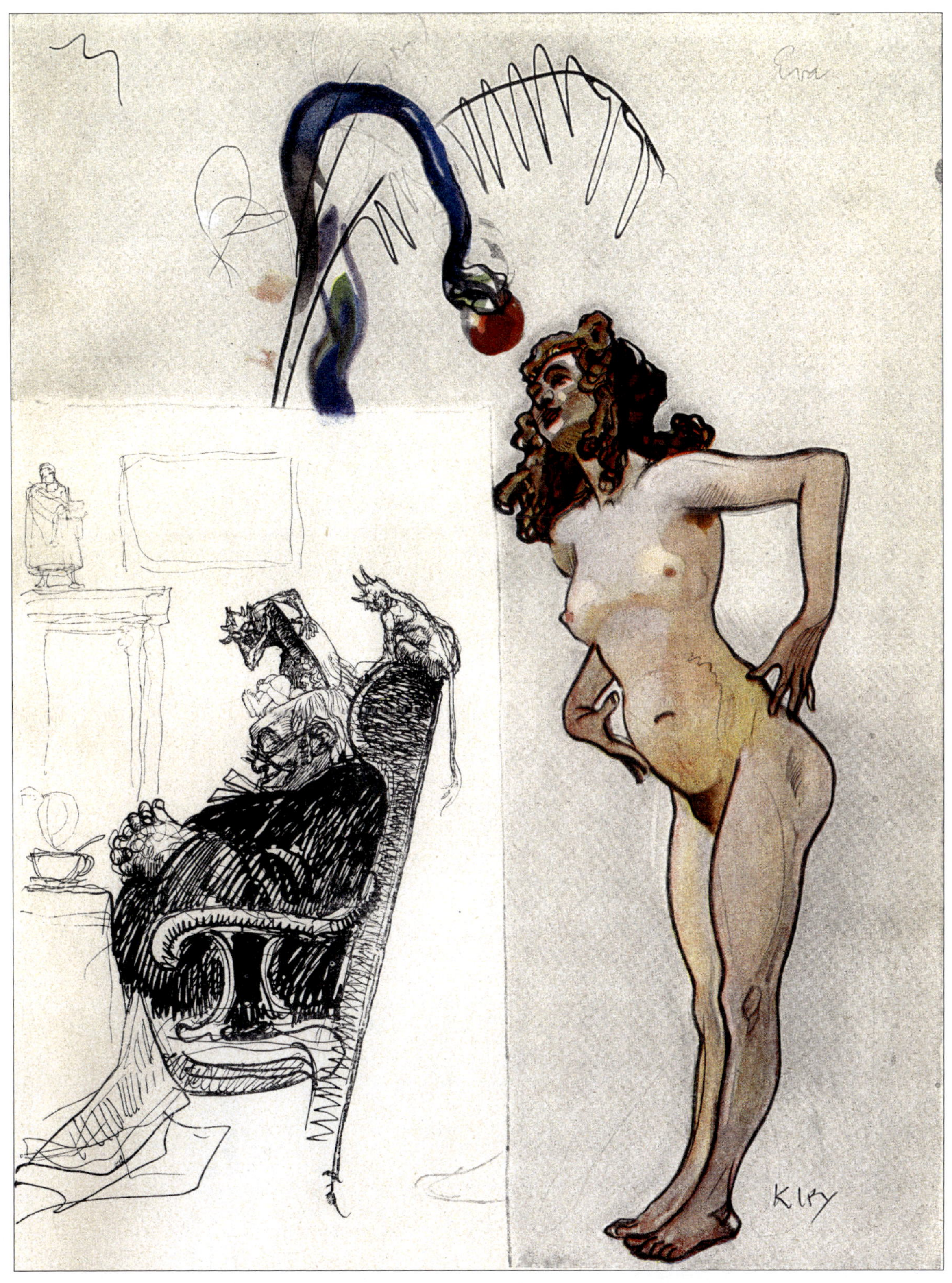

A sketch
Skizzenblatt
Jugend • 1910

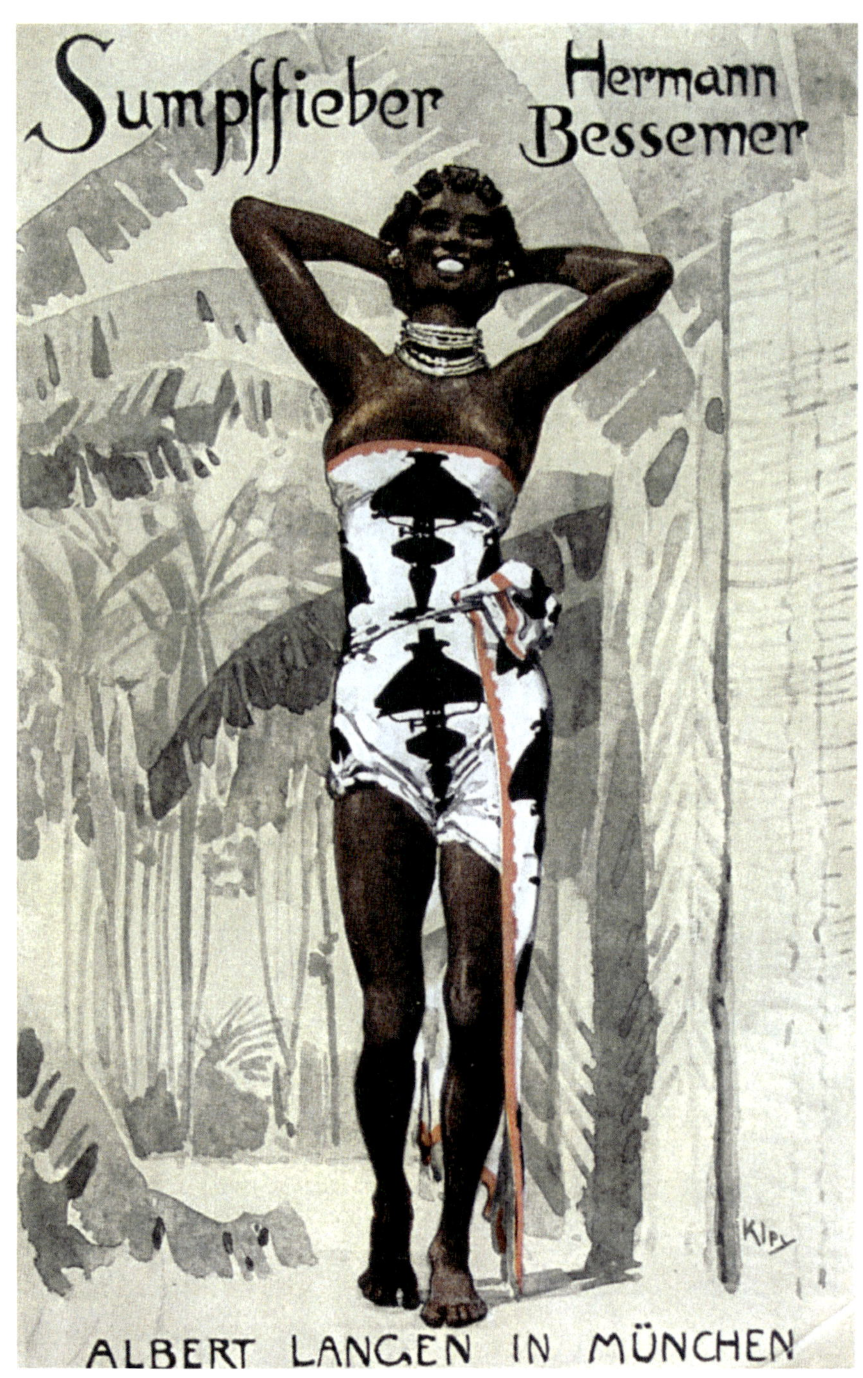

Dustjacket to *Sumpffieber* (*Malaria*)
Hermann Bessemer
Munich • 1908

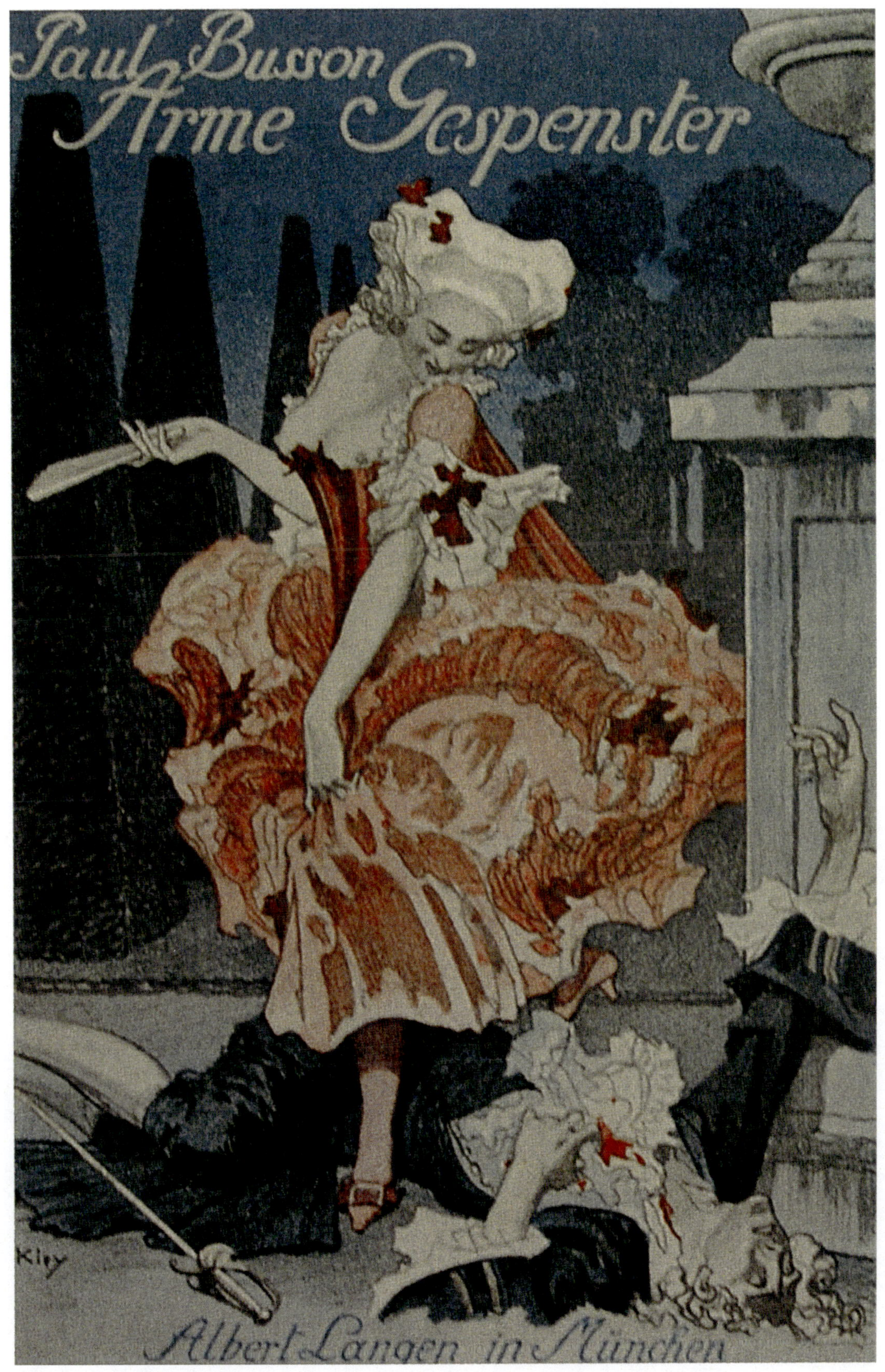

Dustjacket to *Arme Gespenster* (*Poor Ghosts*)
Paul Busson
Munich • 1910

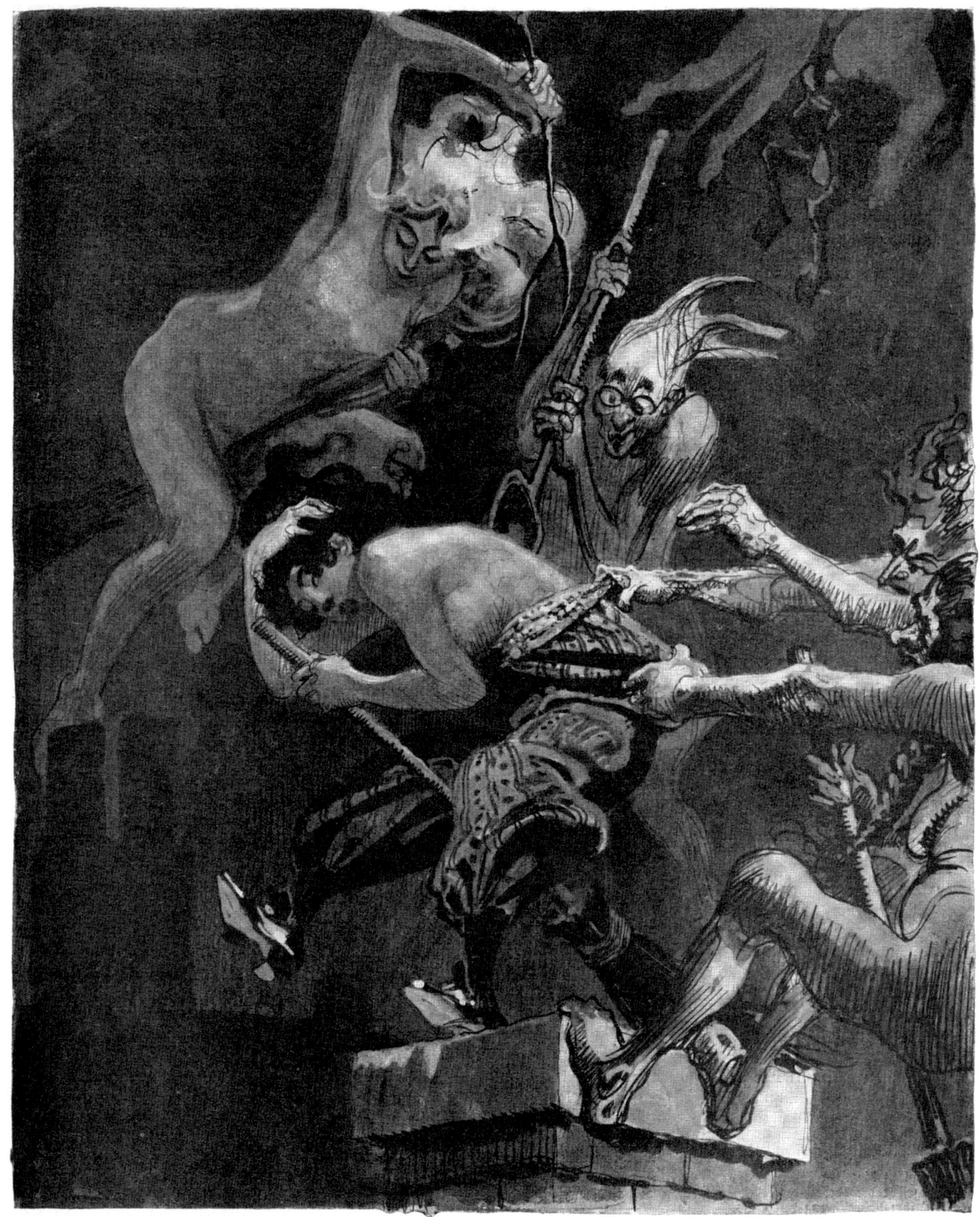

The Latest Fashion
At this year's tour of the Blocksberg mountain, a witch appeared in a pair of harem pants. The poor thing was beaten severely because the other witches didn't yet have harem pants of their own!
Die neue Mode
Bei der diesjährigen Blocksbergfahrt erschien eine Hexe im Hosenrock. Die Ärmste wurde furchtbar verprügelt. Die anderen Hexen hatten nämlich noch keinen Hosenrock!

Jugend • 1911

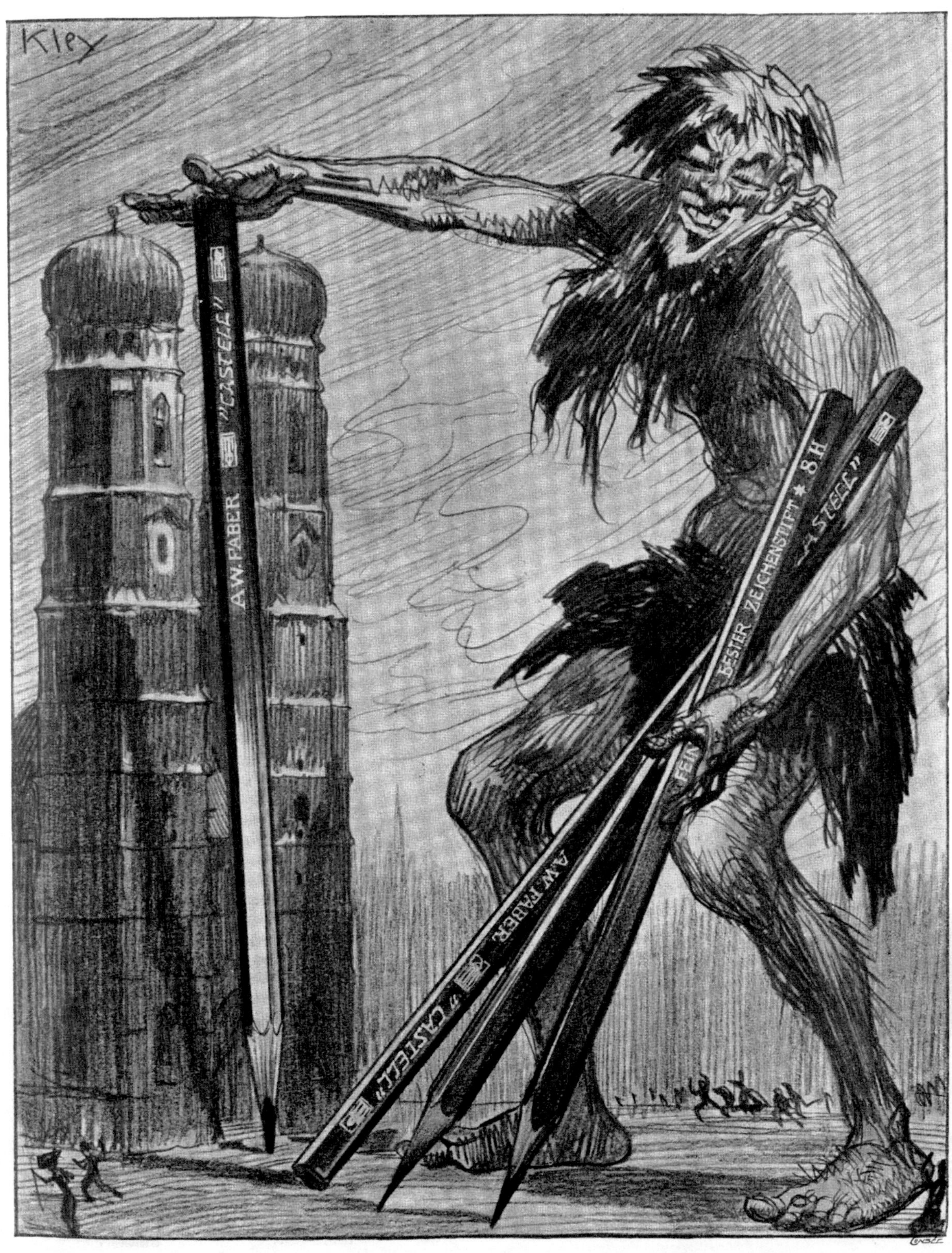

"For the 150th anniversary of the pencil manufacturer A. W. Faber in Stein, near Nuremberg. Drawn by Heinrich Kley with Faber-Castell pencils for the *Jugend* magazine."

"Zum 150jährigen Jubiläum der Bleistiftfabrik A. W. Faber in Stein bei Nürnberg, mit Faber-Castellstiften für die *Jugend* gezeichnet von Heinrich Kley."

Jugend • 1911

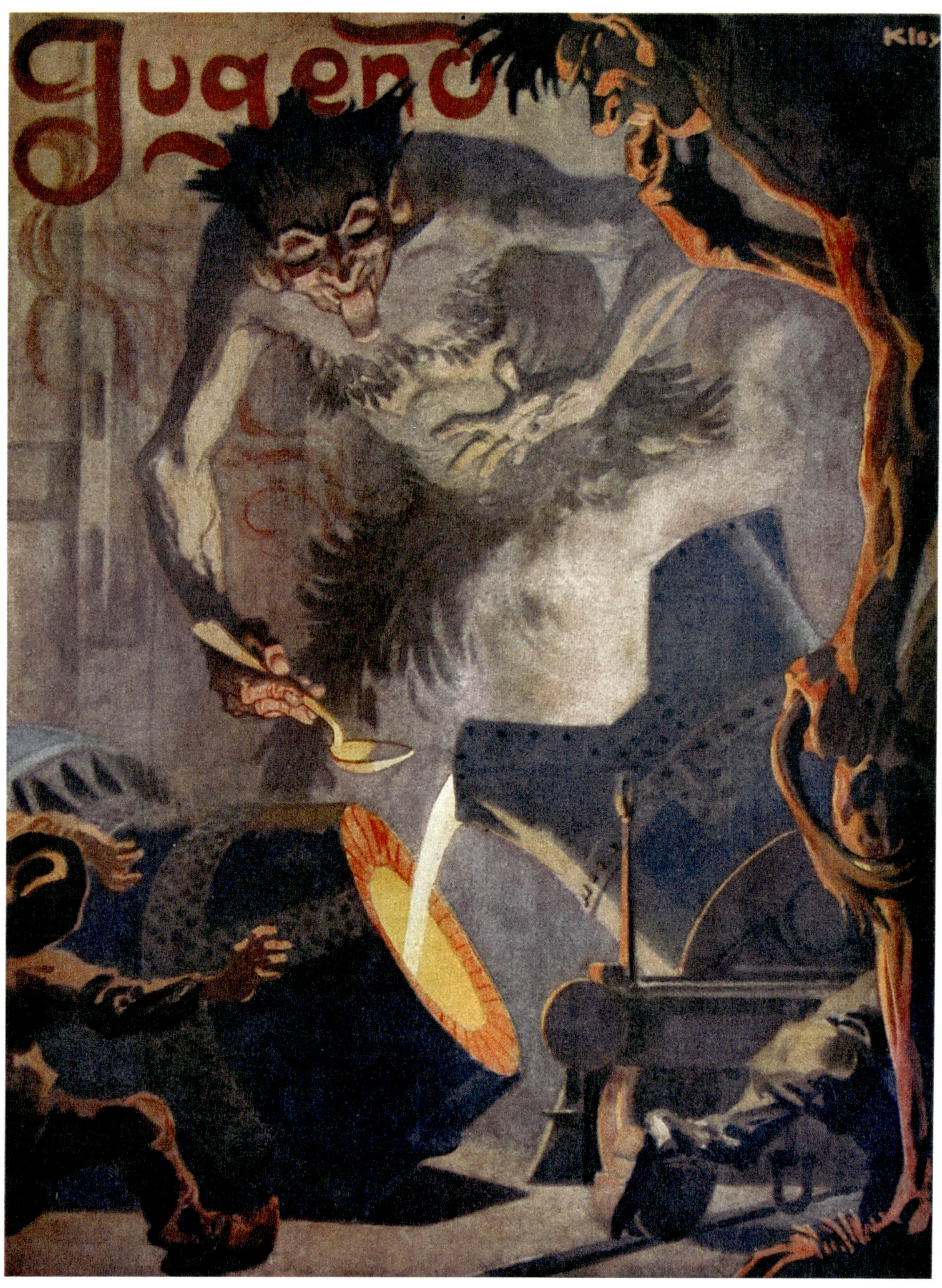

Devil in the Smelting Room
Jugend • 1925

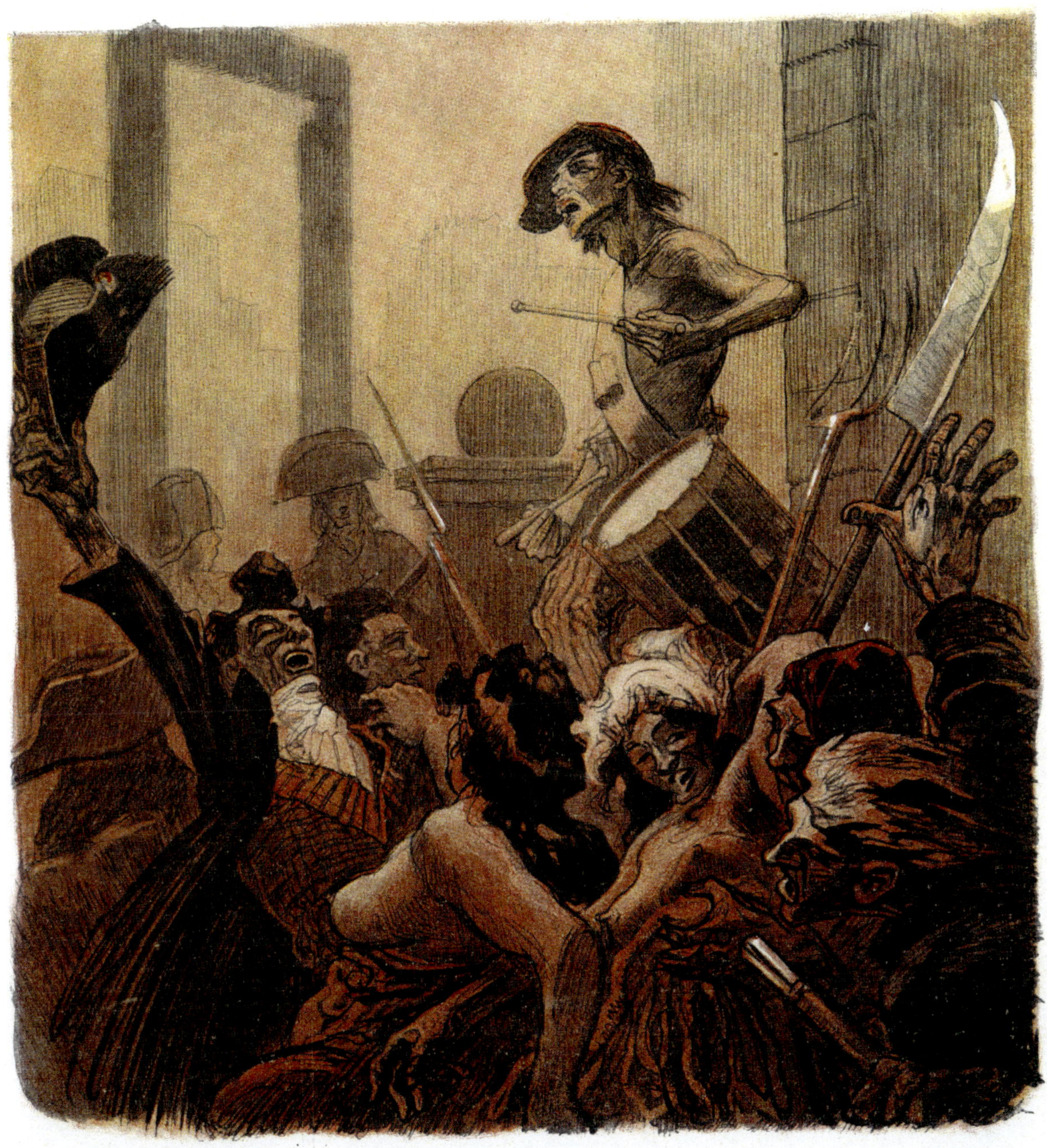

The Carmagnole

Carmagnole

Jugend • 1911

A song and wild dance of the same name popularized during the French Revolution that was triumphantly sarcastic about the fates of the Queen of France, Marie Antoinette, and all who supported the French monarchy.

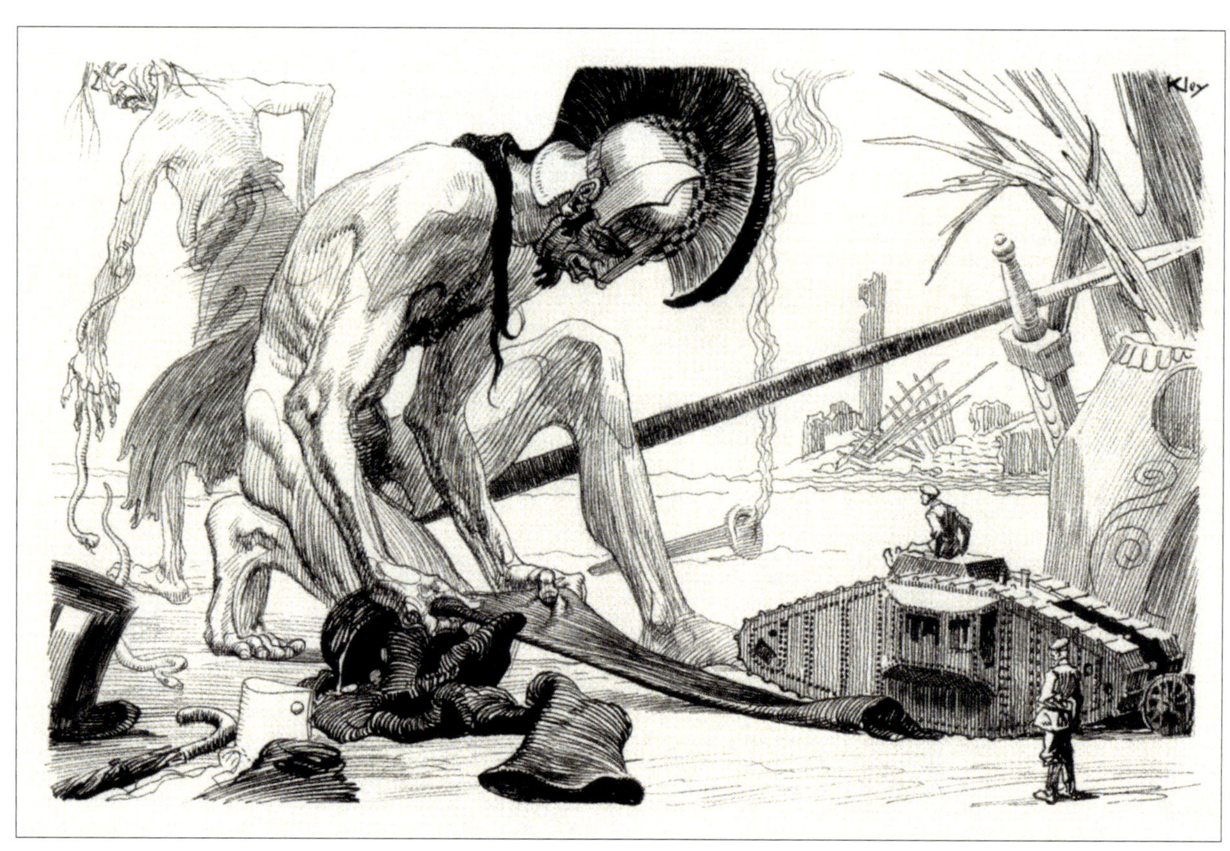

Mars Irons His Civilian Clothes
Mars bügelt sein Zivil
1918

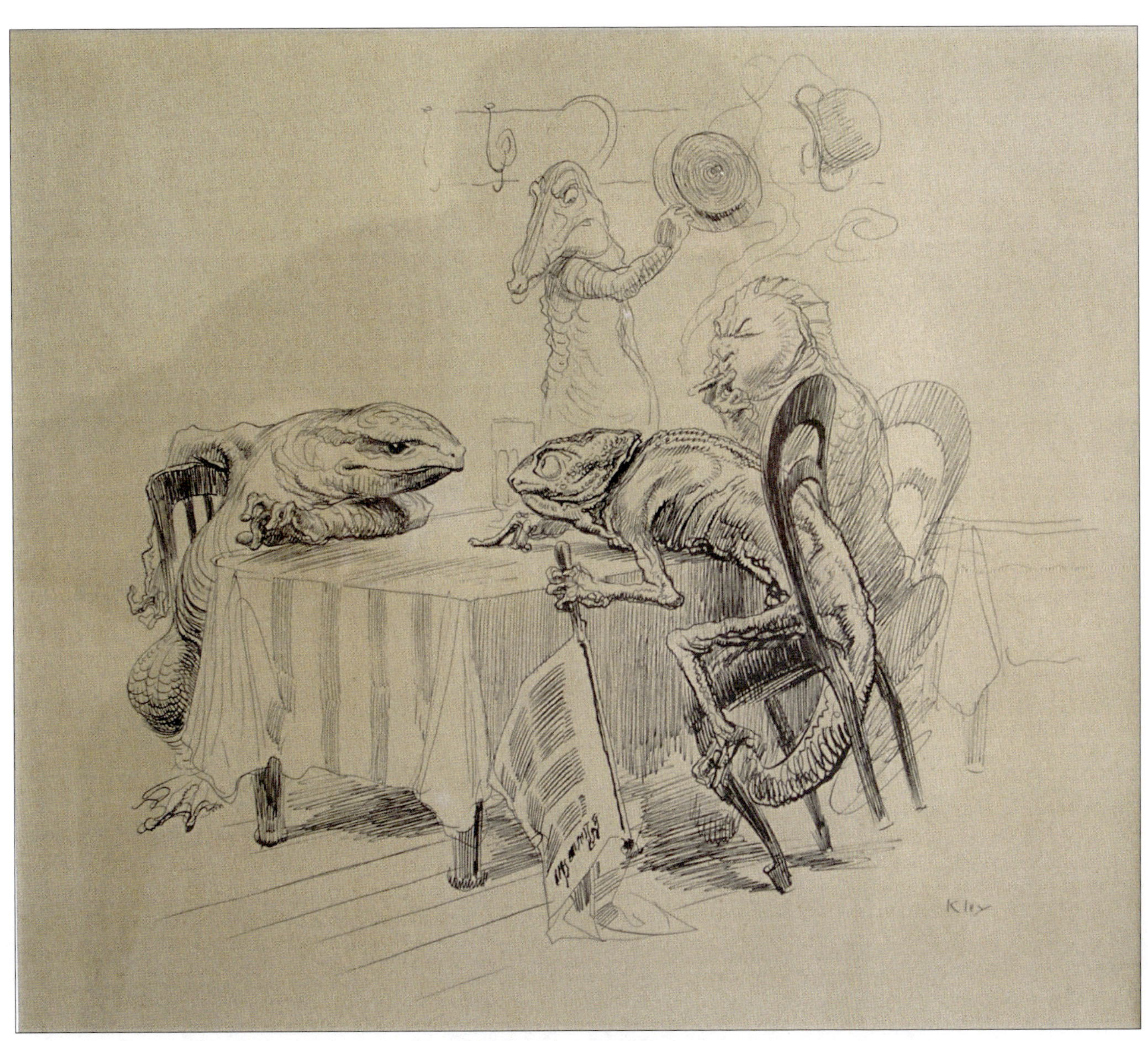

The Politicians
Die Politiker
1910

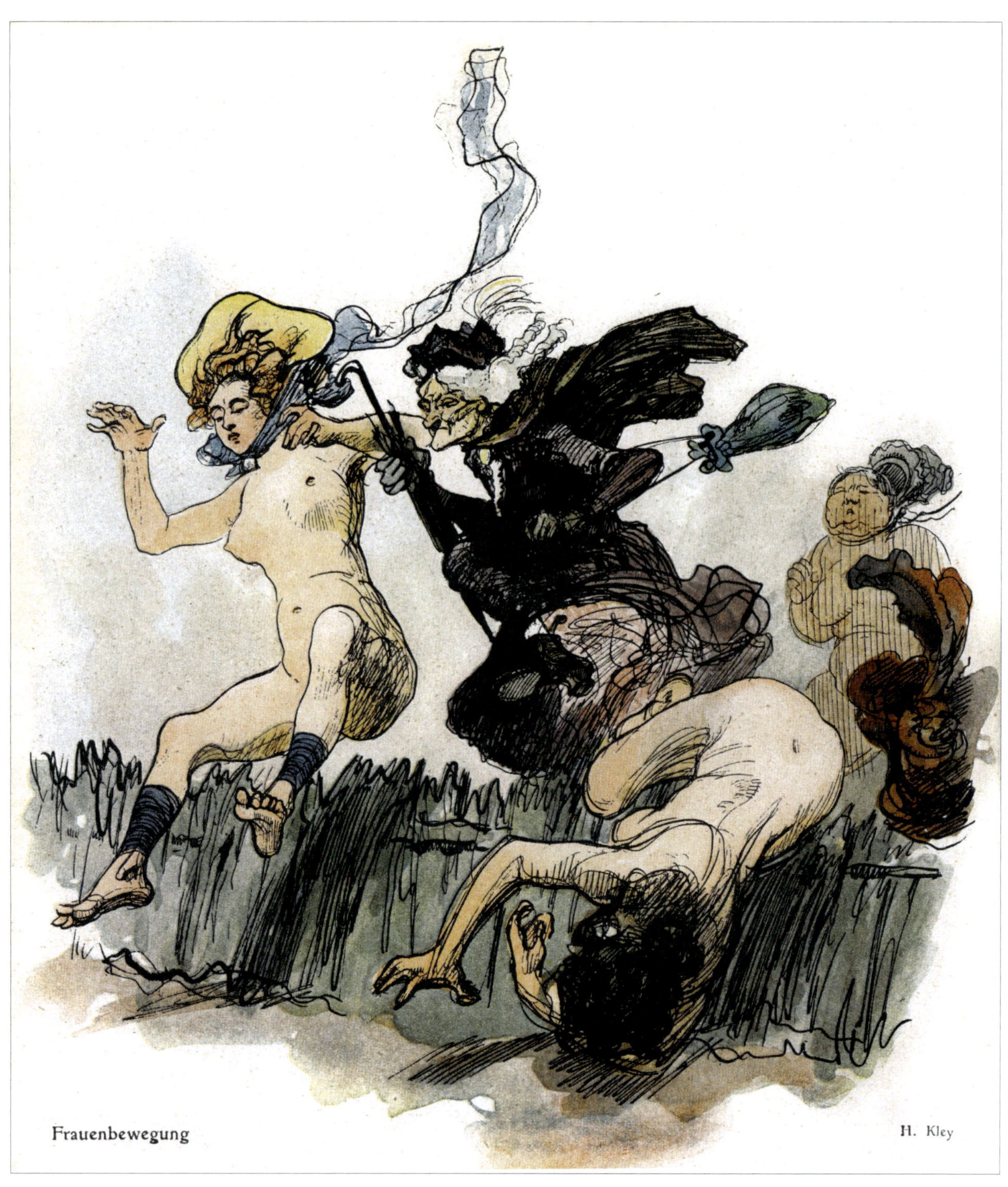

Women's Movement
Frauenbewegung
Jugend • 1910

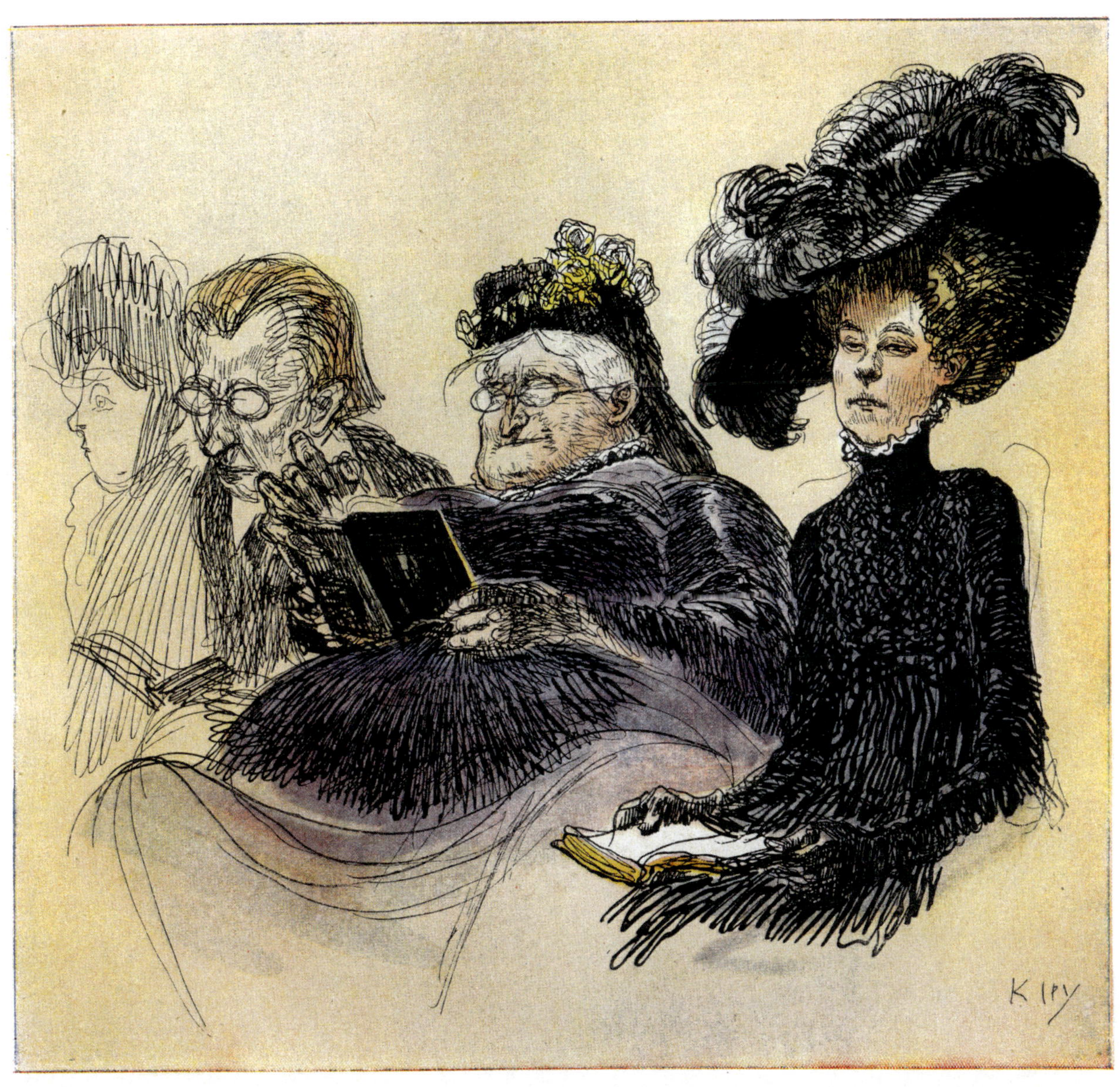

Cause and Effect

"Since they started heating the church, piousness has increased in our town."

Ursache und Wirkung

"Seit die Kirche geheizt wird, hat die Frömmigkeit in unserer Stadt zugenommen."

Jugend • 1910

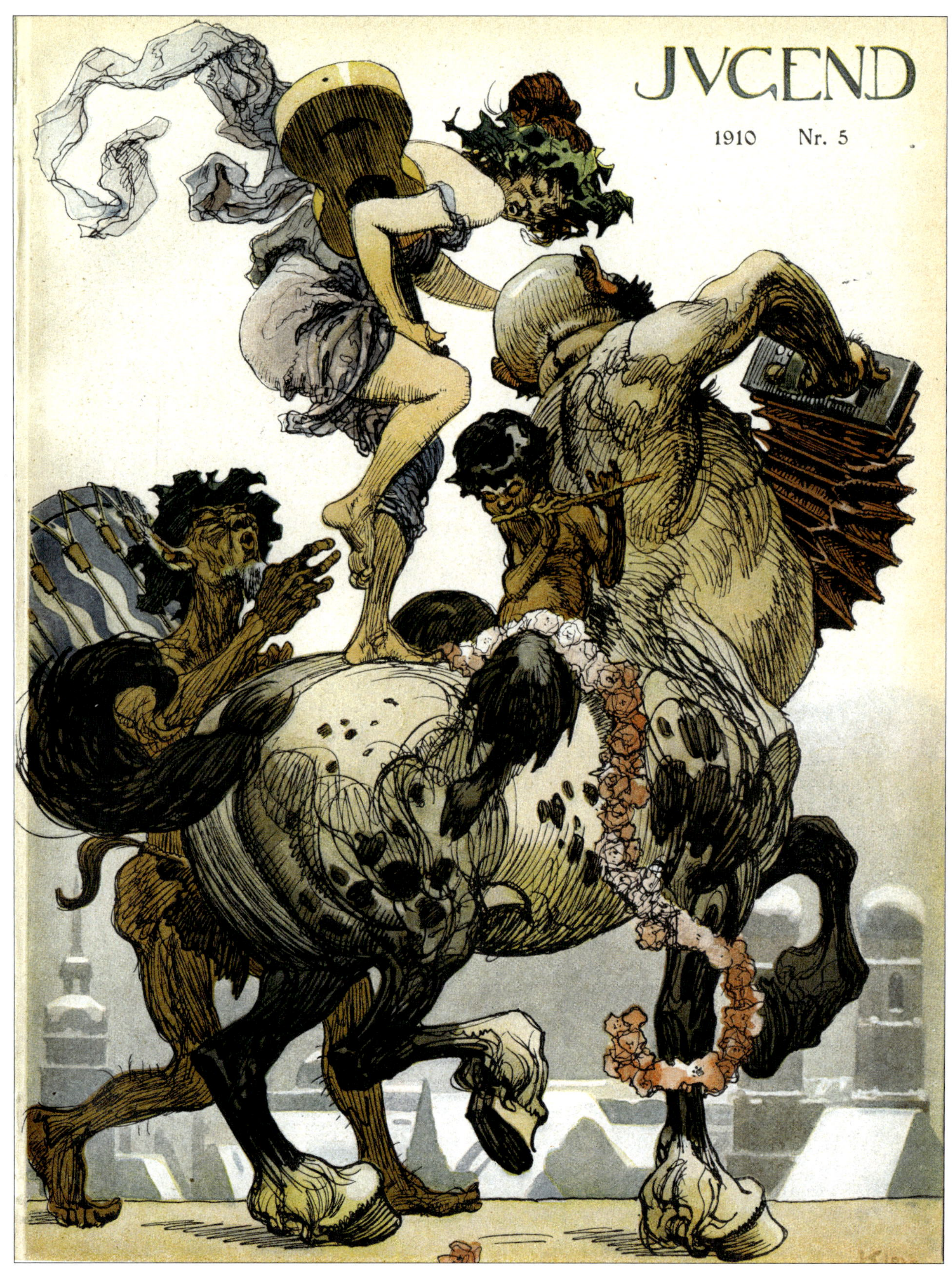

Carnival Comes to Ancient Munich

Jugend • 1910

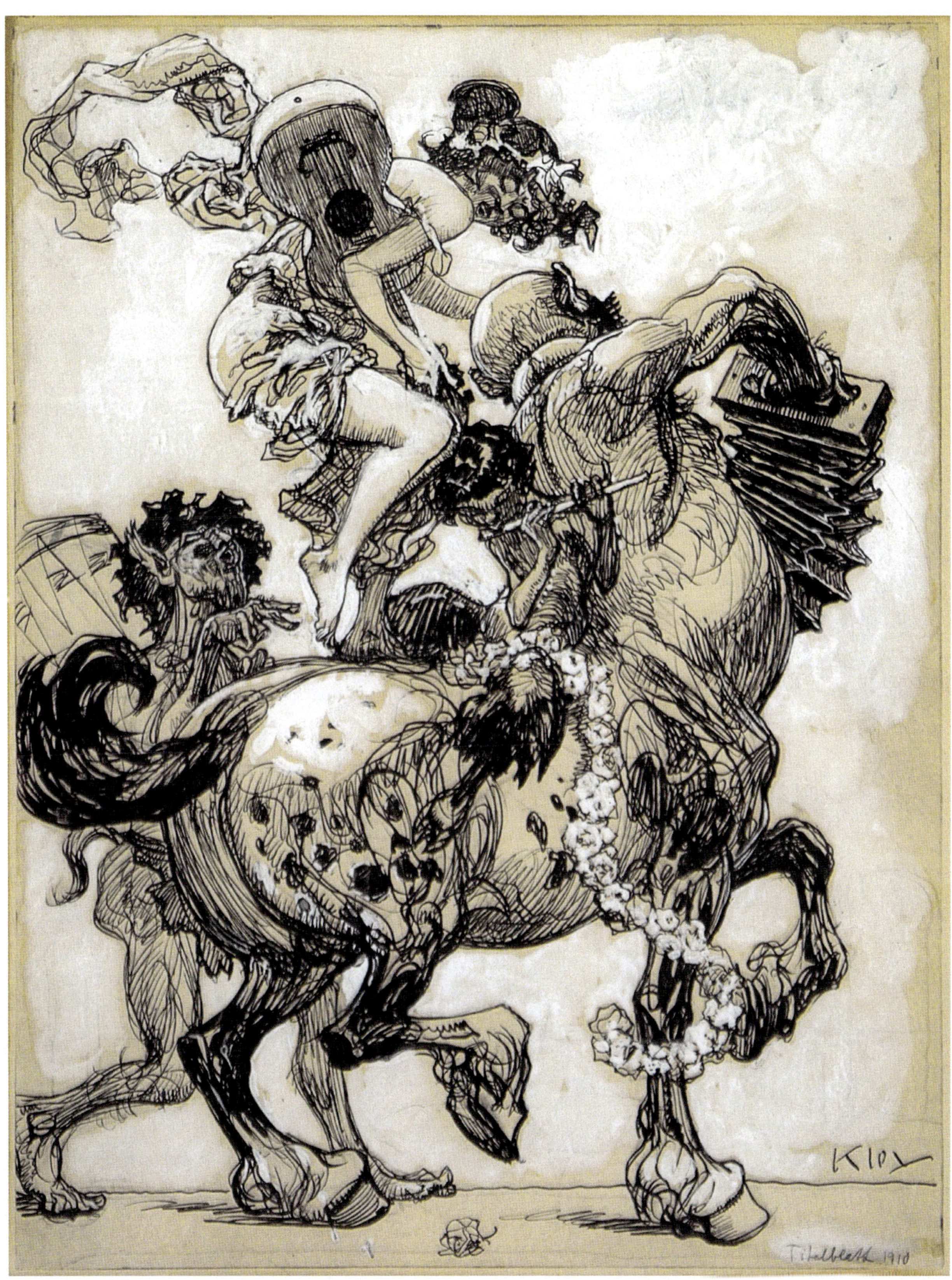
Kley

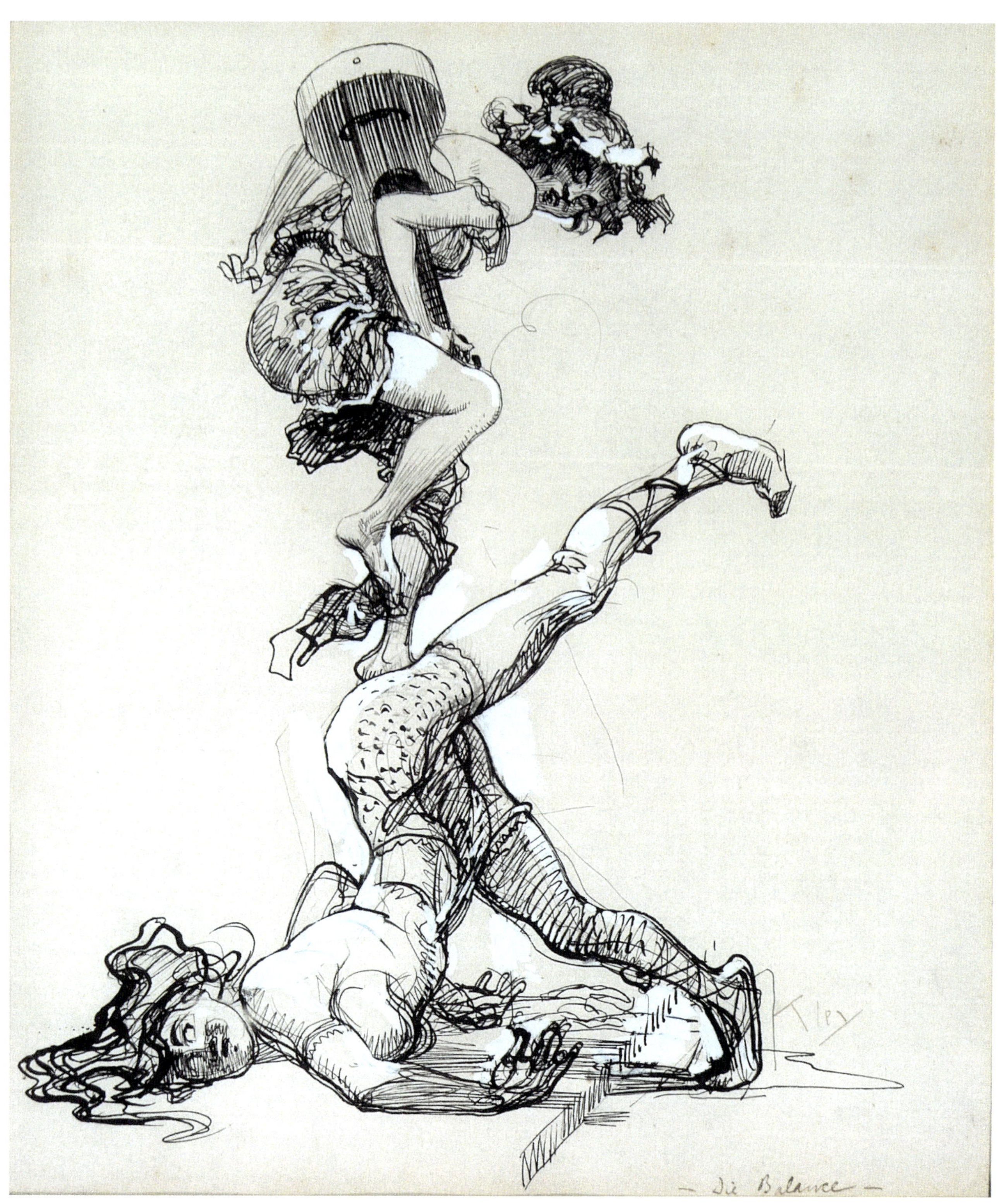
Kley
– Die Balance –

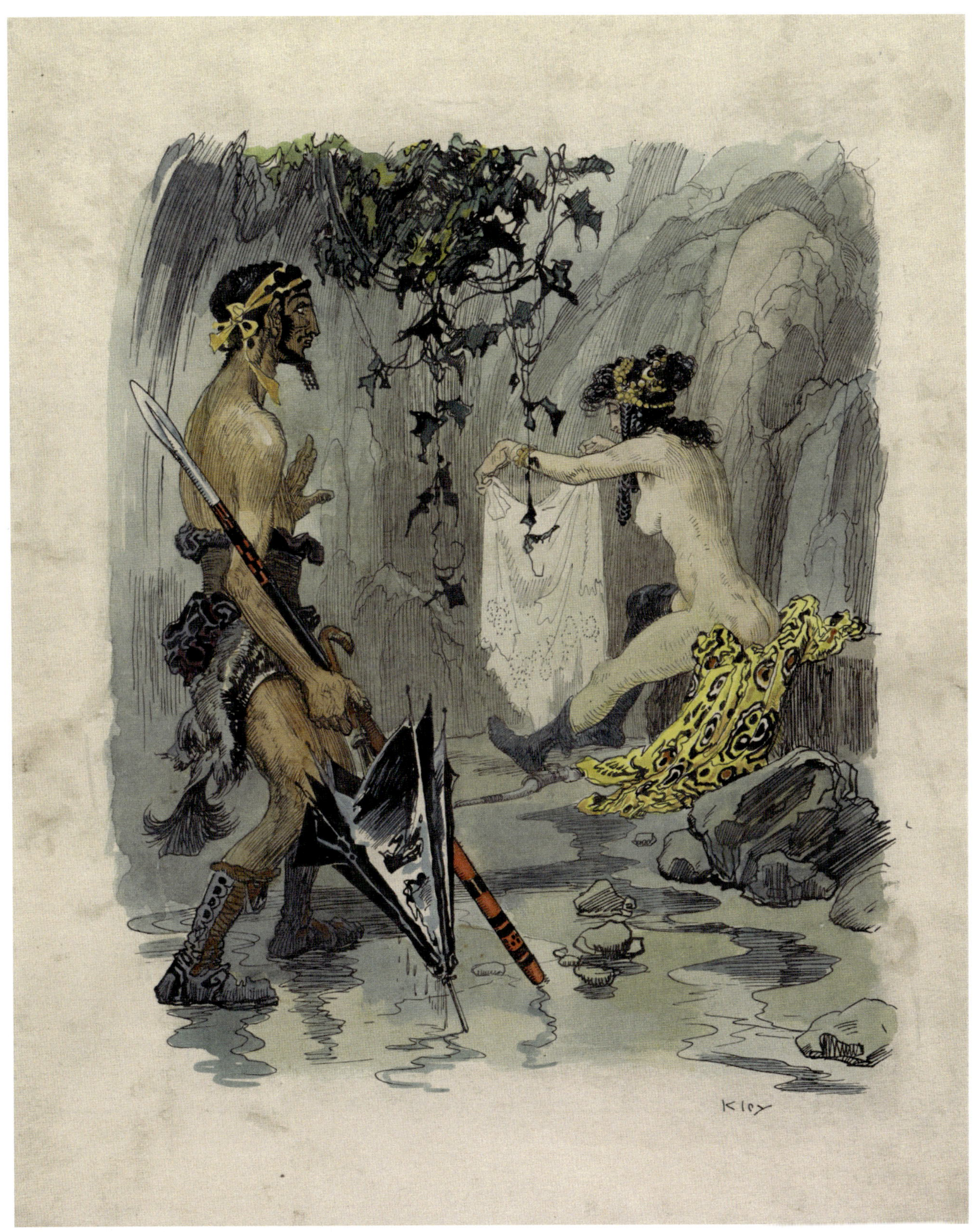

Based on a pen-and-ink illustration
that originally appeared in
***Vergil Aeneis* (*Virgil's Aeneid*)**
possibly circa 1910
(see page 135 in *Volume 1* for the pen-and-ink version of this illustration)

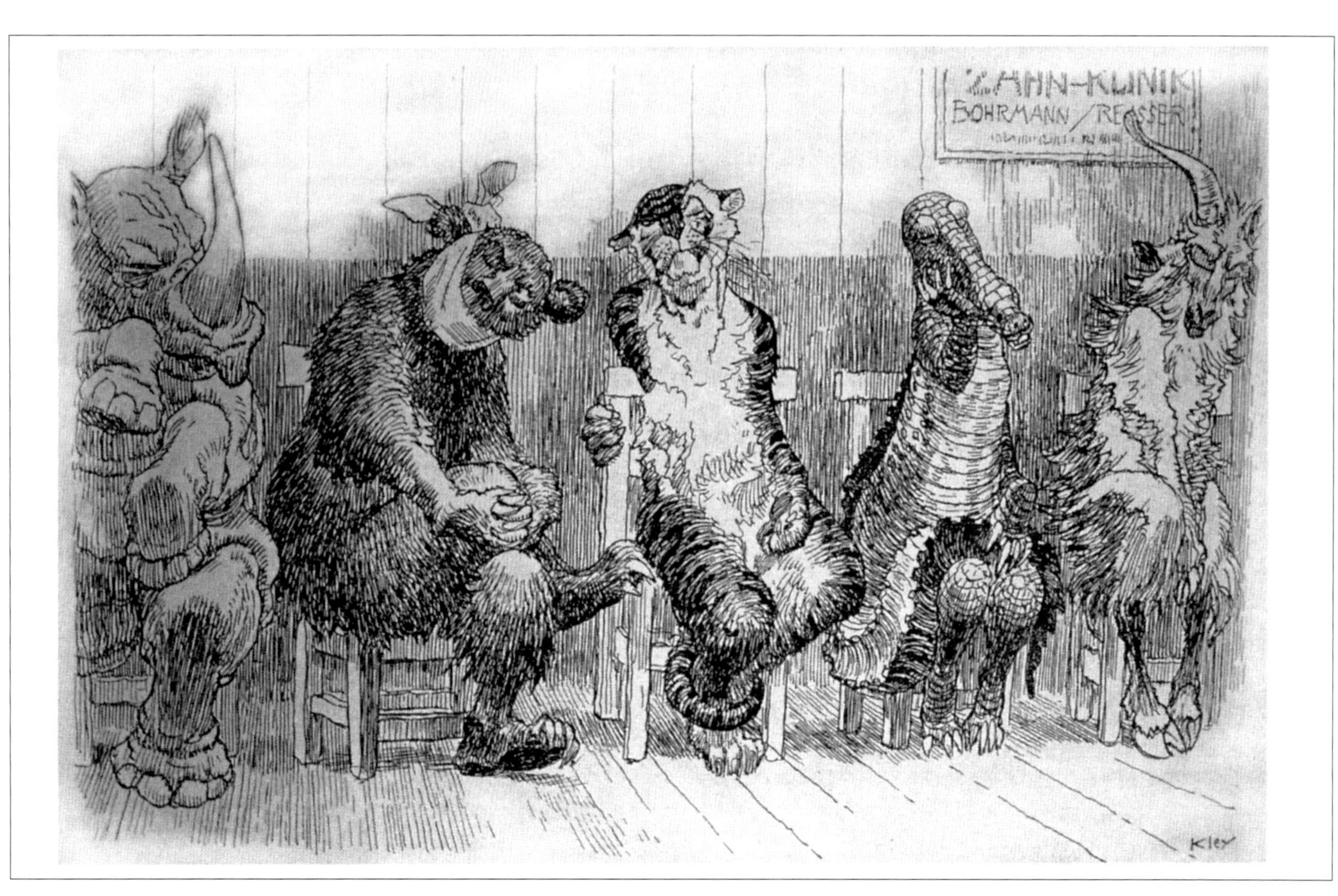

In the Ventrinarian's Waiting Room
Im tierärztlichen wartezimmer
Jugend (No. 8) • 1943

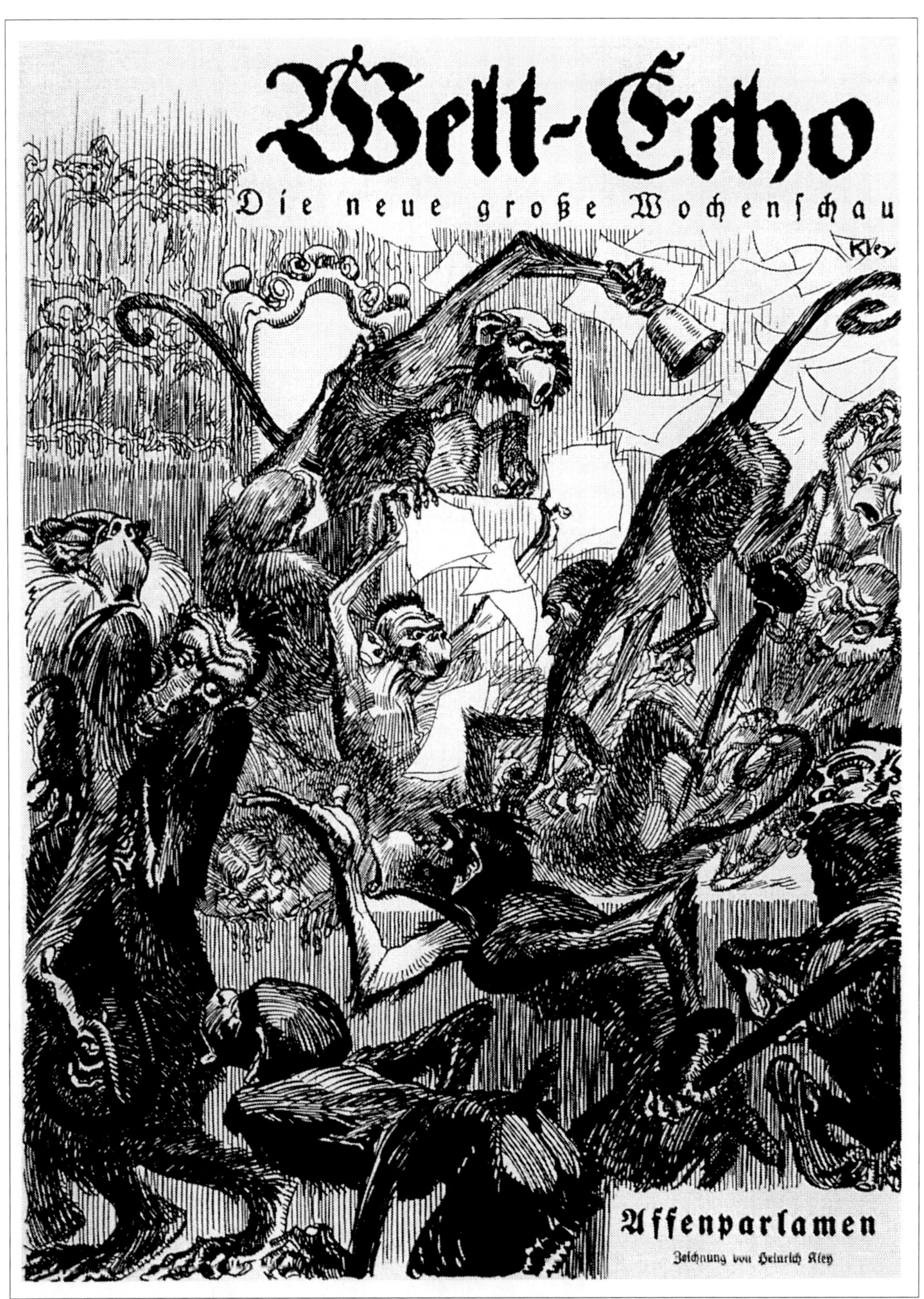

Monkey Parliament

Affenparlament

Welt-Echo (No. 35) • 1919

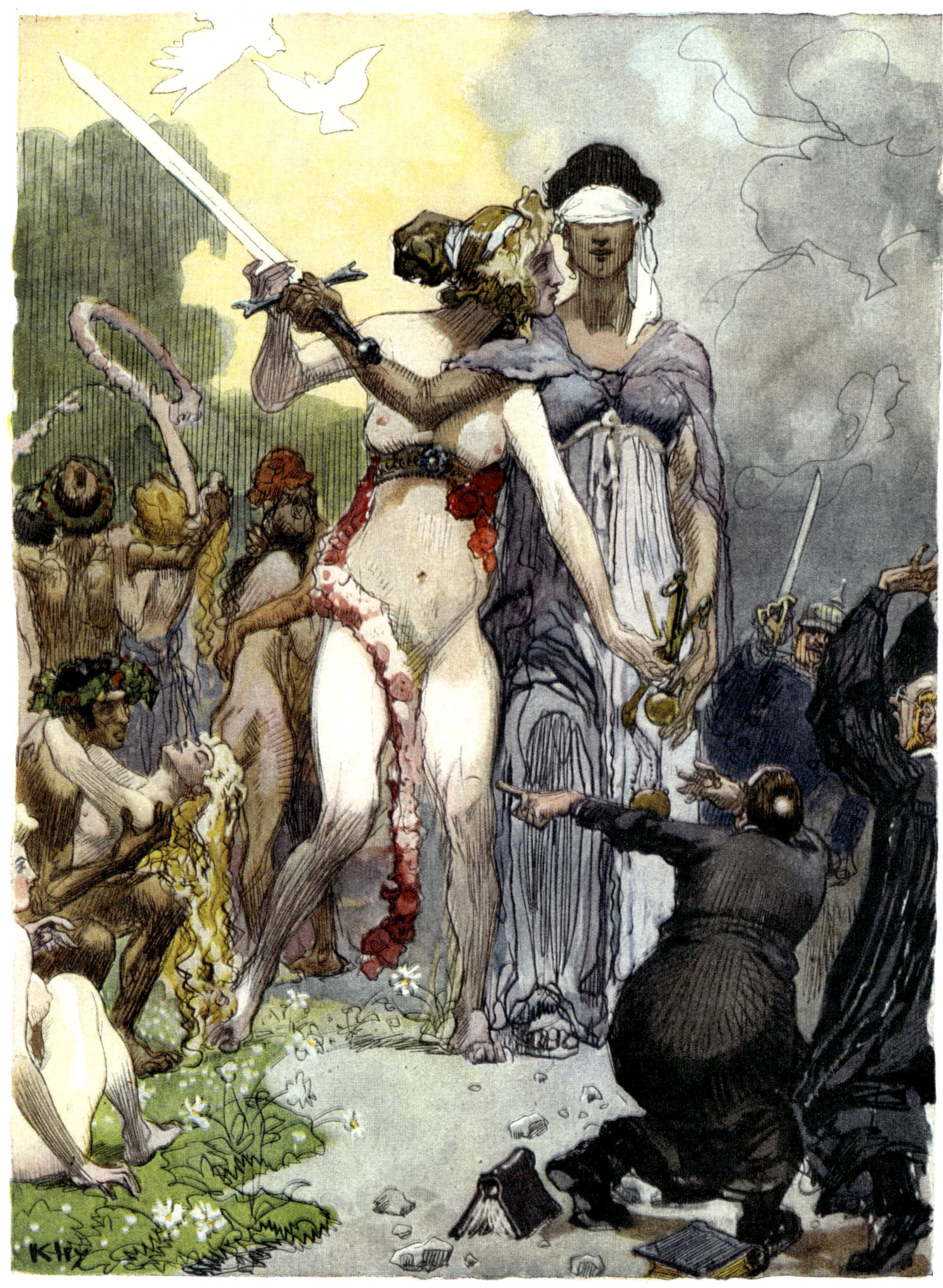

The Right to Eroticism

Jugend • 1911

Inspired by a Friedrich Nietzsche poem

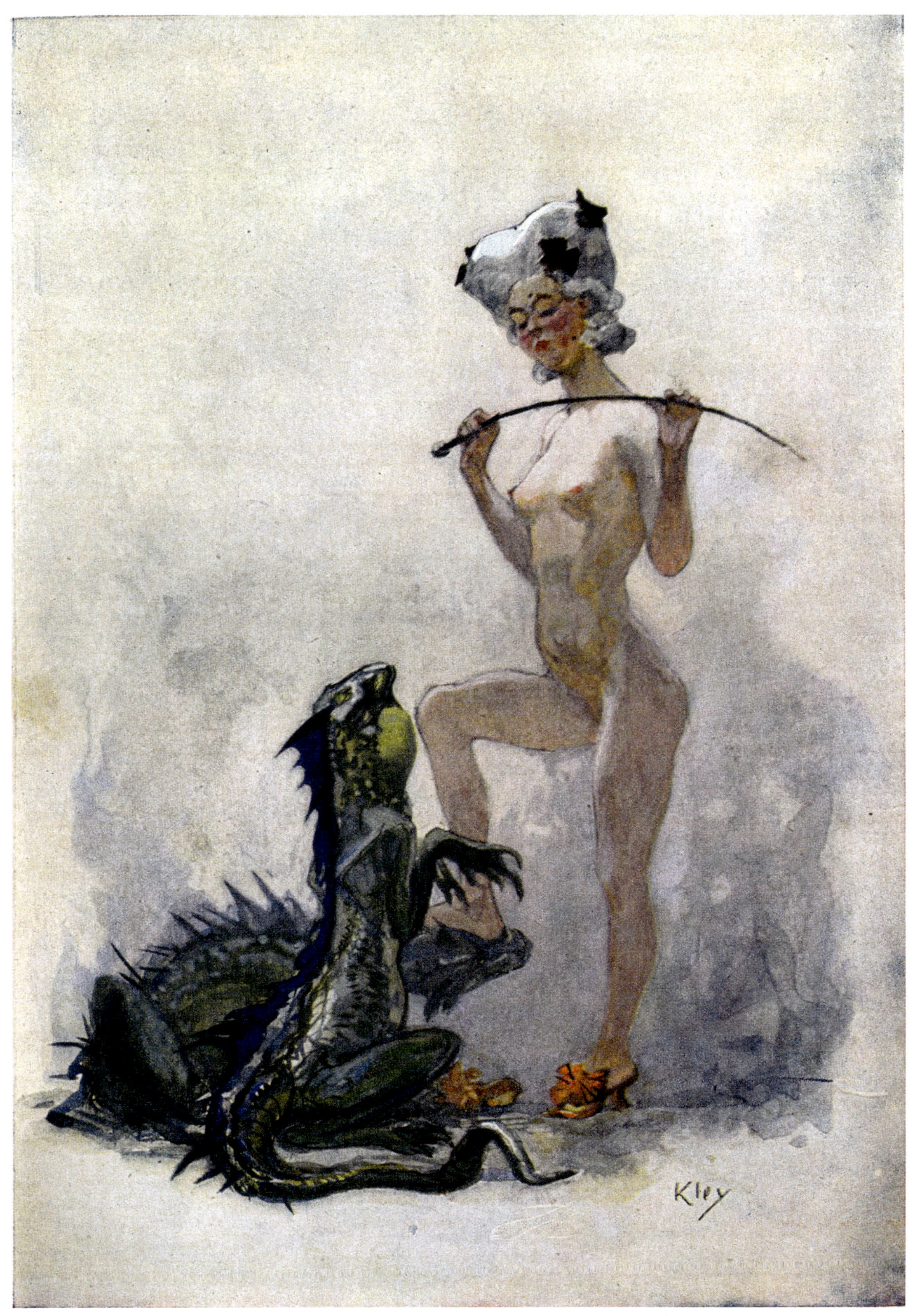

The Tamer
La dompteuse
Jugend • 1910

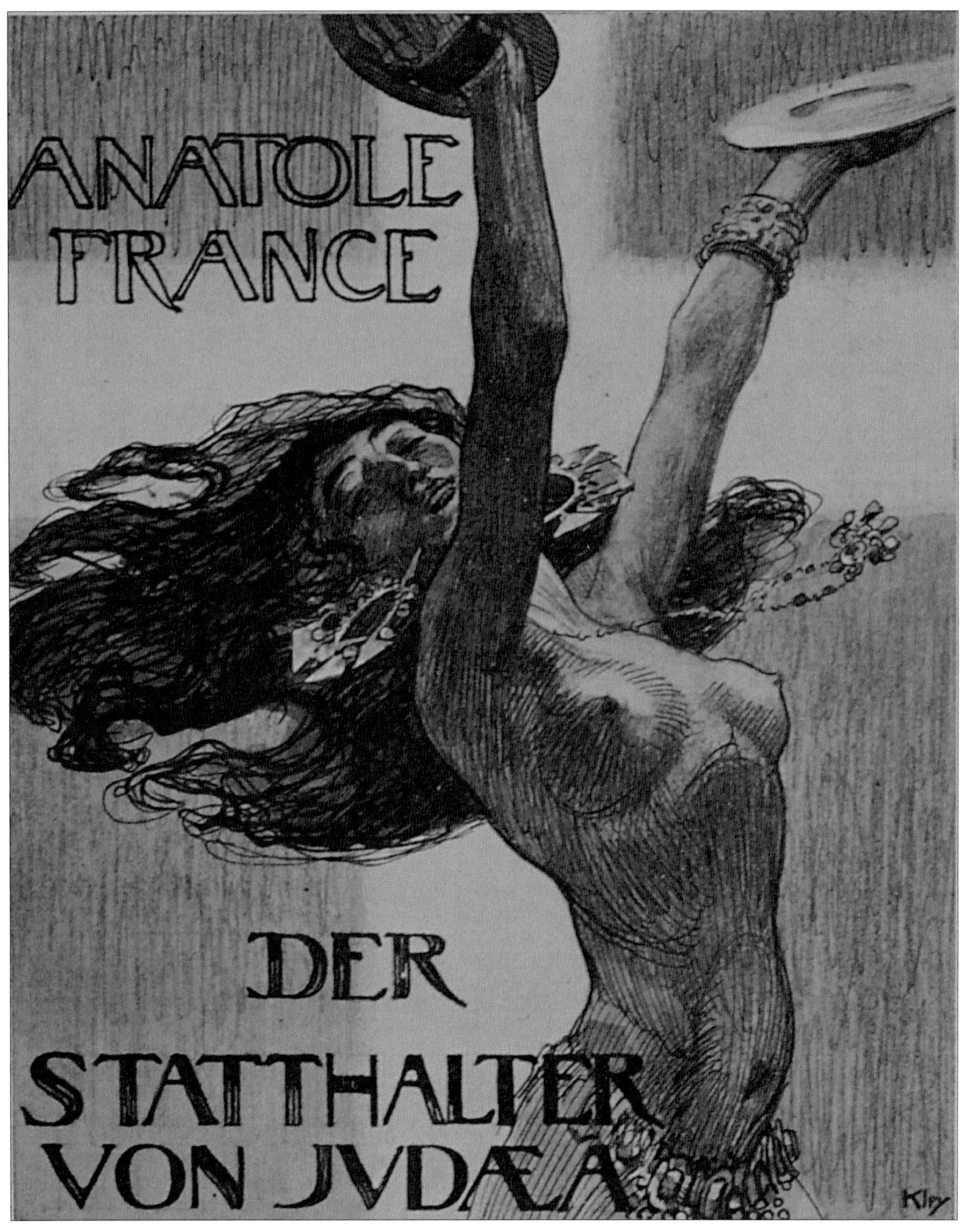

Dustjacket to *Der Statthalter von Judäa* (*The Governor of Judea*)
Anatole France
1910

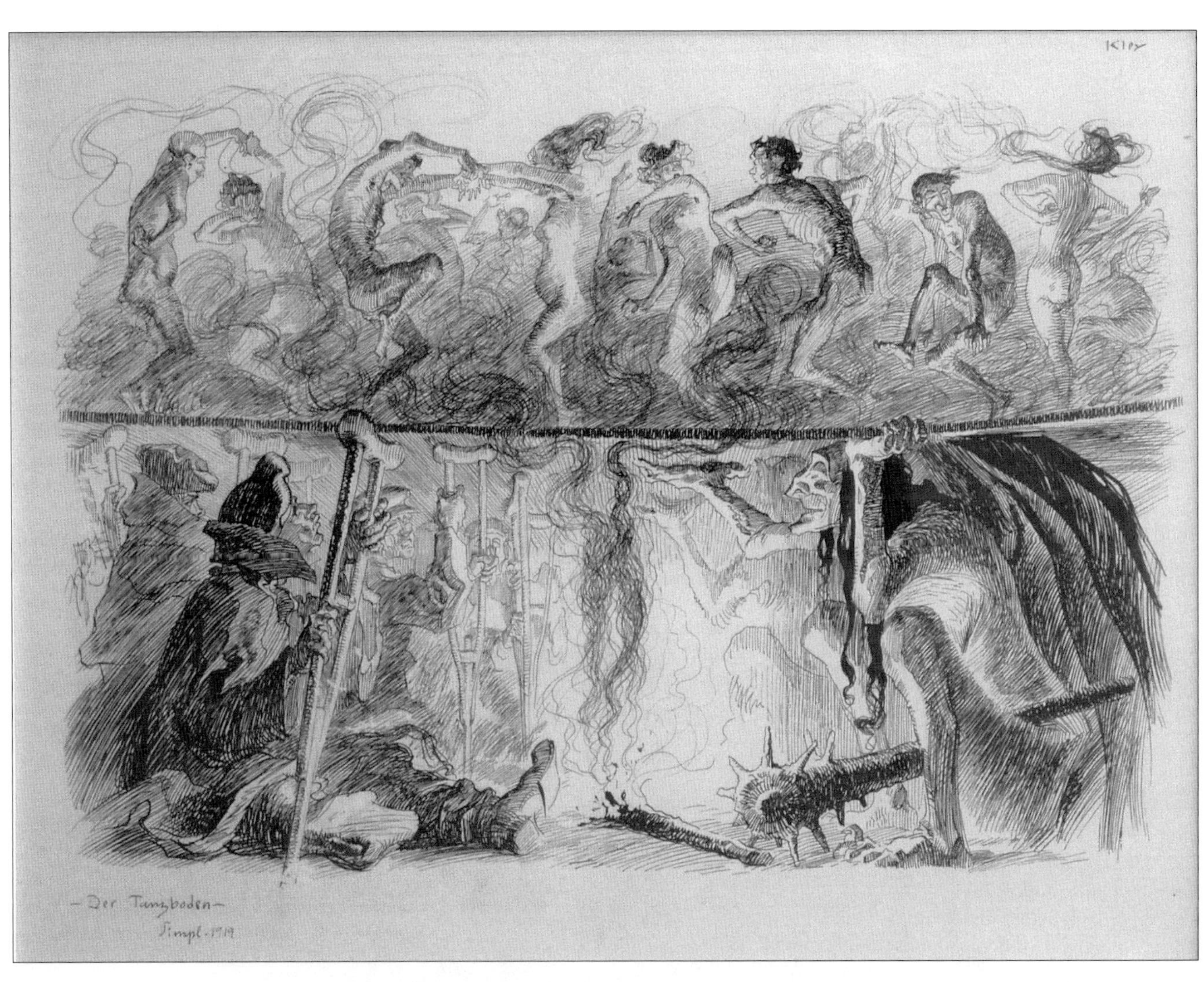

The Dance Floor
Der Tanzboden
1919

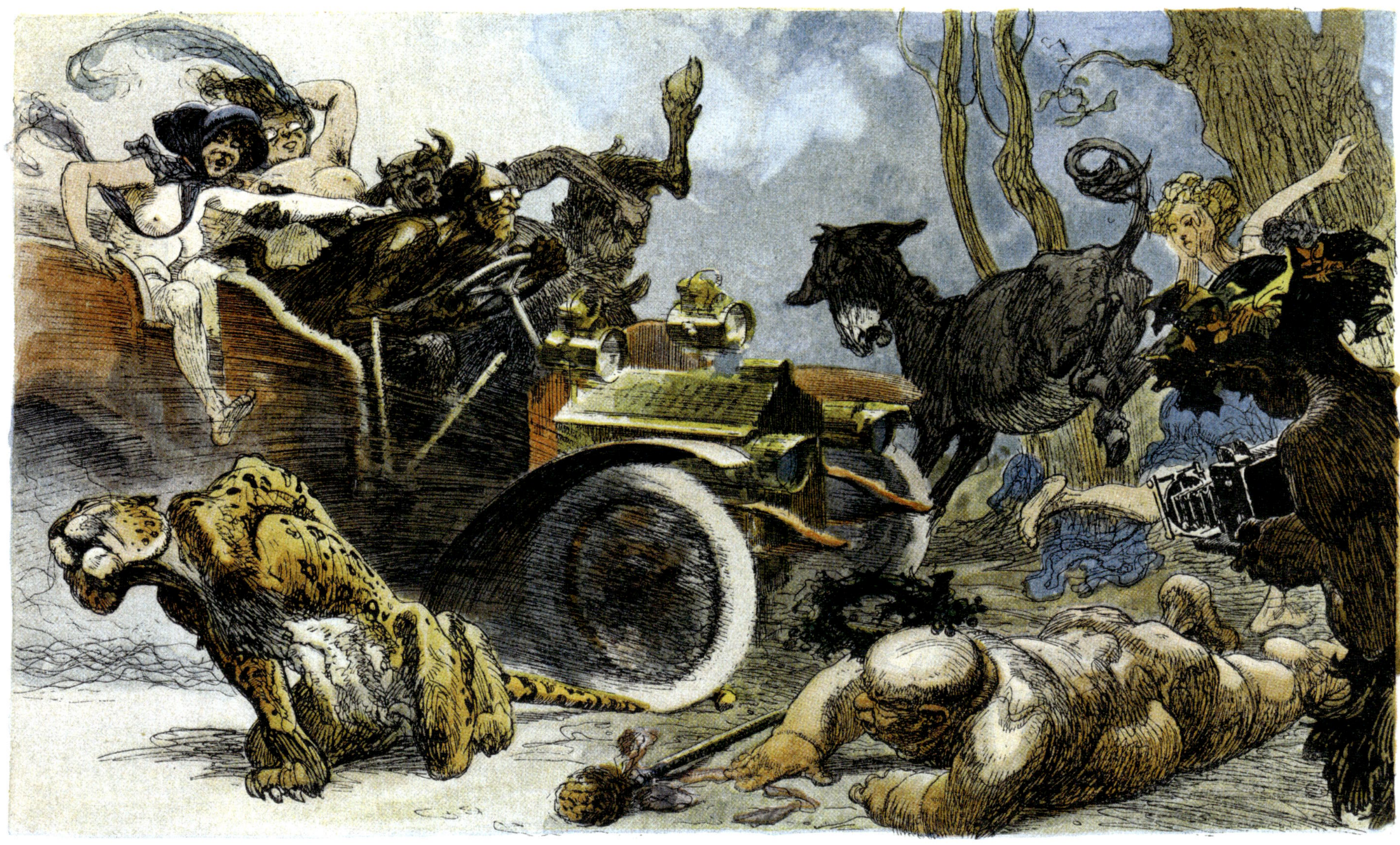

Children of Dionysus
Kinder des Dionysos
Jugend • 1910

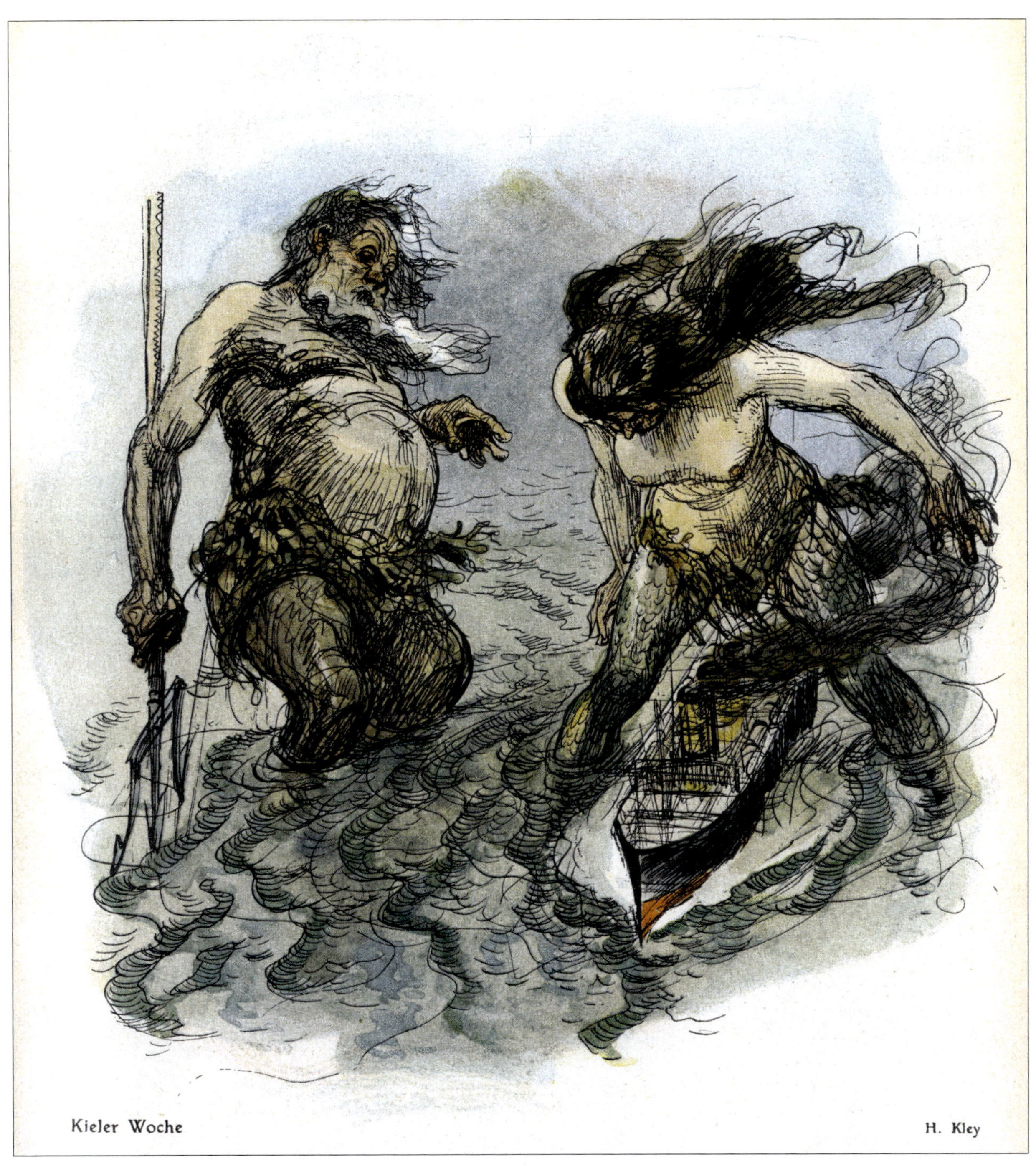

Jugend • 1910

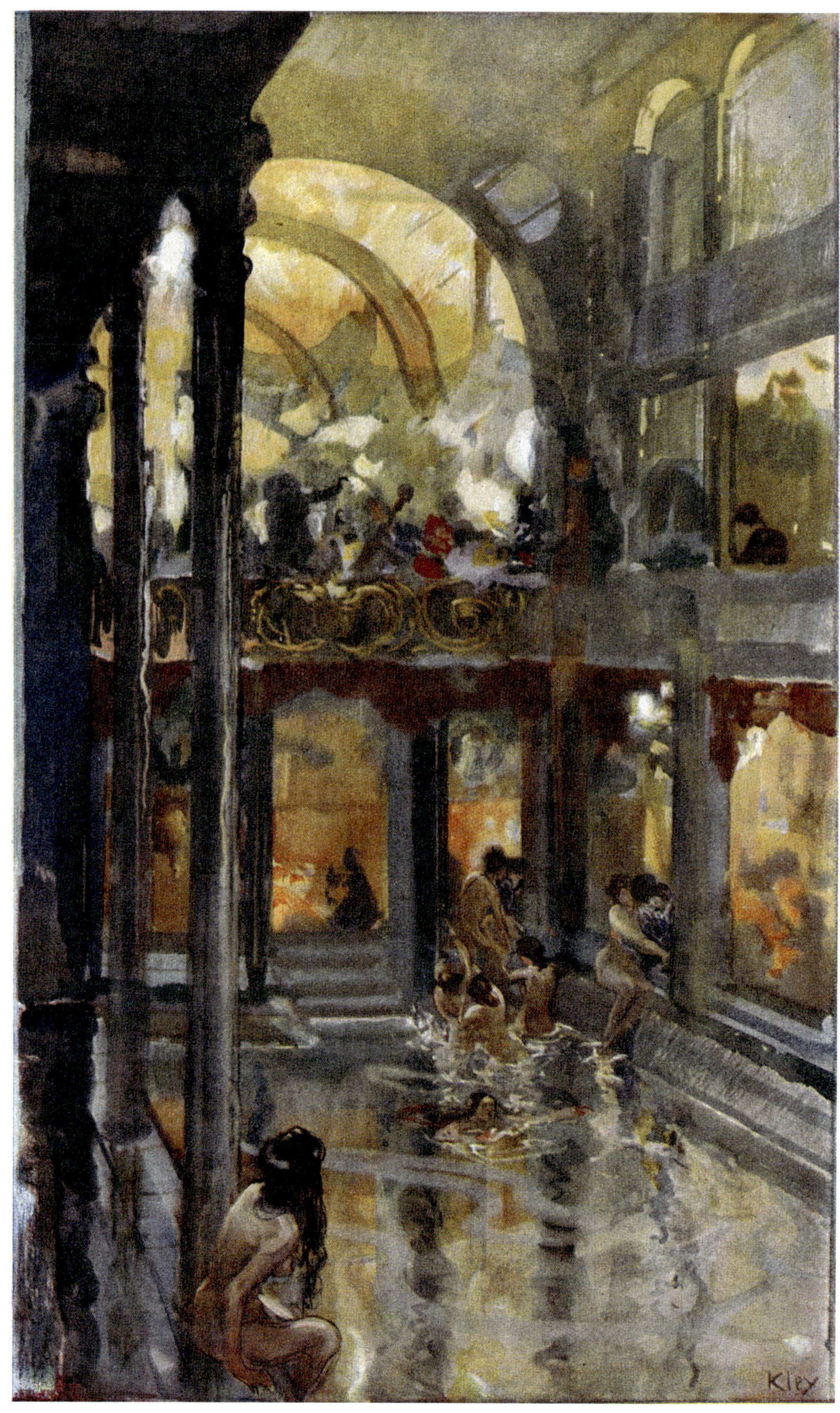

The Palace Bath
Das Schlossbad
Jugend • 1911

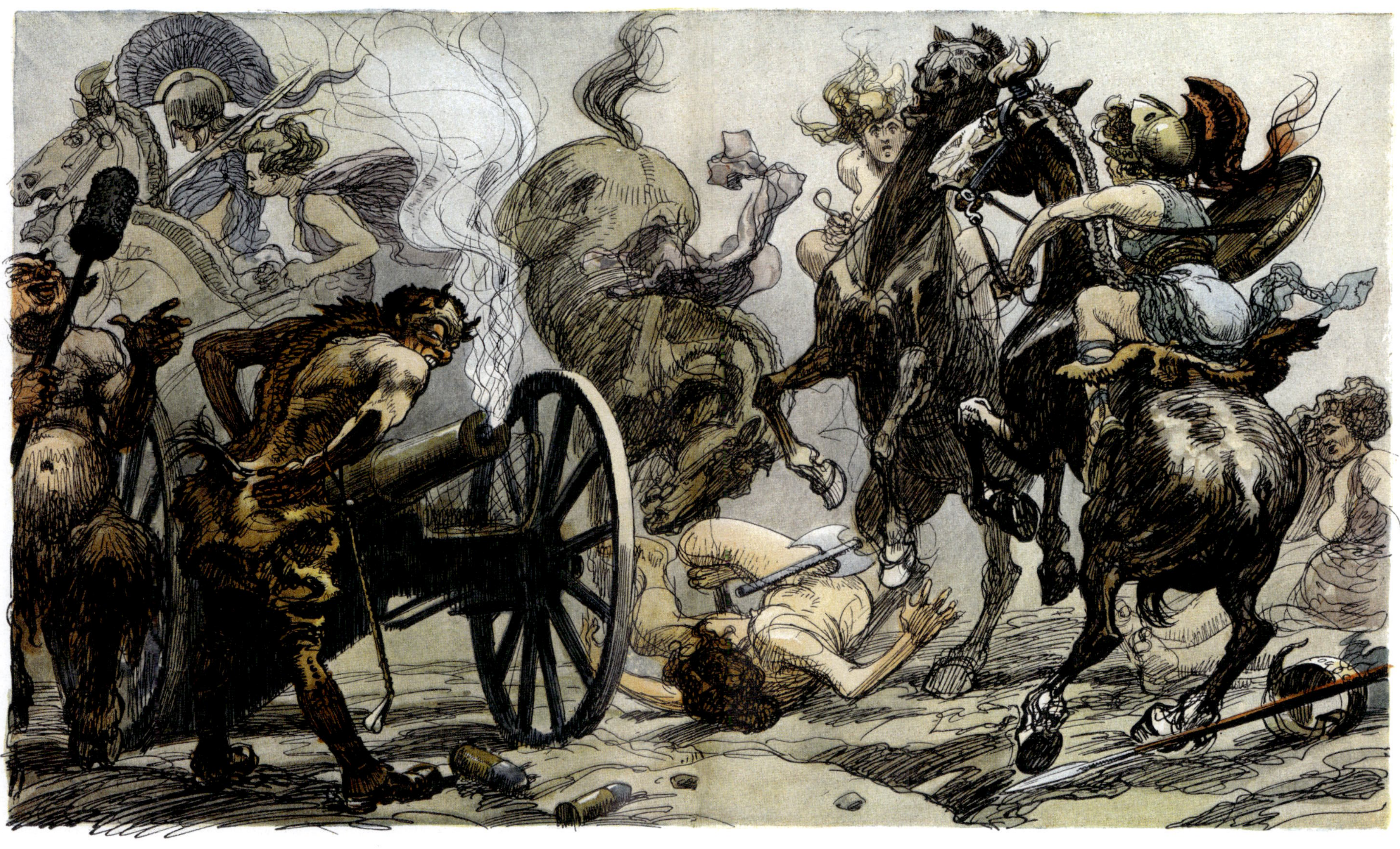

Amazons During Target Practice at the Lechfeld Army Base
Amazonen bei der Schiessübung im Lager Lechfeld
Jugend • 1910

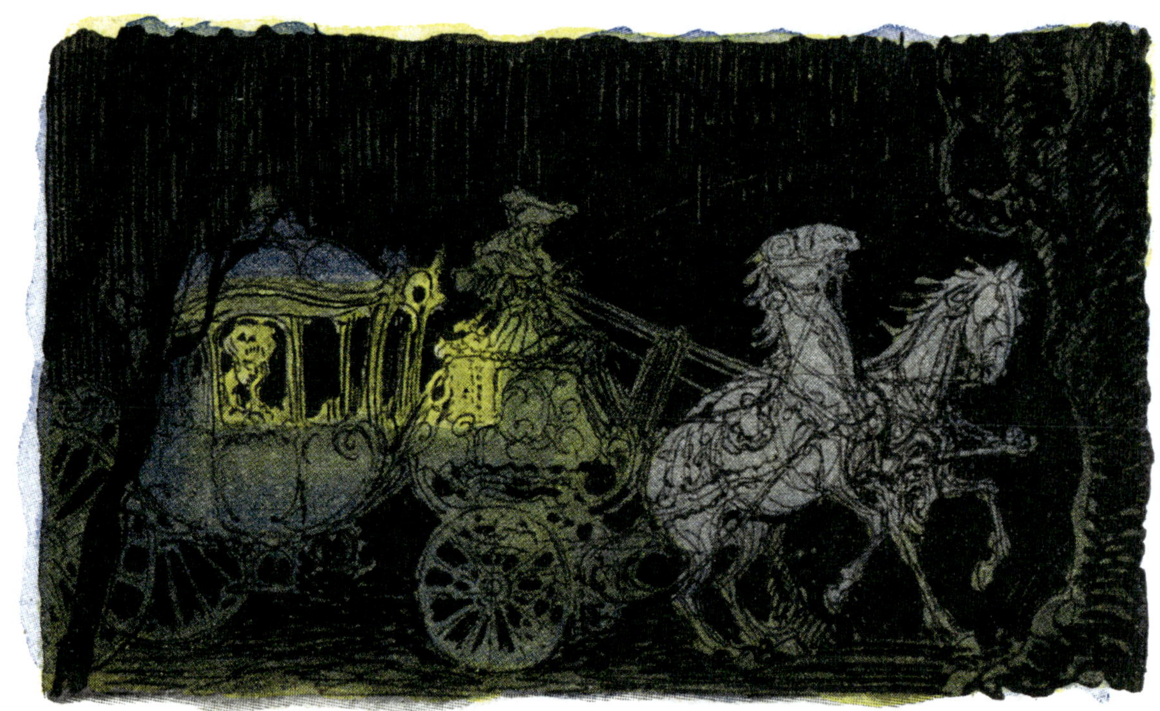

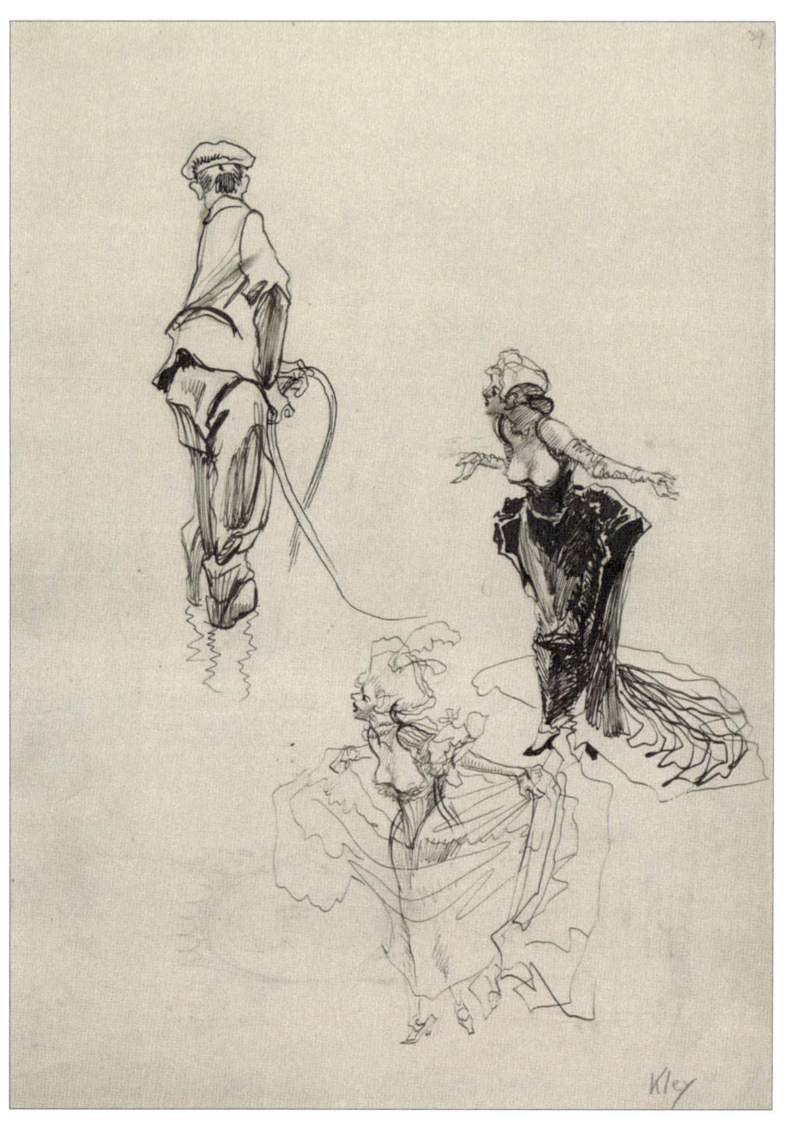
Kley

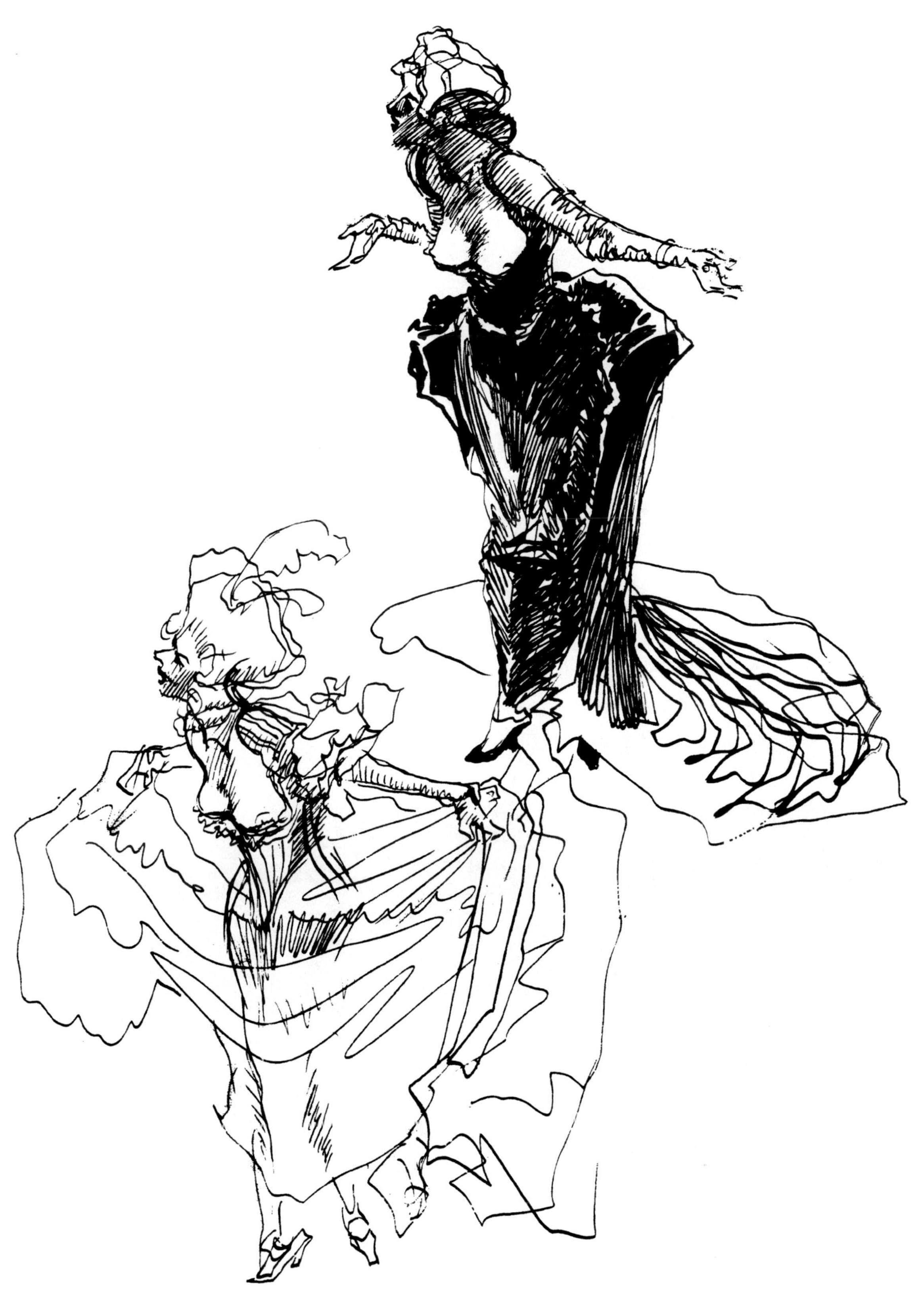

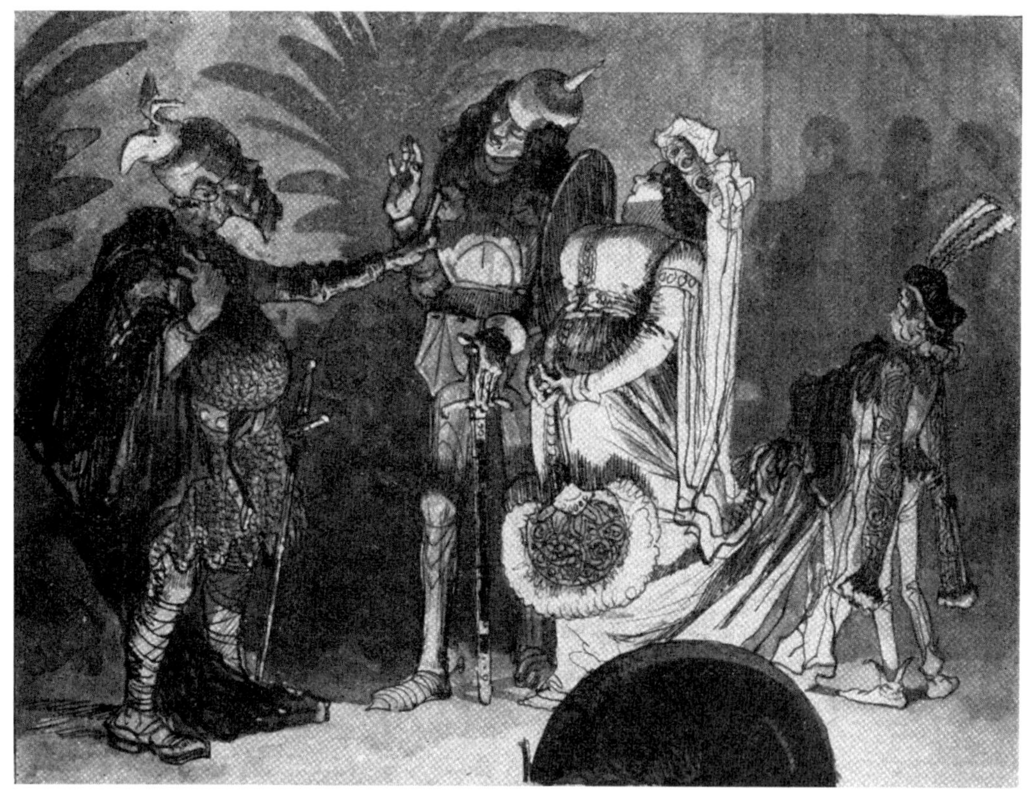

Theater
"We have a new director. He is very cunning and energetic.
The whole theater has already started scheming."
Jugend • 1910

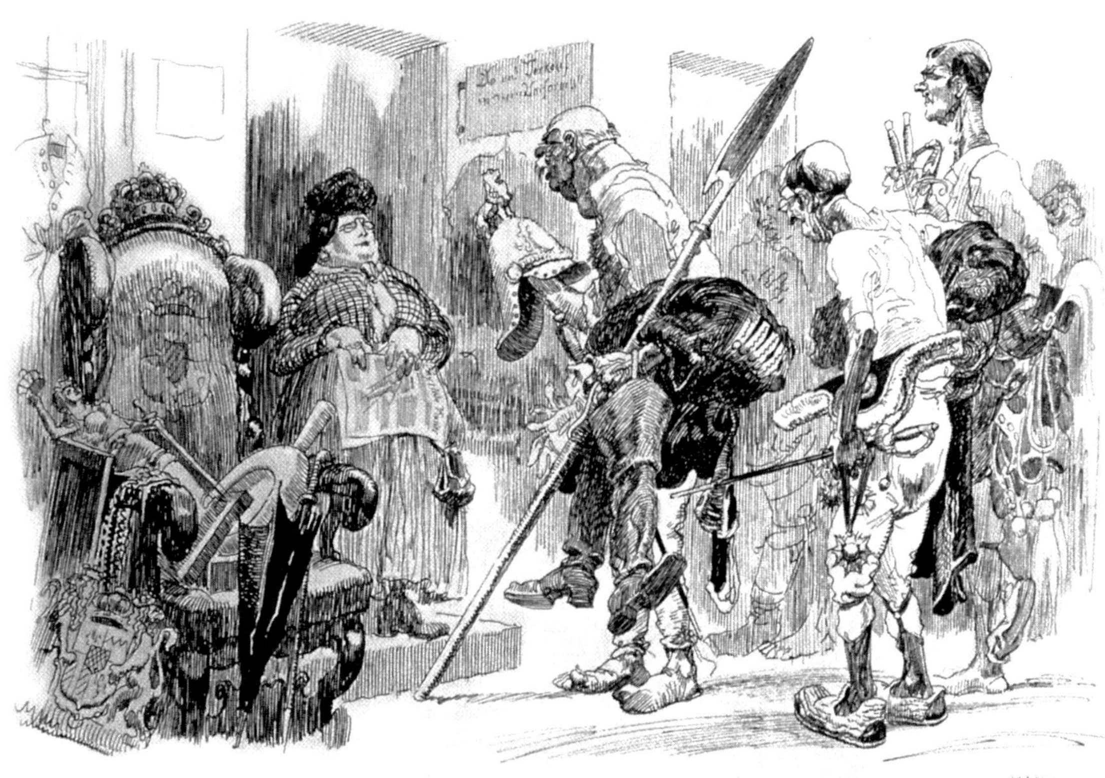

Flea Market
Trödelmarkt
Simplicissimus (No. 37) • 1918

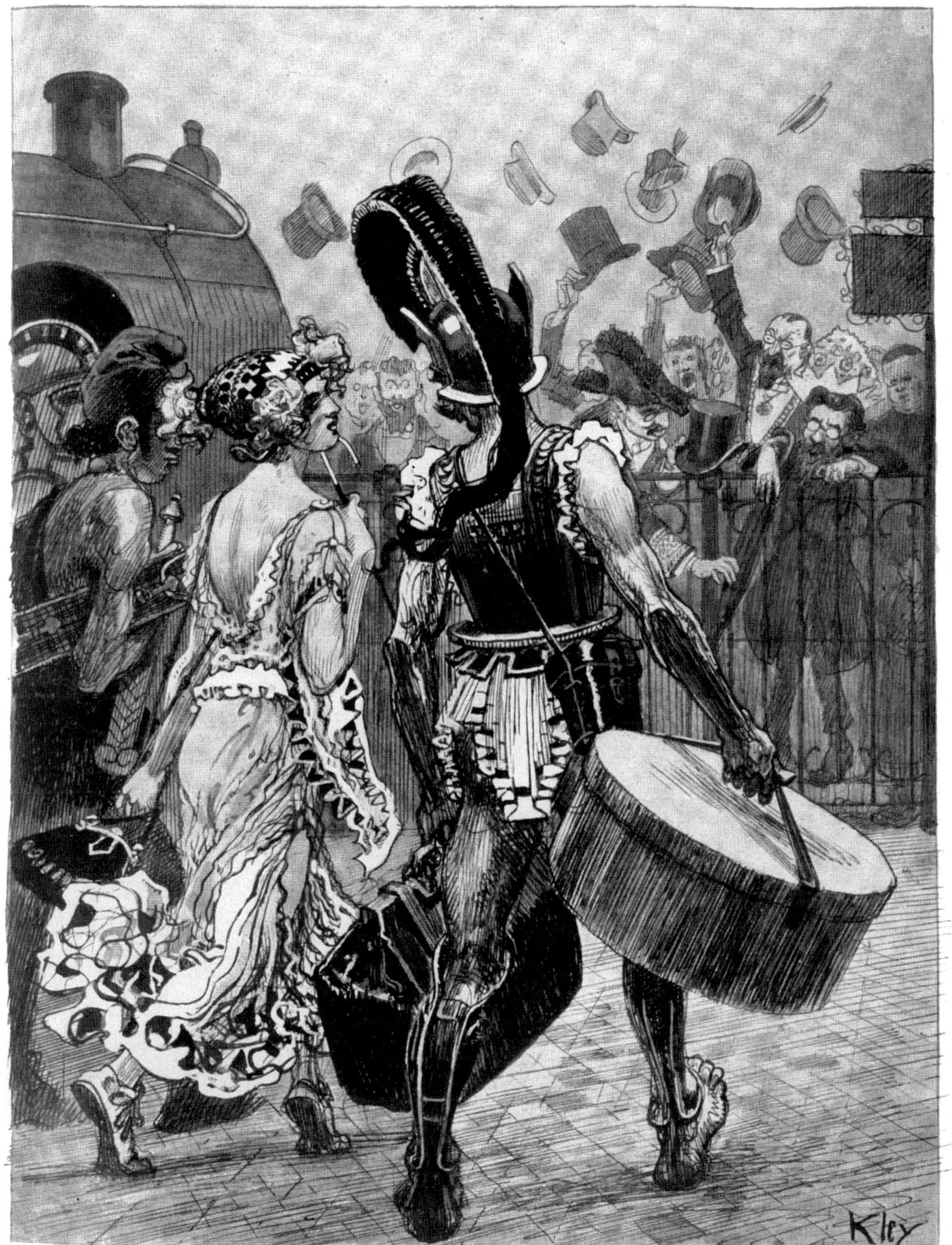

Arrival of the "Beautiful Helen" in Munich
"Achilles, keep Orterer away from me—or else he is going to turn me into a pious Helene!"
Ankunft der "Schönen Helena" in München
Achilles, halt mir den Orterer vom Leibe, -- sonst macht der aus mir noch eine fromme Helene!"

Jugend • 1910

There is a play on names here. "Helen" is referring to "Helen of Troy," while "Helene" is referring to *Die Fromme Helene* (*Pious Helene*), a book by Wilhelm Busch. Georg Ritter von Orterer was a very religious Bavarian politician, so this is to be understood as a dig.

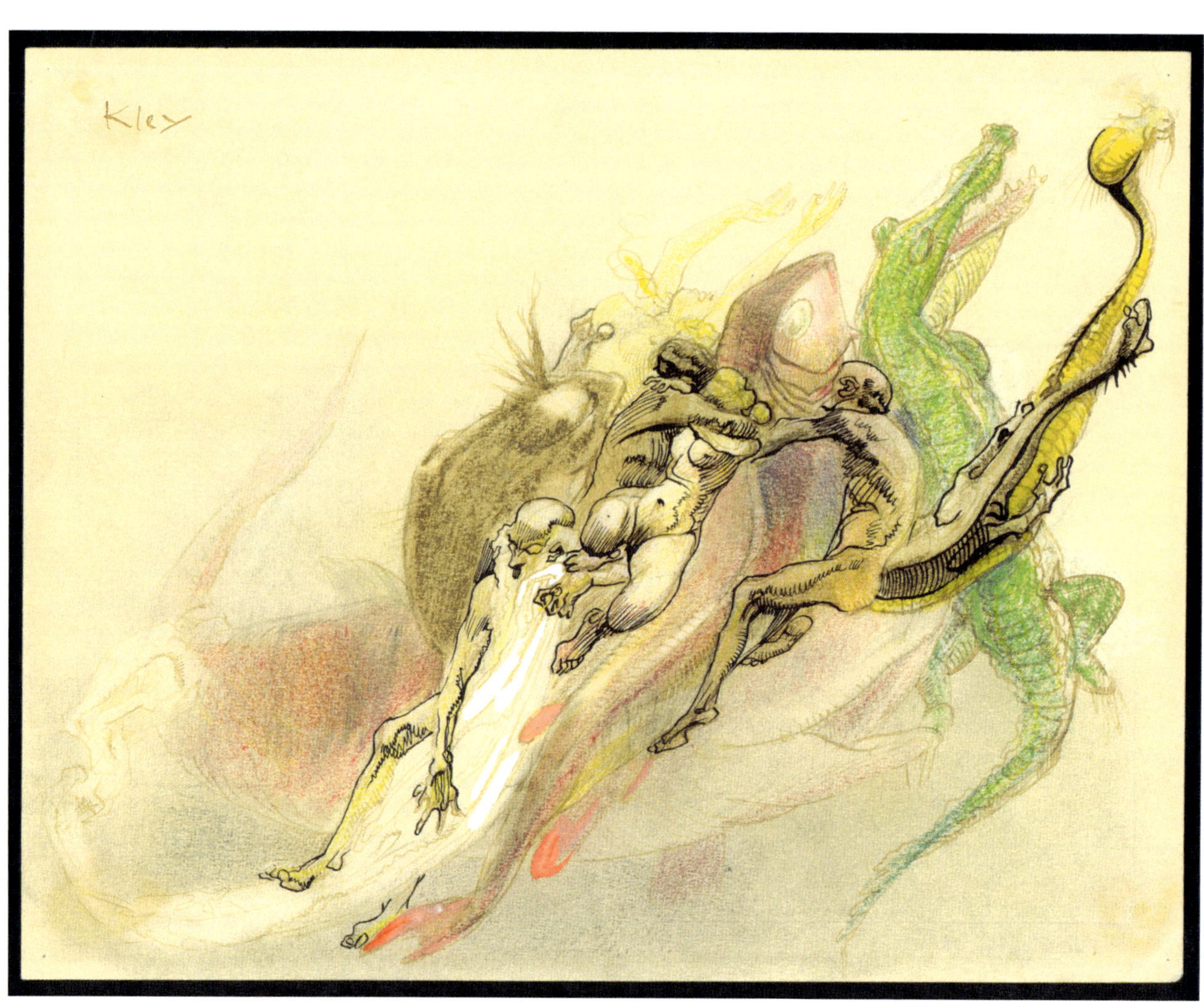
Kley

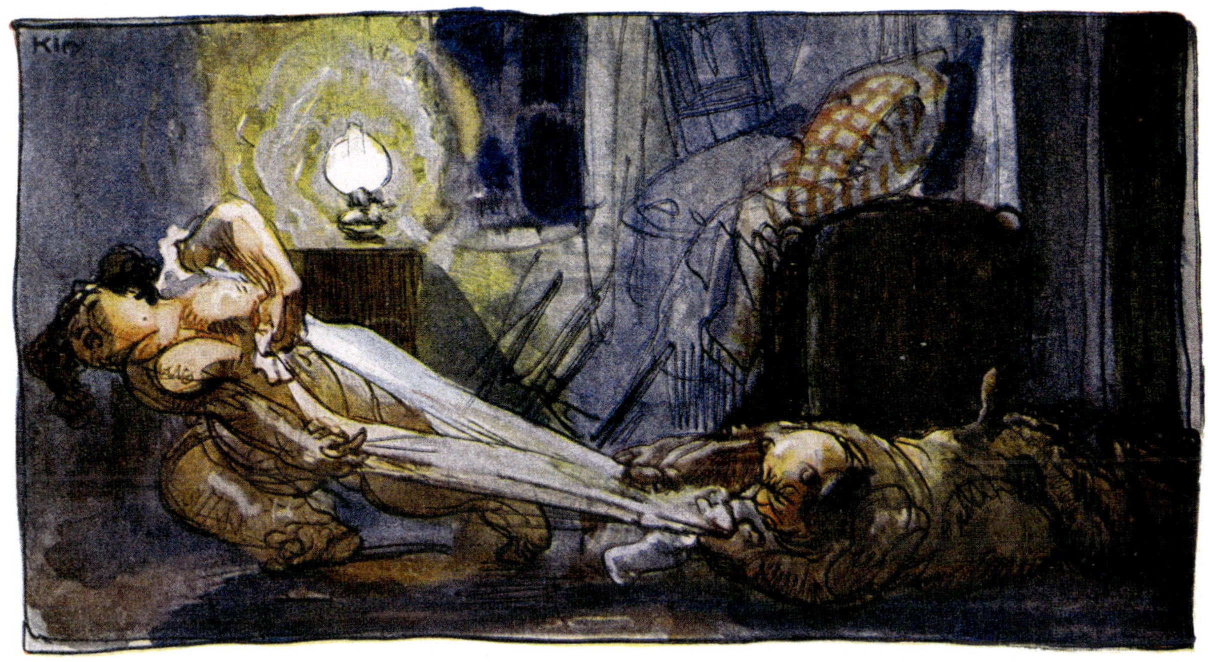

Night Spook
Nächtlicher Spuk
Jugend • 1910

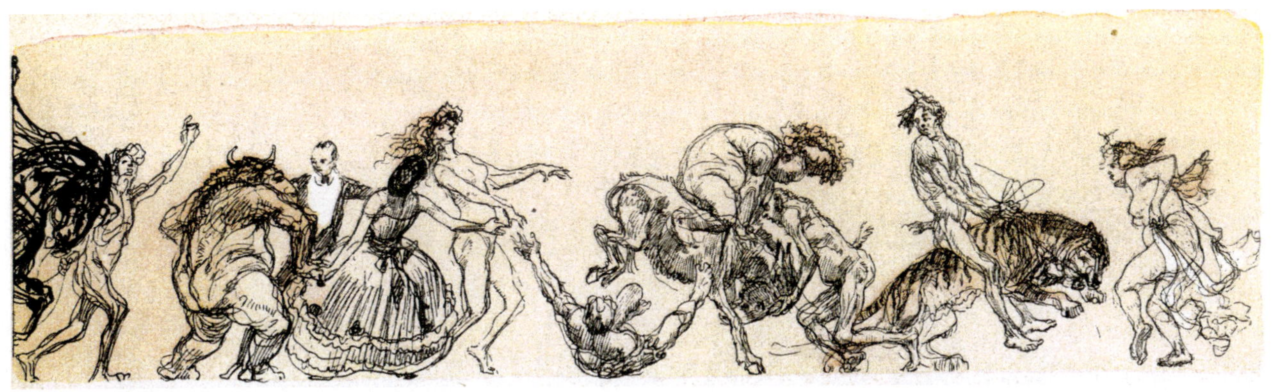

Jugend • 1910

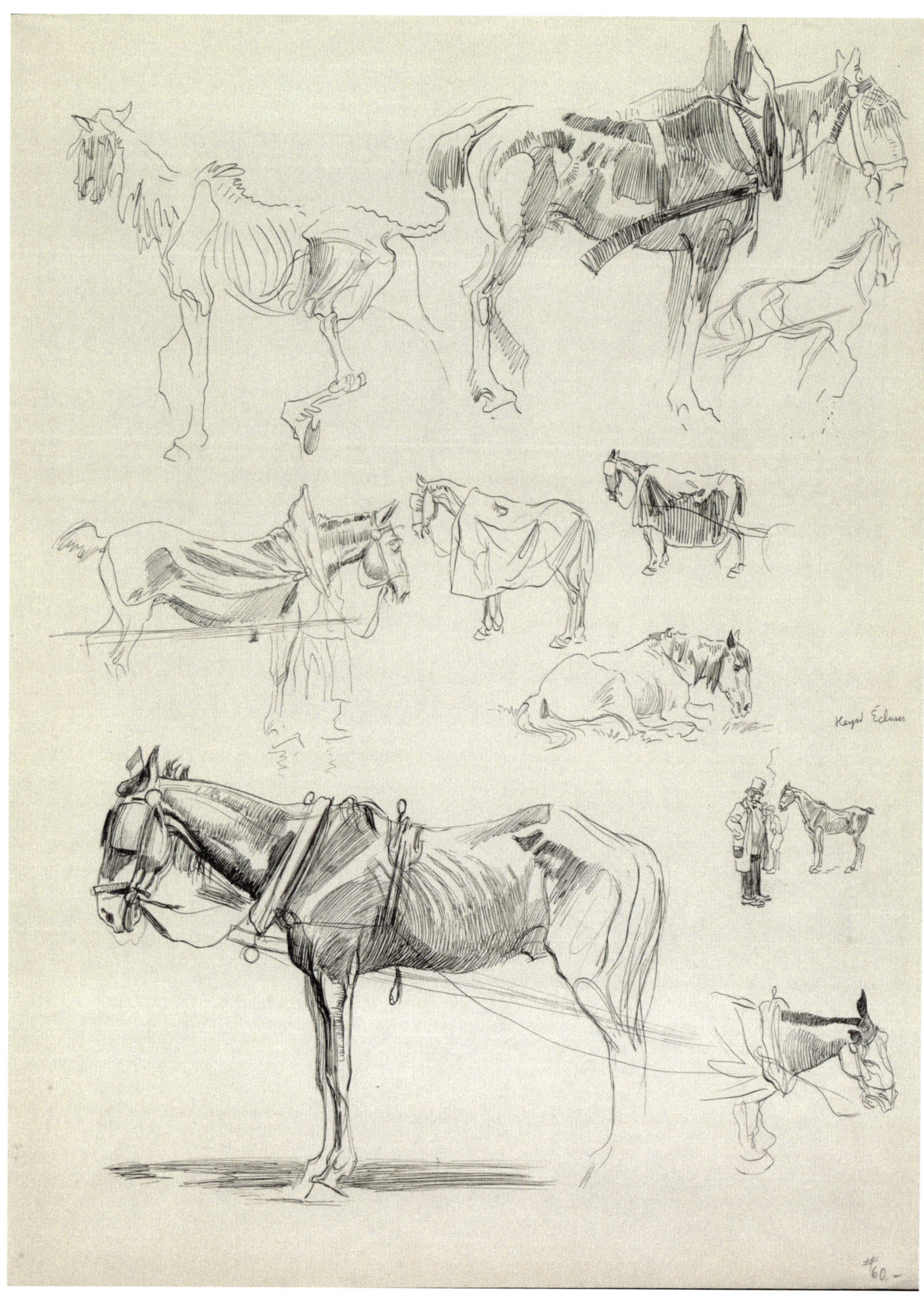

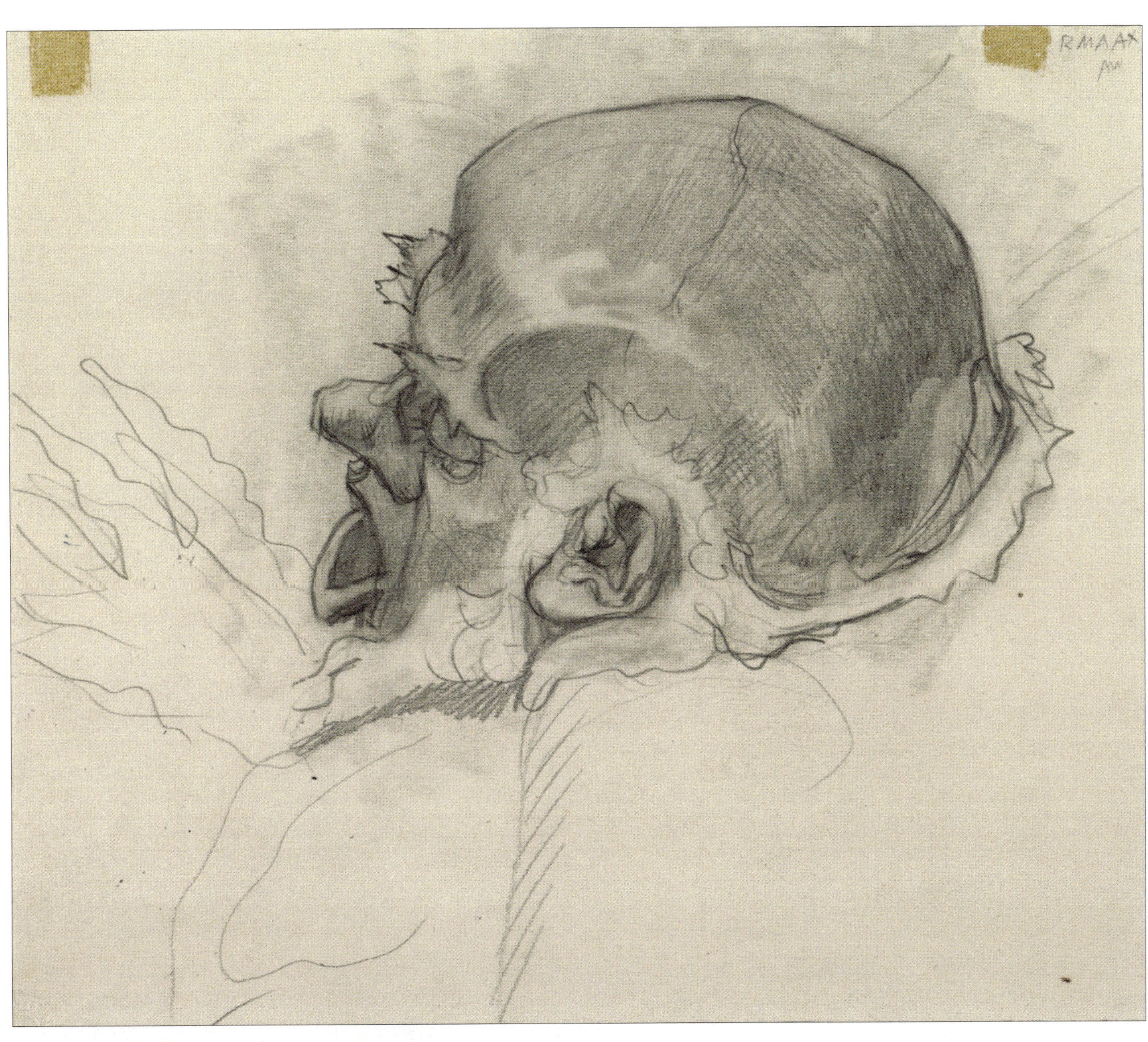

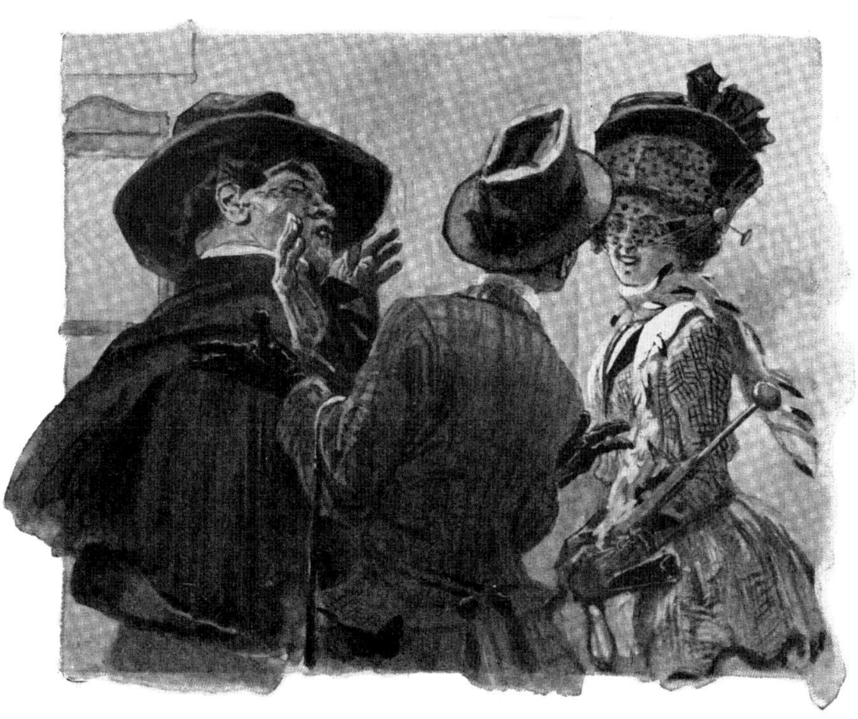

The Homecoming
"You have frostbite? Where did that happen?"
"On our summer vacation."
Jugend • 1910

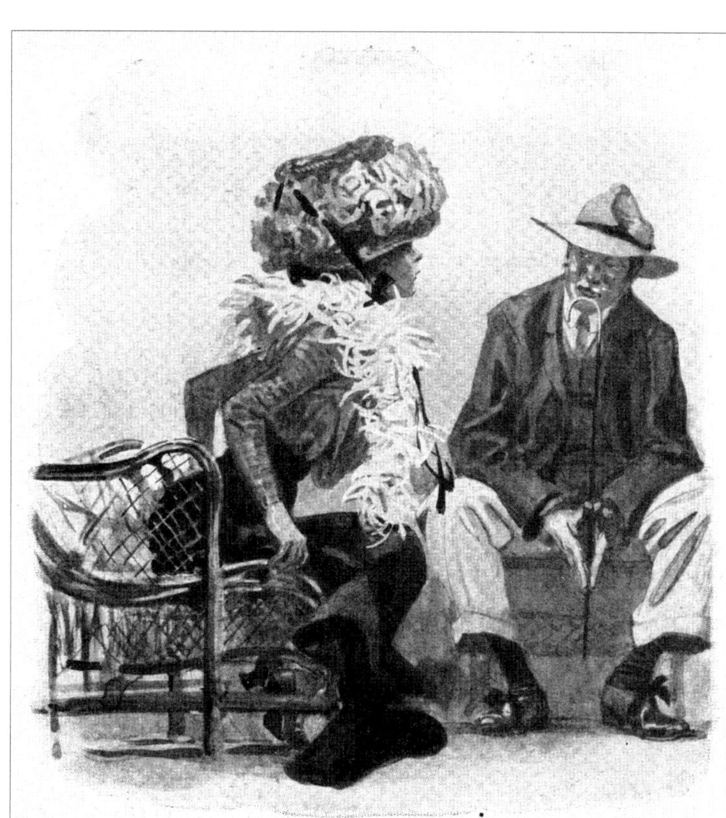

Actresses' Dilemma
"Your director is not opposed to your sudden marriage?!"
"No; I let him know he would have to deal with the joys of fatherhood, otherwise!"
Jugend • 1910

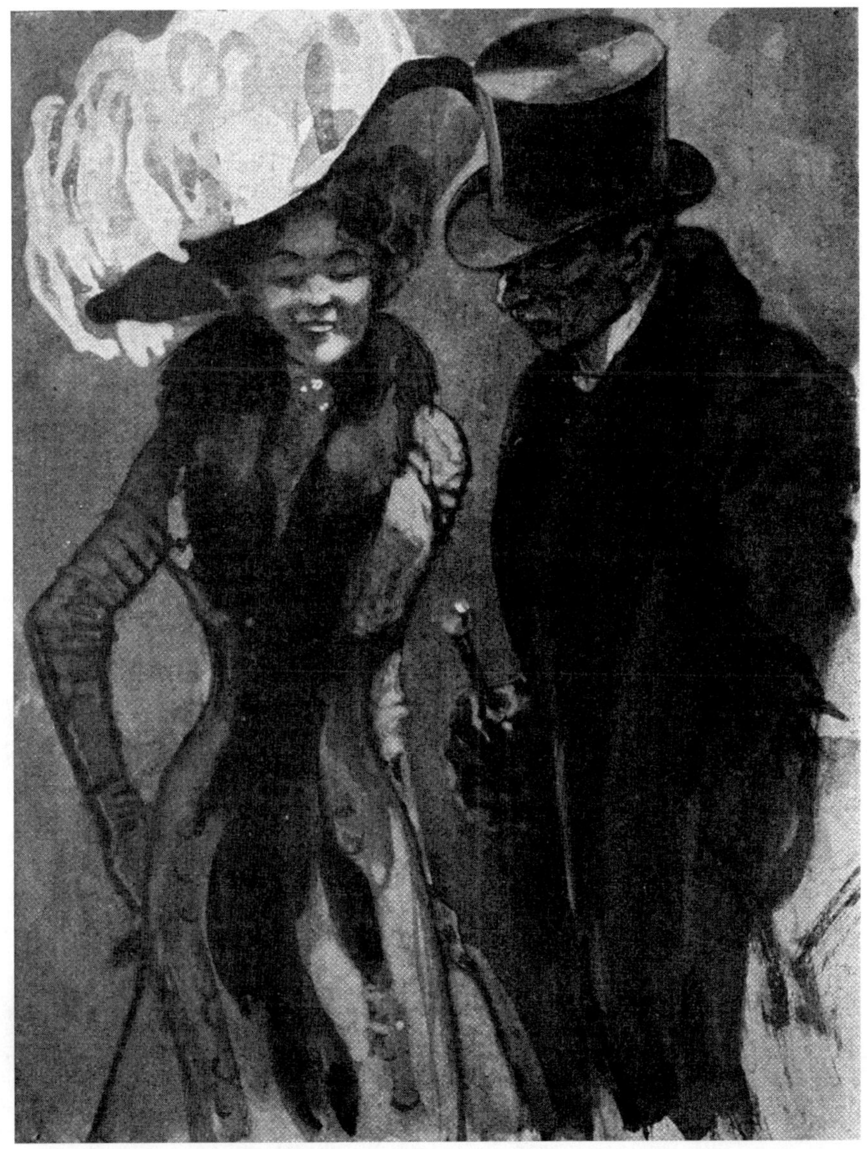

After Singing Practice
"Was this a compliment or not? After singing Philine's aria, the choir master told me I must be good at cooking!"
Jugend • 1910

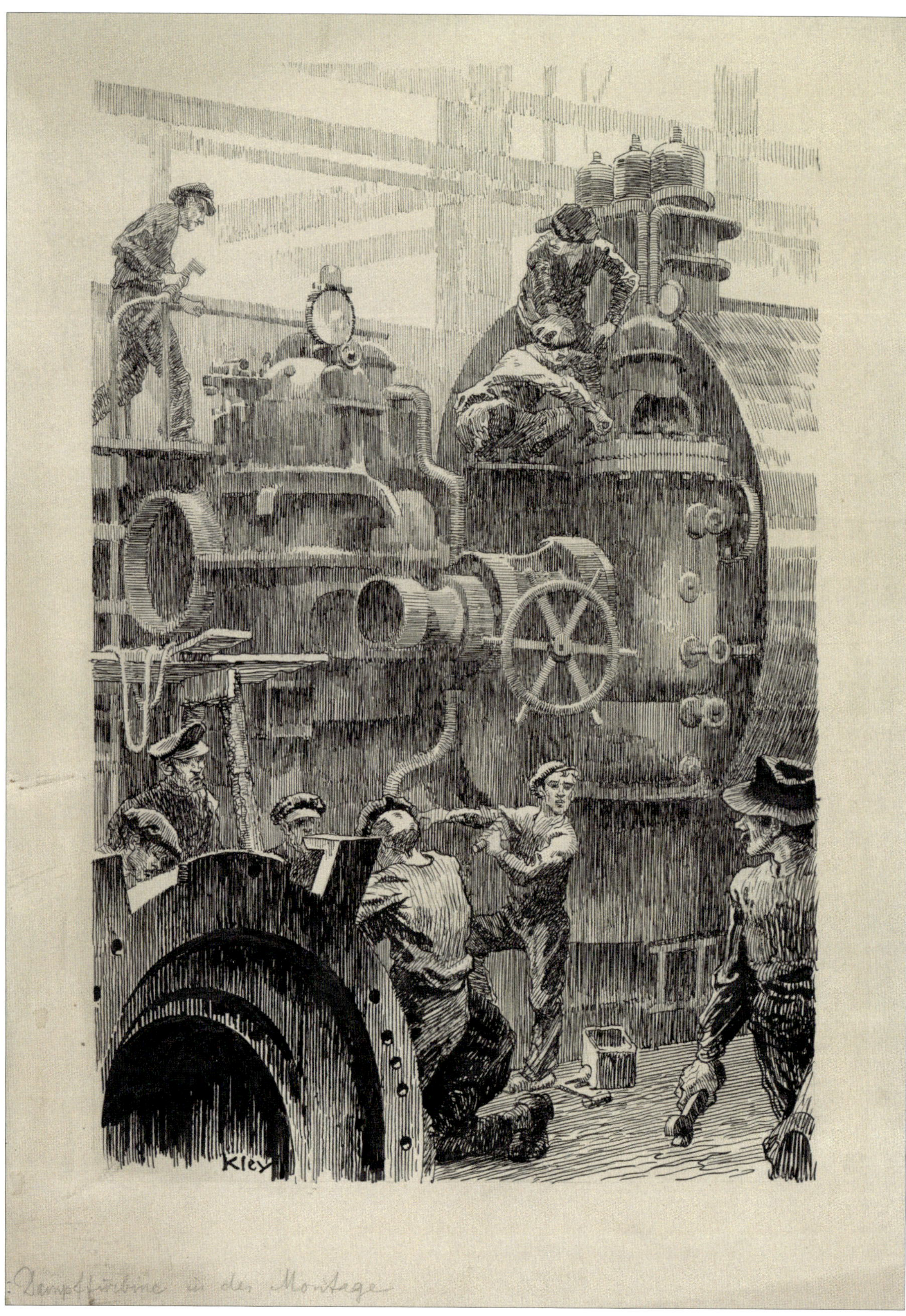
Kley
Dampfturbine in der Montage

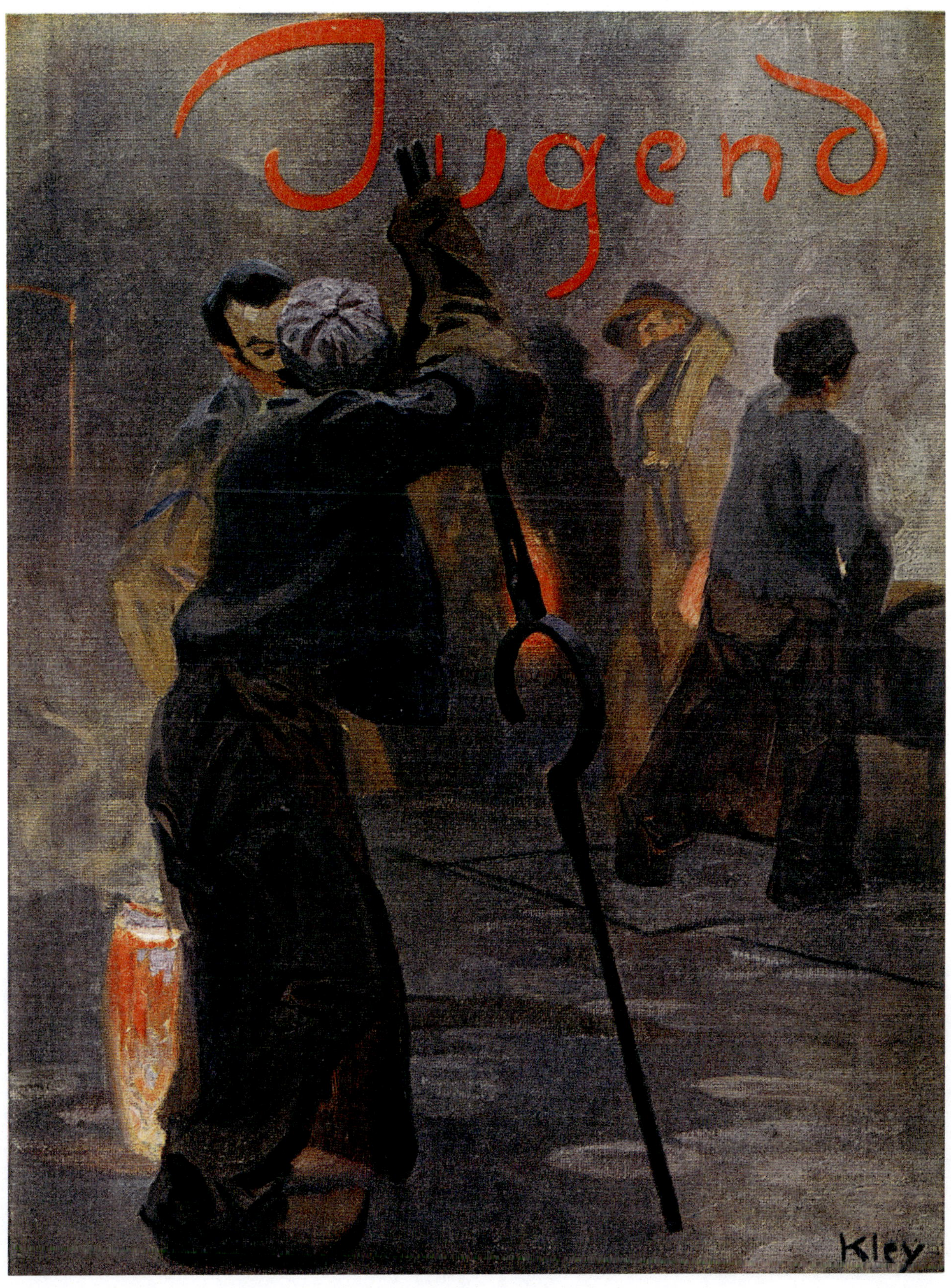

Jugend (No. 5) • 1911
Special "Industry Number"
(pages 131-135)

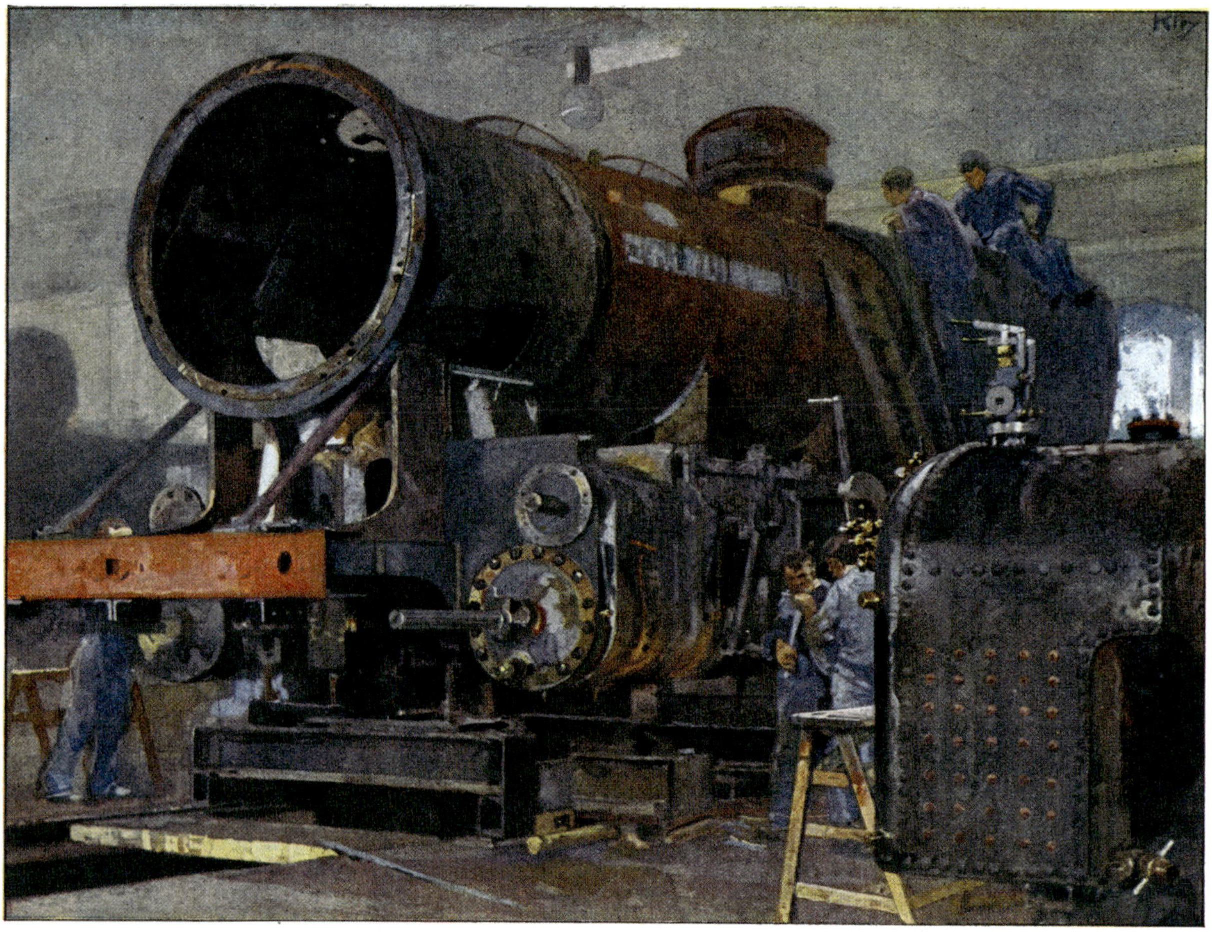

Railway Locomotive Under Construction
Maffei-lokomotive im bau

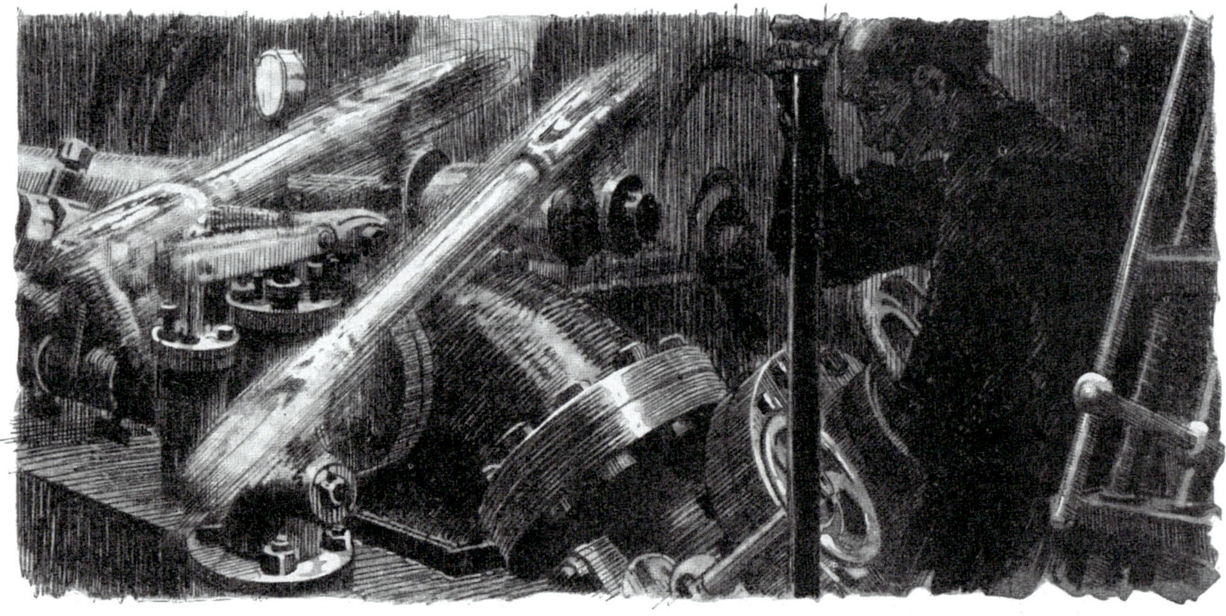

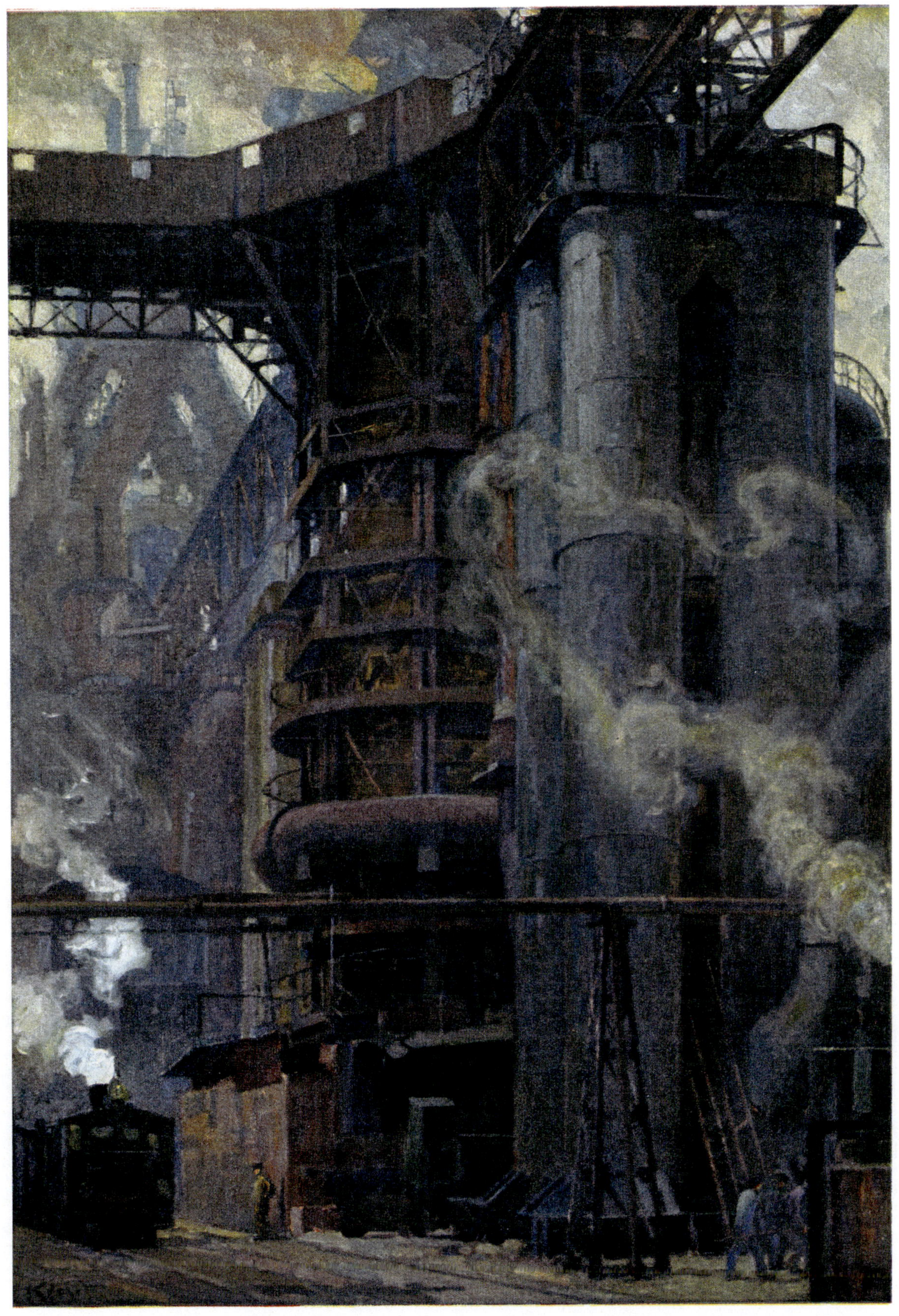

Blast Furnace at Friedrich-Alfred-Hütte
Hochofen der friedrich-alfred-hütte

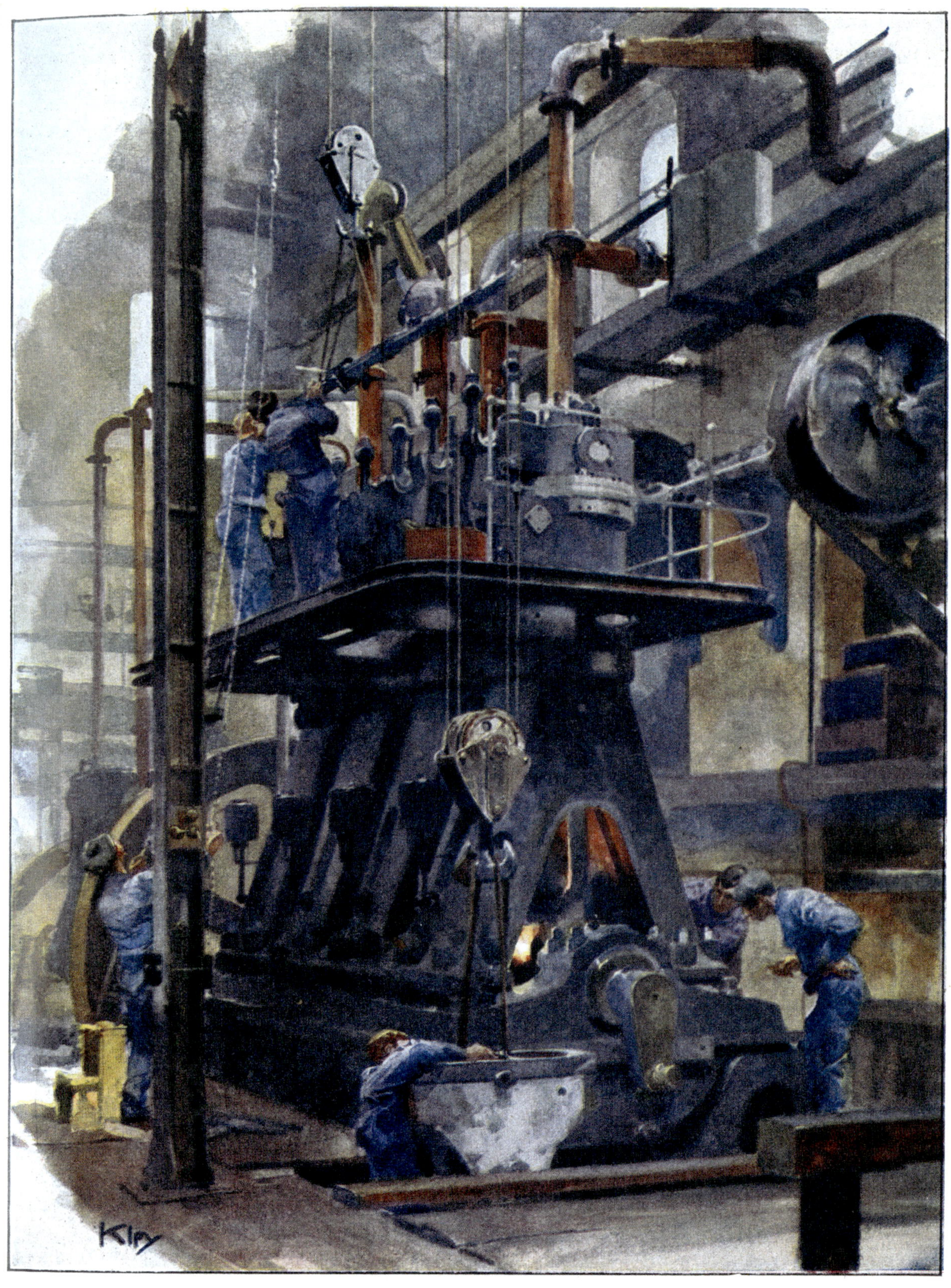

Diesel Engine
On the test bench of the Augsburger mechanic

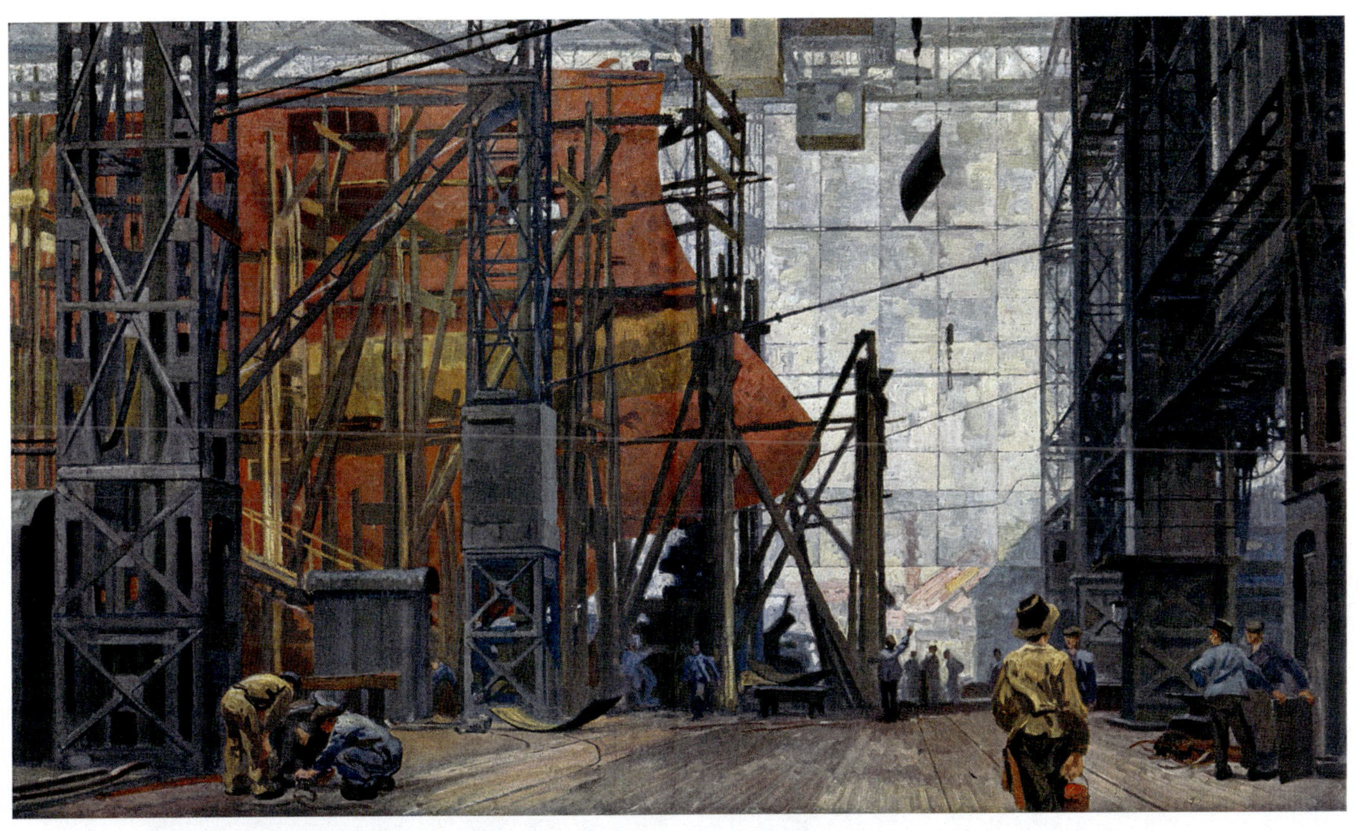

Liner on the Covered Slipway of a German Shipyard
Linienschiff auf gedecker Helling der Germania-Werft

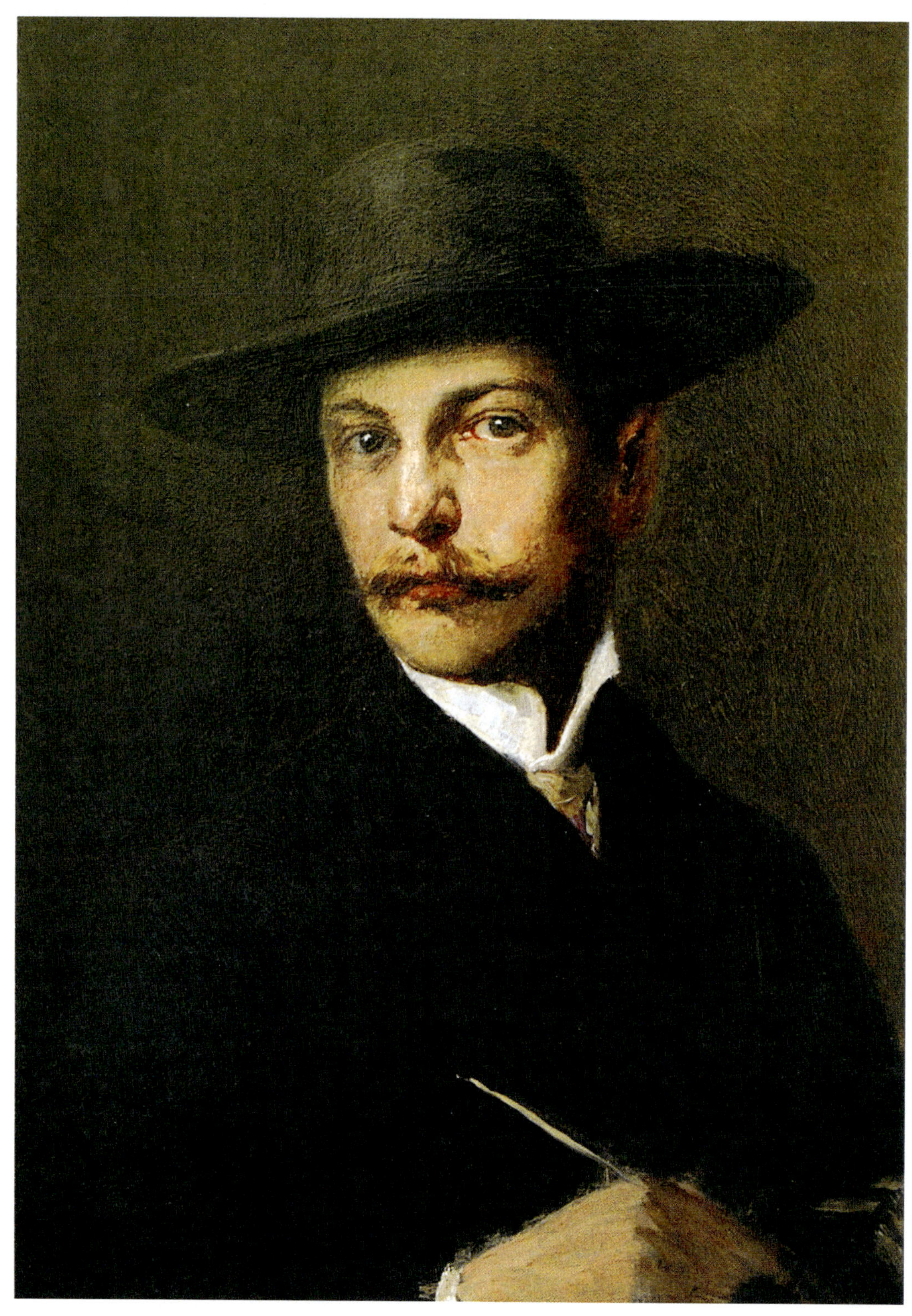

Self Portrait
1885

Made in United States
Orlando, FL
25 January 2023